Trials of Nation Making

This book offers the first interpretive synthesis of the history of Andean peasants and the challenges of nation making in the four republics of Colombia, Ecuador, Peru, and Bolivia during the turbulent nineteenth century. Nowhere in Latin America were postcolonial transitions more vexed or violent than in the Andes, where communal indigenous roots grew deep and where the "Indian problem" seemed so daunting to liberalizing states.

Brooke Larson paints vivid portraits of Creole ruling elites, mestizo middle sectors, and native peasantries engaged in ongoing political and moral battles over the rightful place of the Indian majorities in these emerging, but still inchoate, nation-states. In this story, indigenous people emerge as crucial protagonists through their prosaic struggles for land, community, and "ethnic" identity, as well as in the upheavals of war, rebellion, and repression in rural society.

At the level of synthesis, this book raises broader issues about the interplay of liberalism, racism, and ethnicity in the formation of exclusionary "republics without citizens" over the nineteenth century.

Brooke Larson is Professor of History and the former director of the Latin American and Caribbean Studies Center at Stony Brook University. Her books include *Cochabamba, 1550–1900: Colonialism and Agrarian Transformation in Bolivia* (2nd ed., 1998), and the co-edited volume *Ethnicity, Markets and Migration: At the Crossroads of History and Anthropology* (1995).

Trials of Nation Making

Liberalism, Race, and Ethnicity in the Andes, 1810–1910

Brooke Larson

Stony Brook University

CAMBRIDGE
UNIVERSITY PRESS

CAMBRIDGE UNIVERSITY PRESS
Cambridge, New York, Melbourne, Madrid, Cape Town, Singapore,
São Paulo, Delhi, Dubai, Tokyo, Mexico City

Cambridge University Press
32 Avenue of the Americas, New York, NY 10013-2473, USA

www.cambridge.org
Information on this title: www.cambridge.org/9780521567305

First published 2004
Reprinted 2005, 2007, 2008

A catalog record for this publication is available from the British Library.
Library of Congress Cataloging in Publication Data
Larson, Brooke.
Trials of nation making : liberalism, race and ethnicity in the Andes,
1810–1910 / Brooke Larson.
p.   cm.
Includes bibliographical references and index.
ISBN 0-521-56171-X – ISBN 0-521-56730-0 (pbk.)
1. Indians of South America – Andes region – Government relations.
2. Andes region – Politics and government – 19th century.
3. Andes region – Race relations. I. Title.
F2230.1.G68L37   2003
980′.004′98–dc   2003041956

ISBN 978-0-521-56171-6 Hardback
ISBN 978-0-521-56730-5 Paperback

*To my Stony Brook graduate students,
for wonderful years of collegial friendship,
inspiration, and dialogue.*

Contents

vii

Illustrations

MAPS

FIGURES

Acknowledgments

As with any interpretive synthesis, this book builds largely on the fine-grained archival work of many scholars. Footnotes are kept to a minimum, although the extended Bibliographic Essay offers an overview of the historical and anthropological literature that has shaped, or is currently shaping, our understanding of indigenous societies under modernizing Andean republics during the nineteenth century. However, this book is not intended as an historical survey in the conventional sense. In keeping with the original aims of the *Cambridge History of the Native Peoples of the Americas*, it offers a "synthesis of current knowledge and approaches that is accessible to a wide range of scholars [and students], as well as to experts in the field." Necessarily this book is somewhat idiosyncratic – reflecting my own scholarly background, concerns, and lapses, as well as the richly suggestive but still extremely fragmented "state of the field." Even if set against the larger field of Latin American Studies, the subfield of Andean Studies remains relatively neglected, especially for the nineteenth century. But its rich interdisciplinary tradition in history and anthropology (and more recently in literary studies) has immeasurably enriched my own work in Andean Studies over many years. My approach in this book tends to privilege two sorts of scholarly literature: a classic historical and anthropological literature on Andean peasant history, political economy, and state formation (produced mainly in the 1970s and 1980s) and the recent turn toward cultural forms of power, representation, and contestation that, in turn, influence "new political histories from below" currently flourishing among historians of postcolonial Latin America. Where possible, this study also weaves nineteenth-century sources and images into the book's four case studies of Indians and nation making in the Andes.

My greatest debt lies with those Andean scholars whose scholarly work and political commitment have continued to inspire me since I first encountered Andean Studies in the early 1970s. It is their ongoing research, as well as my own, that forms the basis of this interpretive synthesis. Although the focus of my own research has shifted across time, my enduring fascination with Andean history and contemporary peasant politics has kept me anchored to this spectacular region long after I might ordinarily have gotten restless and moved on. My commitment to Andean Studies also springs from the enduring friendships and collegial support that have sustained me in this and other research projects. I continue to draw deep inspiration from my Bolivian colleagues, for whom the recovery of the past continues to guide their ongoing struggles for social justice in the present. And what would I do without the wonderful companionship of other Andean scholars in the United States and Europe who share these idiosyncratic inquiries and passions? (You know who you are!) I am also grateful to my original editors of the South American volumes of the *Cambridge History of the Native Peoples of the Americas,* Frank Salomon and Stuart Schwartz, for giving me an opportunity to move in new intellectual directions, as well as for undertaking the monumental project in the first place. I also thank Stuart Schwartz, in particular, for his enthusiastic support of the idea of expanding the original essay into a book. That process was guided by Cambridge Social Science editor, Frank Smith, and by the expert editorial work of Camilla Knapp and Sara Black. I also appreciate Brenda Elsey's help with the book's index. I thank them all.

Closer to home are the wonderful friends, colleagues, and graduate students with whom I have been so privileged to work in the History Department at Stony Brook over the past many years. There have been so many graduate students with whom I have worked inside and outside the classroom that I dare not try to name them all. But may they know how much they have nurtured and inspired me by their own research projects, critical commentary, honest questioning, and warm collegiality over many years. This study is the richer for my having studied Latin American history and anthropology with them.

Finally, as most scholars realize, it takes a village not only to raise a child but also to write a book. And no acknowledgment would be complete without loving recognition of the many friends, both near and far, who inhabit my everyday life and help yank me out of the cloistered isolation of scholarly writing. Above all, I am grateful to my extended and immediate family – to my loving parents and step-parents; my dear sisters, Kim and Jodie, and brothers-in-law, Mike and Johnny; my wonderful sons, Josh and Devon; and my life's companion, Carter Bancroft. They continue to mean the world to me.

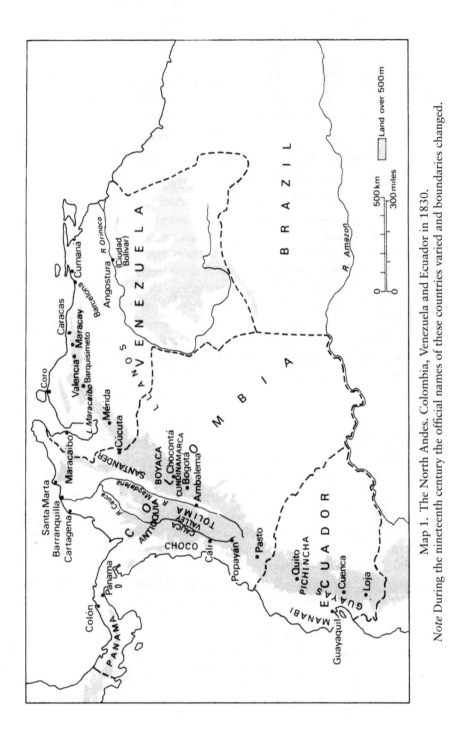

Map 1. The North Andes. Colombia, Venezuela and Ecuador in 1830.

Note During the nineteenth century the official names of these countries varied and boundaries changed.

Map 2. The Central and South Andes. Peru and Bolivia after Indepedence.

Trials of Nation Making

Introduction

This book is a much expanded and revised version of an essay originally published in the *Cambridge History of the Native Peoples of the Americas: South America* (edited by F. Salomon and S. Schwartz [Cambridge, 1999], III: 2, 558–703), which is part of a multi-volume study of indigenous histories and cultures throughout this hemisphere from ancient times to the present day. My original assignment was to write about indigenous responses to independence and liberal reforms throughout South America's western highlands, interior jungles, and southern pampas. Notwithstanding my editors' confidence in me, I immediately recognized my own limitations of time and expertise and convinced them to "carve up" South American ethnic territories, leaving me with the broad swath of territory that once formed the core regions of the Inca empire. My colleagues Jonathan Hill and Kristine Jones brought, respectively, their own talents and expertise to the Amazon lowlands and the Araucanian plains of the far south.[1] By contrast, this study focuses

---

[1] See Jonathan Hill, "Indigenous Peoples and the Rise of Independent Nation-States in Lowland South America," and Kristine Jones, "Warfare, Reorganization, and Readaptation at the Margins of Spanish Rule: the Southern

1

specifically on native peoples of the Andean highlands, stretching from the Chibcha peoples of northern Colombia to the Quechua and Aymara communities of southern Bolivia. Most were peasants who lived in sedentary villages or on Spanish estates, where they eked out a living from agriculture and herding. Many peasants also engaged in a variety of other subsistent activities, including barter and trade, pack driving, textile spinning and weaving, and day wage labor. Since highland peasants had lived under centralized states since before the Spanish conquest, they continued to provide a significant portion of their surplus labor or crops in the form of tribute and other obligations to their political overlords. These native peasantries, however remote or unchanged they might have seemed to nineteenth-century European travelers, were the bearers of a culture and social organization so transformed by conquest, colonialism, and later the violent transition to republican rule that "the depth of change still challenges the historiographic imagination."[2] With such a statement, the late Thierry Saignes advances an implicit challenge to historians to contemplate the depth of social and cultural change in the Andes, set in motion by European currents. To some extent, this book takes up that challenge by exploring the history of rural highland Andean people swept into the vortex of modernizing global, national, or regional economies and who, one way or another, "engaged their wider political world."[3]

Margins (1573–1882)," in F. Salomon and S. Schwartz, eds., *Cambridge History of the Native Peoples of the Americas: South America* (Cambridge, 1999), III: 2, 704–64 and 138–87, respectively.

[2] Thierry Saignes, "The Colonial Condition in the Quechua-Aymara Heartland (1570–1780)," in F. Salomon and S. Schwartz, eds., *Cambridge History of the Native Peoples of the Americas: South America* (Cambridge, 1999), III: 2, 59–137, quotation on 59.

[3] The phrase comes from Steve Stern's edited collection on peasant politics and political cultures in the Andes, *Resistance, Rebellion, and Consciousness in the Andean Peasant World, 18th to 20th Centuries* (Madison, 1987), 5–6.

But why confine the chronological scope to the nineteenth century? Social and economic historians have long been interested in tracing continuities across the conventional political divide between colony and republic. Some have reorganized historical time around the idea of the "long nineteenth century," stretching from the latter part of the eighteenth century to well into the early twentieth century, say from 1780 to 1930. Their "long nineteenth century" has the advantage of encompassing cultural continuities and structural constraints that shaped postcolonial history. Certainly this time frame accommodated anthropologists' interest in the extraordinary resilience of Andean cultural practices. But as Saignes warned, too much emphasis on issues of "cultural survival" tends to reify the singularity of Andean political culture in its mountainous environment while removing it from messy historical contexts of flux and change.[4] Recent theoretical problems of "postcolonialism," emanating from cultural theorists interested in the endurance of colonial hierarchies, knowledges, and representations in African and Asian societies emerging from long histories of formal colonialism under the West, have pointed to the continuity and contestation of colonial polarities in the process of forging modern nationhood.[5]

---

[4] The conceptual struggle to balance cultural continuities against historical forces of change in long-term studies of native Andean societies has been a vital source of interdisciplinary conversation and debate among Andeanists since the 1970s. For a synthesis of that debate, see Brooke Larson, "Andean Communities, Political Cultures, and Markets: the Changing Contours of a Field," in Brooke Larson and Olivia Harris with E. Tandeter, eds., *Ethnicity, Markets and Migration in the Andes: At the Crossroads of History and Anthropology* (Durham, 1995), 5–53, and various contributions in Segundo Moreno Yánez and Frank Salomon, eds., *Reproducción y transformación en las sociedades andinas, siglos XVI–XX* (Quito, 1991), 2 vols.

[5] See the influential volume edited by Gyan Prakash, *After Colonialism: Imperial Histories and Postcolonial Displacements* (Princeton, 1995). *Post-Colonial Studies Reader*, B. Ashcroft, G. Griffiths, and H. Tiffin, eds. (London, 1995) reveals the breadth and variety of "postcolonial" topics,

Among Latin American scholars, a renewed interest in the question of "the colonial legacy" has provoked a broader conceptual argument about the "problem of persistence" in Latin American history.[6] As Jeremy Adelman notes, too much emphasis on the deep structures and discourses of colonialism leaves out of the picture the power of people, and especially subaltern groups, to alter the course of nation making.

Perhaps more than almost anywhere else in the Americas, Andean peasant history has taught us differently. For even after interminable centuries of colonial rule, it was the Andean peasantries of highland Colombia, Ecuador, Peru, and Bolivia who rose up against symbols of colonial oppression and brought the emerging transatlantic "Age of Revolution" into the interior of South America. Comparable to the slave-led upheavals of Haiti in the 1790s, Andean peasant insurgency in the 1770s and 1780s forever changed the configuration of colonial power, at the top, and local

approaches, and concerns, all of which are loosely bound by their critical approaches to questions of power, meaning, and culture in societies where modernity encounters imperialism, or internal colonialism. Subaltern studies, an offshoot of postcolonial theory, shifts the locus of analysis to peasant and other "subaltern" groups as subjects of history in counter-hegemonic narratives. See the recent critical appraisal by Dipesh Chakrabarty, *Habitations of Modernity: Essays in the Wake of Subaltern Studies* (2002). Postcolonial and subaltern questions are creatively engaged in the Andean context by Silva Rivera, "La raíz: colonizadores y colonizados," in Xavier Albó and Raúl Barrios, eds., *Violencias encubiertas en Bolivia. Cultura y Política* (La Paz, 1993), 27–142, and Mark Thurner, *From Two Republics to One Divided: Contradictions of Postcolonial Nationmaking in Andean Peru* (Durham, 1997).

[6] Jeremy Adelman, ed., *Colonial Legacies: The Problem of Persistence in Latin American History* (New York, 1999). I implicitly refer to the older "structural" analyses of colonial heritages, legacies, and continuities in the larger context of Latin America's position of "economic dependence" in the world economy. For example, the flagship study of Stanley and Barbara Stein, *The Colonial Heritage of Latin America: Essays on Economic Dependence in Perspective* (New York, 1970).

indigenous polities and forms of ethnic mediation, at the bottom of society. At the level of the state, the Bourbon reforms, and a particularly harsh persecution of all things Inca, were tangible outcomes of the Andean rebellions. Equally significant was the bitter impact of that historical period for indigenous people. Collective peasant memories of rebellion and repression, although discontinuous and latent for much of the nineteenth century, lay buried just under the surface of quotidian consciousness until well into the twentieth century. In moments of political crisis and rupture, local indigenous peoples might tap into those long-term historical memories, or they might conjure Inca or Andean utopias, as armament in local struggles for land and justice. On this conceptual level, therefore, there is no logical case to be made for severing deep genealogies of Andean communal memory and struggle or, for that matter, for dichotomizing Andean political history into the familiar time units of colonial and republican. Indeed, this book will have occasion to reach back into late colonial history, and particularly to that historical juncture of crisis and transformation in the late eighteenth-century Andean highlands, in order to understand developments in the period after independence. Yet that late colonial "Age of Andean Insurrection" is itself a critical historical moment that needs to be set apart from national narratives and examined in its own right. Indeed, it was thought that the "Age of Andean Insurrection" was significant enough to warrant its own extended treatment in the Cambridge volumes,[7] and there is a flourishing new historical subfield reappraising that era of upheaval (see the Bibliographic Essay).

This book approaches the history of highland Andean peoples as fundamentally intertwined with a larger set of economic, political, social, and cultural processes, not as a set of inert peasant

---

[7] See Luís Miguel Glave, "The 'Republic of Indians' in Revolt, c. 1680–1790," in F. Salomon and S. Schwartz, eds., *Cambridge History of the Native Peoples of the Americas: South America* (Cambridge, 1999), 3 vols., III: 2, 502–57.

communities or cultures to which world-historical forces suddenly arrived. Contrary to nationalist renderings of the independence wars along the Pacific seaboard of South America, my premise is that popular and peasant uprisings fundamentally conditioned the undulating movement of revolution and counterrevolution during the first quarter of the nineteenth century, making the would-be Creole patriots ever more ambivalent about the prospects and promises of independence. Thus, as many historians have argued, it seems that the wars for independence followed a contrapuntal logic – to rupture colonial rule without unleashing another "age of insurrection" in the interior peasant highlands. Where that perilous project could not be secured, Creole elites often preferred to forgo independence altogether. In the greater Andean region, the political destiny of the colonies seemed to hang in the balance for a quarter of a century. Even after formal independence came, the fear of bandit hordes, no less than full-scale Indian rebellion, cast deep shadows across Creole political ambitions for the rest of the nineteenth century.

Like much of the rest of Spanish America in the aftermath of war, the Andean republics succumbed to other threats, more structural in nature – economic recession, political instability, elite fragmentation, militarized haciendas, and deep regional rivalry. On the other hand, the chaos of war and economic retrenchment did not shatter colonial forms of power and extraction in the countryside, nor even mark the end of the colonial institution of Indian tribute. Bolivarian ambitions and rhetoric aside, three insolvent republics promptly reverted to the Indian head tax, levied primarily on land-based *ayllus,* or indigenous communities. Creole statesmen only began to dismantle their nations' tributary regimes under the converging material and ideological pressures (and opportunities for new revenue sources) emanating from export-driven capitalism after 1850. State reforms to end tribute at midcentury thus created a crucial material and symbolic turning point, as Creole politicians began to prepare their republics for (what they hoped would be) the onset of liberalism, capitalism, and modern state making.

Although liberal political leaders heralded the abolition of African slavery and Indian tribute as the triumph of modernity over the colonial past, indigenous peasant leaders took a more cautious, ambivalent stance. However hated, abused, and onerous the institution of tribute, it had imparted traditional colonial rights and obligations to native peoples by virtue of their status of "Indian" vassal under the protective laws of Spanish absolutism. Abolition of tribute under modernizing republics may have lifted the onerous head tax (although it was rapidly reimposed under new guises), but it also removed the formal right of indigenous people to claim communal lands, local self-rule, and state protection. In the eyes of modernizing elites, this particular colonial heritage (i.e., inherited colonial-Andean rights to communal land access) stood in the way of economic progress, particularly in the South Andes where traditional communities still held on to large swaths of highland. In accord with liberal and capitalist precepts, Indian land and labor needed to be converted into transferable commodities, whose redistribution would be mediated by the play of market forces and secured by individual property rights. The abolition of communal landholding was no mere theoretical threat, for by 1870 powerful world-historical forces did begin to pose massive threats of land divestiture and labor extraction to highland communities. In many parts of the Andean highlands, liberalism and modernity seemed to unleash a new cycle of territorial and cultural conquest, which set in motion a series of intense conflicts between peasant groups, regional overlords, and the centralizing modernizing state. At a deeper level, these converging pressures of modernity created *an arena of interpretive struggle* over indigenous political rights, social memory, location, and identity, which reflected the postcolonial predicament of so many native Andean peasants caught between the contradictory legal-political discourses of colonialism, liberalism, and racism. My aim in this book is to trace the layered contours of struggle, adaptation, and contestation among highland Andean peasants that lay at the very core of nation-building processes in Colombia, Ecuador, Peru, and Bolivia.

Before we set off on this journey, we might rightfully ask ourselves why we should conjoin the ideas of liberalism, racism, and ethnicity? After all, independence ruptured the old imperial order and opened up the possibility of creating societies built on all-encompassing constitutions and ideals of individual equality before the law. The short answer to this question is to suggest that such political possibilities engendered deeper anxieties and unresolved tensions inherent in the generic postcolonial situation, but especially in places where colonialism, slavery, and caste had been deeply entrenched for several centuries. In regions like Mexico, the Caribbean, or the Andes, the institutional and normative apparatus of coerced labor would not soon be dismantled. And as Paul Gilroy has so beautifully studied, the institutions of labor coercion, colonialism, and racism gave those subordinated people who experienced them a vantage point on Western modernity that starkly exposed the limits and contradictions of universalist and nationalist ideals. Both the Caribbean and the Andes, and other regions where internal cultures of colonialism prevailed, thus became "critical transformative sites[s] of that modernity," not the least because of the ambiguous encounter of African and Andean populations with it.[8] By anchoring these four historical cases of postcolonial Andean republics deep in the subsoil of colonial heritages,

---

[8] Paul Gilroy, *The Black Atlantic: Modernity and Double Consciousness* (Cambridge, 1993); see also Ann Laura Stoler and Frederick Cooper, "Between Metropole and Colony: Rethinking a Research Agenda," in their edited volume, *Tensions of Empire: Colonial Cultures in a Bourgeois World* (Berkeley, 1997), 1–56, quotation on 8.

fractious states, and subaltern subjectivities, this book offers a corrective counterpoint, perhaps, to an earlier tendency in the historical literature to grant too much agency to the power of the "hegemonizing" state to bind subordinated popular cultures to the dominant state through discursive and institutional means in the late nineteenth and early twentieth centuries. By bringing popular culture and state formation into a tense relational "field of force," the late Bill Roseberry suggested that we think about "cultural hegemony" as a multilayered process through which dominant and subordinated groups argued over the terms of power and justice within a "common discursive framework."[9] Like many recent interpreters of Gramsci's notions of power, culture, and social practice, Roseberry envisions hegemony not as a static state of consent, but rather as a lived "language of contention" through which subaltern classes actively challenged dominant discourses, symbols, and state institutions. It is this analytical framework, highlighting mediations between power and meaning, social practice and state formation, that has guided historical work on the theme of nation making in postcolonial Latin America in recent years.[10]

[9] William Roseberry, "Hegemony and the Language of Contention," in Gilbert Joseph and Daniel Nugent, eds., *Everyday Forms of State Formation: Revolution and the Negotiation of Rule in Modern Mexico* (Durham, 1994), 355–66.

[10] To sample this approach to the problem of cultural hegemony in Latin America, there is no better example than Joseph and Nugent's 1994 volume, *Everyday Forms of State Making*, although the historical literature is voluminous by now. Much of this historical literature borrows its conceptual starting point from cultural Marxism, including the applied re-readings of Antonio Gramsci's *Selections from the Prison Notebooks* (London, 1971) by such non-Latin Americanist scholars as Stuart Hall, Raymond Williams, James Scott, Philip Corrigan, and Derek Sayer. See especially Kate Crehan's clear and insightful study of how Gramscian notions of culture and power have informed recent anthropological studies, *Gramsci, Culture and Anthropology* (Berkeley, 2002).

Early-twentieth-century Mexico has provided an especially salient case for exploring the hegemonic capacity of postrevolutionary "mestizo nationalism" to absorb and deploy indigenous and popular politics in a common framework of meaning, albeit in a singularly fluid political and social context. But the framework also lends itself to broad comparative studies of "everyday forms of state formation" and the sort of societies, polities, and political cultures those tense hegemonic processes eventually produced. Florencia Mallon's searching comparison of peasant struggles over land, power, and meaning in Mexico and Peru immediately comes to mind.[11] Analyzing the interactions of alternative discourses of liberalism and justice in comparable contexts of state formation, peasant land divestiture, and foreign invasion, Mallon argued that in certain instances the liberalizing Mexican state was forced to come to terms with radical peasant projects and to partially incorporate them into nationalist discourses in order to tame, or submerge, them during the mid- to late nineteenth century. She then uses the Mexican template to draw comparative insights from the Andean case of republican Peru, arguing that colonial legacies, civil war, and rural rebellion ended up producing a highly authoritarian, profoundly racist, and exclusionary political culture in Peru. Just as Gramsci used the idea of hegemony to explain the *failure* of the Piedmont bourgeoisie to construct a common language of rule, so Mallon explores the incapacity of Peruvian politicians and intellectuals to broaden notions of national belonging in the late nineteenth century. Rather, the Peruvian state constructed a "new system of neocolonial domination,... built once again on the principles of an ethnic and spatial policy of divide and rule."[12]

---

[11] Florencia Mallon, *Peasant and Nation: The Making of Postcolonial Mexico and Peru* (Berkeley, 1995).

[12] Ibid., 328.

By most measures, both comparative and historical, it seems apparent that the Andean republics had uncommon difficulty negotiating power and legitimacy within a common framework of liberalism or nationalism during the late nineteenth century. Neither the turn away from colonial-tributary traditions to liberal free-trade doctrines around midcentury, nor the emergence of "civilizing" discourses at the end of the nineteenth century, succeeded in binding indigenous cultural values or identities to the discursive domain of the nation-state in the greater Andean region. To argue the contrary viewpoint is to grant too much agency to liberal or republican discourses and their putative capacity to rupture internal colonialism or to contain contestatory Andean cultures and identities. On this last point, we must take particular care in the Andean region because, as Mark Thurner has shown for the case of Huaylas, Peru, both Andean Creole elites and indigenous peasantries engaged in a discursive mirror-game of ambivalent *republicanismo*, which reflected its radical polyvalence. Urban elites and peasant communities inscribed varied political meanings and moral expectations in that word – as they tried to negotiate postcolonial arrangements that would govern Indian-state relations.[13] On the other hand, such ambiguities of meaning opened up all sorts of possibilities for local forms of negotiation and maneuver under the right circumstances. The general condition of statelessness in the Andean countryside following the wars of independence, and the official restoration of Indian tribute (often thinly veiled by universalistic euphemisms), went a long way toward postponing the rupture of Indian-state dialogues and local understandings of *republicanismo*. By midcentury, however, liberalizing states began to discard the juridical remnants of the colonial "dual republic" in their halting efforts to bring all Indian subjects under one unifying rule of law. As mentioned earlier, this turn toward liberal discourse

---

[13] Thurner, *From Two Republics to One Divided*, chap. 2.

had blunt material roots, as world market conditions opened up channels of commercial and industrial capitalism. In the rural hinterlands, liberal policy involved the redrawing of lines on a map, the redefinition and allocation of land ownership, and the conversion of communal forms of landed possession to individual property. All across Amerindian regions, the advent of liberal reforms intensified the ongoing competition for legitimacy, not just for the right to claim contested lands but also for the right to define the political rules of the game in the first place. Popular readings of *republicanismo*, particularly as they pertained to colonial entitlements to communal lands and lifeways, gradually lost ground to metropolitan discourses of liberalism, racism, and civilization.

But it would be a mistake to reduce peasant politics to the proverbial polarity of Indian resistance or accommodation to the forces of liberal reform during the mid- to late nineteenth century. To do so would be to deduce peasant political subjectivity simply from class determinants or, even more speciously, from putative cultural attributes. The four Andean case studies in this book reveal the dynamic, unpredictable interplay between social contexts and subaltern subjectivities, between individual and communal agendas, between momentary configurations of power and possibilities of social action. Clearly, the advent of "popular liberalism" among certain groups of peasants at key political moments did not necessarily signify Indian endorsement of free-trade doctrines, the sovereignty of the individual, propertied citizenship, or assimilation through *mestizaje* (i.e., race mixing). In the same way, native Andeanness did not preclude local *intracommunal* forms of struggle and conflict, individual opportunism, or the plasticity of ethnic self-identity. Market and export resurgence in the late nineteenth century did open up new spaces for individual smallholding, migration, and social mobility through *mestizaje* toward the end of the nineteenth century, and many peasants followed those routes out of their condition of rural Indianness into the ambiguous racial-spatial domain of urban underclass life.

Nor, on the other hand, did indigenous people make reflexive use of the colonial law and discourse (the Hapsburg legal construct of the "*república de indios*") in order to advocate the wholesale restoration of colonial rule – complete with its regulatory institutions of extraction, social control, and hierarchy. But in those regions where indigenous material experience, social connections, and political understandings were largely defined by the *ayllu*-community, there often ensued a dangerous disjuncture between the political aspirations of liberalizing elites and the moral expectations of native Andean leaders. And with the breakdown of a common language of contention, state reform could easily turn into threat, peasant grievance into violence, local conflicts into "ethnic mobilization," and elite anxiety into military repression. So it was that the Andes entered the twentieth century without having built a hegemonic "language of contention" to replace the shattered colonial heritage of "dual republics" or to contain the resurgence of ethnic politics.

Fundamental to the failure of the Andean republics to negotiate cultural hegemony was the profound ambivalence that fissured the dreams and discourses of Creole nation-builders themselves. Postcolonial theory has gone a long way toward exposing the dialectics of inclusion and exclusion that lay at the very core of cultural nationalism and Western modernity in a variety of contexts. For the central paradox of Western modernity was to impose universal definitions of free labor and citizenship, as well as to mold national cultures into homogeneous wholes (along Eurocentric ideals), while creating the symbols and categories of innate difference in order to set the limits on those "universalistic" ideals.[14] In citing Ben Anderson's felicitous metaphor of cultural nationalism as imagined

---

[14] Etienne Balibar, "The Paradoxes of Universality," in David Goldberg, ed., *Anatomy of Racism* (Minneapolis, 1990), 283–294; and Partha Chatterjee, *The Nation and Its Fragments: Colonial and Postcolonial Histories* (Princeton, 1993).

community, we must pay equal attention to the ways in which Andean Creole elites (re)produced, or reconfigured, the enduring structures of colonial class and racial domination.[15] A major task of this book is to consider the production of racialized values, images, and discourses normalizing new colonial-racial hierarchies designed to fill the vacuum left by the old tributary/caste system.[16] Creole nation-builders did so, however, not by producing a dense and coherent canon of scientific doctrines or *indigenista* literatures. Positivist ideologies burst onto the national scene in the late 1880s and 1890s, but with a few pioneering exceptions, *indigenista* writers did not gain national influence until well into the early twentieth century. Even so, it is important to examine emerging elite articulations of liberalism, nationalism, and racism in messy political contexts of rural struggle, market expansion, and political crisis. This study seeks to do so by exploring how nineteenth-century racial imagery, thinking, and practice were embedded in, and in turn reorganized, internal colonial hierarchies subordinating Indianness (and its variant racial admixtures) to the Creole domain of power, civilization, and citizenship. Just as colonial ideology and law once codified a tripartite hierarchy on the basis of racial purity and mixture (white, mestizo, Indian), so now did modern race thinking reinforce biocultural and spatial distinctions designed to locate Indians, and hybrid

---

[15] Benedict Anderson, *Imagined Communities: Reflections on the Origins and Spread of Nationalism* (London, 1991), esp. chaps. 6 and 8.

[16] In thinking about the intersection of racial representation, liberal ideology, and/or the development of nationalism in the west, I have drawn on numerous conceptual and historical studies, many of which are cited later. But see especially, David Goldberg, *Racist Culture: Philosophy and the Politics of Meaning* (Oxford, 1993); Etienne Balibar and I. Wallerstein, *Race, Nation Class: Ambiguous Identities* (London, 1991); and Michael Omi and H. Winant, *Racial Formation in the USA from the 1960s to the 1980s* (New York, 1986). For synoptic discussions of "racial and ethnic" relations and discourses in Latin America, I often have relied on Peter Wade's synthesis, *Race and Ethnicity in Latin America* (London, 1997).

popular cultures, on the boundaries of national belonging. The quandary for Andean Creole elites was precisely how to build an apparatus of power that simultaneously incorporated and marginalized peasant political cultures in the forced march to modernity.

The book brings closure to these overlapping national narratives of Indians and nations around 1910, perhaps as arbitrary a cut-off point as any other year might seem to be. Certainly, there is no obvious benchmark, since the Andes experienced no convulsive event approaching the 1910 Mexican Revolution. But as I hope to illustrate, the converging pressures of modernization and modernity (the latter refers broadly to discursive struggles over the idea of a universal modernizing process) profoundly redefined the ideological climate, brute power relations, agrarian conditions, and Andean identities vis-à-vis emerging nation-states in ways that endured well into the twentieth century. Retrospectively, it is possible to calibrate the myriad material and ideological changes that came about in the transition from tribute-based Andean republics to racially polarized nation-states over the second half of the nineteenth century. And yet if we project ahead in time to the 1920s and 1930s, it is also possible to appreciate the advent of new forms of peasant, labor, and populist politics; the rise of nationalist and populist state projects, armed with rural outreach programs of educational, hygienic, and moral reform; and, not least, the economic and political consequences of the tectonic shifts in world market capitalism after 1930. The study of Andean indigenous history and politics during the first half of the twentieth century necessarily becomes more involved in broader national and transnational processes, as Bolivian anthropologist, Xavier Albó, has so insightfully demonstrated.[17]

---

[17] See his essay, "Andean People in the Twentieth Century," in F. Salomon and S. Schwartz, eds., *Cambridge History of the Native Peoples of the Americas: South America*, III: 2, 765–871.

The question of historical legacies, or persistence, is almost a prerequisite of any colonial or postcolonial history of the Andes, or for that matter, of Latin America. As I argued earlier, it is perilous to explore the shifting terrain of Indian-state relations in the nineteenth-century Andes without at least a cursory look at the tremors and transformations that shook the rural Andean world in the eighteenth century, or without a sense of how colonial-racial divisions persisted at the level of both ideology and practice. Yet unlike most examinations of colonial legacies, the historian's grasp of liberalism's multiple legacies for post-1910, or post-1930, Latin America is usually more tenuous. Be that as it may, this book brings closure by examining the "burden of race" that the modernizing Andean republics carried into the early twentieth century. My argument is that stark binary discourses of race and space not only informed late nineteenth-century liberal and civilizing projects but implicitly framed the later *indigenista* grammar of race and ethnic difference (in ways that tended to redeem Indians in order to promote binary schemes of racial uplift and purity). Racial binarism was starkest in the southern Peruvian and Bolivian highlands. Marisol De La Cadena's recent work on the politics of race and culture in twentieth-century Cuzco, for example, elucidates this distinctive Andean variant of *indigenismo*, which searched for regional and historical identity in the cultural achievements of the Incas and, more ambiguously, in the exoticism of insulated rural Indian peasants who were to be preserved and uncontaminated by *mestizaje* and other urban influences.[18] Drawing on the research of De La

---

[18] Marisol De La Cadena, *Indigenous Mestizos: The Politics of Race and Culture in Cuzco, Peru, 1919–1991* (Durham, 2002). Other recent works that explore discourses of anti-*mestizaje* in the Andes include Benjamin Orlove, "Putting Race in Place: Order in Colonial and Postcolonial Peruvian Geography," *Social Research* 60 (1993), 301–36; Marta Irurozqui, *La armonía de las desigualdades. Elites y conflictos de poder en Bolivia* (Cusco, 1994); Brooke Larson, "Redeemed

Cadena and other scholars working on literary, diagnostic, and visual discourses of race and culture, this book explores the binary grammar of race that emerged in many parts of the Andes around the turn of the twentieth century. Only Colombia seemed to entertain an alternative racial project of "whitening" through *mestizaje*. By contrast, myths of *mestizaje* rarely fired the Creole imagination in the rest of the Andean region, where writers and politicians preferred idioms of race, region, culture to reinforce class inequalities and to position its indigenous peoples at the margins of nation and modernity. Indeed, it is plausible to argue that Creole elites deliberately clung to idioms of internal colonialism (newly dressed in fashionable racialized language) precisely in order to control Indian labor and preempt any sort of Mexican-styled upheaval among its rural masses. And if measured against the Mexican revolution, it can be said that in the short run they largely succeeded.

An equally powerful counterlegacy, however, was the vital capacity of indigenous peoples to call upon their own "institutionalized space" in the nation as "Indians" so as to continue pressing for collective rights and recognition.[19] Here is where we can perceive

Indians, barbarianized Cholos: Crafting neocolonial modernity in Liberal Bolivia," in N. Jacobsen and C. Aljovín, eds., *Political Cultures of the Andes, 1750–1950* (Durham, in press). Compare to Central American and Mexican motifs of *mestizaje*, respectively, in Jeffrey Gould, *To Die This Way: Nicaraguan Indians and the Myth of Mestizaje, 1880–1965* (Durham, 1998), and Alan Knight, "Racism, Revolution and *Indigenismo*: Mexico, 1910–1940," in R. Graham, ed., *The Idea of Race in Latin America, 1870–1940* (Austin, 1990), 71–114. Cf. Greg Grandin, *The Blood of Guatemala. A History of Race and Nation* (Durham, 2000), which is more comparable to dominant racial discourses of the Andes.

[19] This insight comes from Peter Wade, who argues that indigenous people occupied a relatively "privileged" institutionalized position in Latin American nation-states, derived from their prior colonial status, in comparison to enslaved Afro-American populations. Wade notes that after tribute and slavery were abolished in the Andean republics in the mid-nineteenth century, "there was a distinct difference between the images of blacks and Indians in

the limits of structural comparison. For if we insist on "measuring" the scope and importance of nineteenth-century Andean peasant politics against, say, the cotemporal upheavals of Mexico, or, for that matter, against the great Andean rebellions of the late eighteenth century, they inevitably come up short. And from there it is easy to slide into assumptions about Andean quiescence, alienation, or defeat toward the end of that century. But just over the temporal horizon, on the other side of 1910, there loomed a new cycle of indigenous mobilization against the threats of landlessness and economic coercion. Even as they increasingly turned to issues and identities of class and citizenship, rural Andean people evolved new discourses and practices of ethnic self-empowerment, which eventually worked their way into the core national political struggles over culture, power, and identity.

Nearly one hundred years later, beginning in the 1980s, transregional indigenous movements in Colombia, Ecuador, and Bolivia have come to permeate all facets of political life, as well as to engage wider transnational issues of indigenous rights, human rights, and ecological conservation. In recent years, rural highland peasants have begun to negotiate coalitions with indigenous peoples of the tropical lowlands in their common search for political and territorial justice in the face of geographic dispersion, cultural homogenization, and global capitalism. Contemporary Indian movements in the Andes are finally thrusting indigenous intellectuals into public life, forcing governments to value, or at least recognize, their

---

debates about the identity of the new nations," in that Indians were seen as superior to blacks and, as such, more worthy of redemptive and assimilative programs of reform (Wade, *Race and Ethnicity in Latin America*, 31). From the point of view of subaltern practice, furthermore, indigenous people could mobilize legal-discursive resources, as well as ethno-cultural lineages, in order to defend their communal lands and other Andean-colonial patrimonies, whereas black populations had few such traditions to invoke or reinvent. There was no Afro-American analogue to the *república de indios*.

nation's heritage of cultural diversity and to promote innovative development projects grounded in a new ideology of "indigenization" (the revitalization of cultural traditions).[20] (The striking Peruvian exception may have to do with the recent Shining Path movement, which had a devastating impact on many peasant regions, produced a powerful military backlash, and led to different sorts of defensive peasant organizations.[21]) Rather than disappearing into *mestizaje* or marginality, contemporary indigenous activists have kept alive communal memories of struggle and hope for redefining the boundaries of belonging in genuinely multiethnic nation-states. Perhaps it is these indigenous aspirations that should be seen as the most enduring legacy of nineteenth-century peasant politics.

[20] For anthropological approaches to ethnicity as a relational category of sameness and difference in varied contexts of subaltern mobilization, national identity making, and class stratification, see Thomas Eriksen, *Ethnicity and Nationalism: Anthropological Perspectives* (London, 1993); and Marcus Banks, *Ethnicity: Anthropological Constructions* (Routledge, 1996). On specific Latin American cases of modern Indian "ethnopolitics" at the international, national, and grassroots levels, see Michael Kearney, "Indigenous Ethnicity and Mobilization in Latin America," *Latin American Perspectives* 23 (1996), 5–16. For an exceptionally upbeat account of grassroots multicultural development, see Kevin Healy, *Llamas, Weavings, and Organic Chocolate. Multicultural Grassroots Development in the Andes and Amazon of Bolivia* (Notre Dame, 2001). On the rise of contemporary indigenous militancy and the new "politics of diversity" in Latin America, see "The First Nations, 1492–1992," *Report on the Americas* 25 (1991); Alison Brysk, *From Tribal Village to Global Village: Indian Rights and International Relations in Latin America* (Stanford, 2000); Donna Van Cott, *The Friendly Liquidation of the Past: The Politics of Diversity in Latin America* (Pittsburgh, 2001); and Kay Warren and Jean Jackson, eds., *Indigenous Movements, Self-Representation, and the State in Latin America* (Austin, 2002).

[21] See Gustavo Gorriti, *The Shining Path: A History of the Millenarian War in Peru* (Chapel Hill, 1999), and Steve Stern, ed., *Shining and Other Paths: War and Society in Peru, 1980–1995* (Durham, 1998).

1

Andean Landscapes, Real and Imagined

It is impossible to tell the story of the struggle to conceive of, and build, modern nation-states in the Andean region without first considering the power of its alpine topography to shape and challenge human endeavors. As Karen Spalding eloquently showed in her study of colonial Huarochirí, "the relationship between human groups and their environment in the Andes is basic to any understanding of the patterns of Andean society."[1] Archaeologists have marveled at the unique ability of Andean civilizations to exert "human mastery over global extremes in environmental conditions" – spanning mountain, marine, desert, and jungle ecologies, all of which required distinctive adaptive strategies.[2] The brilliance of Andean civilizations, culminating with the Inca, was precisely their ability to harness the extraordinary ecological diversity in this part of the world and to turn it to their collective advantage under centralized systems of rule. By setting this context, we are also

---

[1] Karen Spalding, *Huarochirí: An Andean Study under Inca and Spanish Rule* (Stanford, 1984), 9.
[2] Michael Moseley, *The Incas and Their Ancestors: The Archaeology of Peru* (London, 1992), 25.

reminded of the millennial history of human adaptation and florescence in the Andes, even as indigenous cultures were profoundly transformed under successive states, including the Inca and later the Spanish. This was no pristine social landscape of permanent tribes or pure ethnicities. Long before the Europeans invaded the Andes in 1532, Andean chiefdoms inhabited a world of constant flux, tension, and transformation during the dizzying expansion of the Inca empire, Tawantinsuyu.

Beginning in the 1530s, the Andes were drawn onto the unifying stage of Western imperialism, followed by three centuries of colonial rule under Spanish absolutism. Native societies were forced to cope with epidemic, war, emigration, population decline, labor extractions, forced resettlements, cultural regulation, and repression – not to mention all the humiliations, exclusions, and dependencies upon which colonial relationships were built. At the same time, however, indigenous and mestizo people proved capable of exploiting the language and law of Spanish colonialism for their own ends and of locating their own political activities within the context of the wider Spanish-speaking world. Historians have documented in rich detail the fundamental challenges and profound transformations that colonialism brought to the Andes. But to recognize that crucial, if obvious, point is not to deny the central premise of this book: the late nineteenth-century liberal assaults on indigenous forms of subsistence and community threatened, as perhaps only the European conquest had done, the intricate webs that bound most Andean peasantries to their mountainous world and all that it had come to symbolize.

CHARTING THE CONTOURS OF HIGHLAND ECOLOGIES, CULTURES, AND POLITIES

Let us begin by charting the geocultural contours of the northern, central, and southern Andes that compose the four republics

(Colombia, Ecuador, Peru, and Bolivia) under examination (see Maps 1, 2, and 3). For some forty million years, the Andean mountain chain has formed the warped backbone of western South America, stretching some 5,500 miles from Colombia in the north to northern Chile in the south. Its western border was etched by the Pacific coastline, which begins its journey southward as a band of broad lush rainforest before turning into a narrow desert plain in southern Ecuador, around the Gulf of Guayaquil. The desert coast continues southward into Peru, where it gradually broadens into the Atacama desert of northern Chile. This moonscape bordering the gray Pacific Ocean would be unfit for human habitation were it not for the rivers that traverse the sands on their way from the *cordillera* (or mountain chain) to the sea. In fact, these fertile valleys cradled several millennial civilizations, ancestors of the Inca.

Looming over the coastal plain is the western *cordillera*, which rise to an average elevation of more than 12,000 feet above sea level. Yet just as the tropical coast of the north turns arid as it moves southward, so do the mountains shed their vegetation as they twist and thrust their way down the western edge of the continent. Ecuador's green humid mountains reemerge as massive jumbles of mountain shaded in hues of copper, yellow, and brown and crowned by jagged, snow-capped peaks. But where the mountainous land-scape is more breathtaking, the climate is harsher, and subsistent farming is all the more challenging.

Along its northern reaches in Venezuela and Colombia, the Andes divide into three parallel ranges, carved by the fast-flowing Cauca and Magdalena Rivers. This broken terrain, sliced by river gorges and walls of mountain, created isolated pockets of human habi-tation, which continued to defy Creole dreams of imposing order and unity on Colombia's broken mosaic of indigenous, African, and white populations long after the great liberator, Simón Bolívar, had given up hope in 1826. Ecuador's mountainous topography was not quite so formidable to its nation-builders. There, the Andes merge

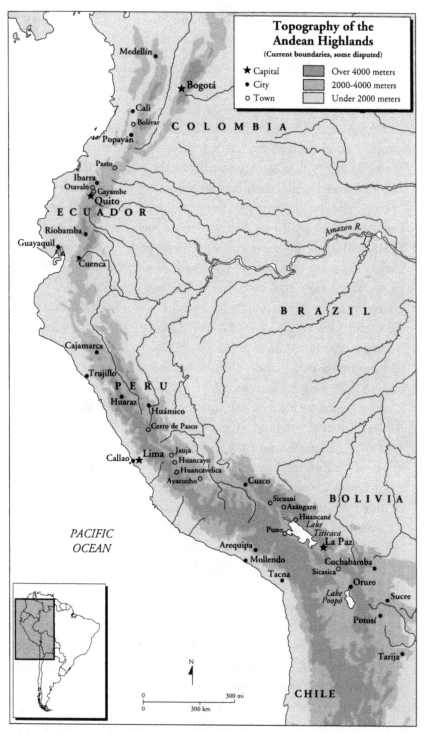

Map 3. Topography of the Andean Highlands

into two columns and shelter a series of broad intermontane basins (Quito, Riobamba, and Cuenca), as well as several high-altitude plateaus (*los páramos*).

Taking a giant leap southward into Peru, we see the mountains morph into giants and the fertile land disappear into deep ravines sliced by rivers flowing eastward into the upper Amazon basin. Every once in a while, there is some relief from this alpine labyrinth in irrigated temperate valleys. For example, in the central sierra of Peru, the Mantaro River Valley offers a vast horizontal expanse of land, ideal for intensive cultivation and pastoral activity. It also carved the main passageway into the interior mountains en route from coastal Lima to Cuzco during Inca and colonial times. Other intermontane valley networks in central and southern Peru cleaved the region's high-altitude landscape, creating ecological pockets of warm, moist, fertile land at midrange altitudes. These ecological niches proved indispensable to the economic organization of life among successive Andean societies.

If we were to identify the ancient heartland of the southern Andes, it probably would have to be situated on the *altiplano* surrounding the vast inland Lake Titicaca, lying at 12,000 feet above sea level. A thousand years before the Inca empire, the shores of Lake Titicaca were the site of a flourishing civilization, probably centered around the religious and political center known today as Tiawanaku. During later periods of political dispersion and decentralization, the vast *altiplano* surrounding the lake was home to powerful and far-flung ethnic chiefdoms (*senoríos*). Still later, the Inca regarded the Collasuyu (as this area was known), with its Pukina- and Aymara-speaking chiefdoms, as one of the richest regions in the Andean world. And the Inca were quick to covet, and then to conquer, these highland polities, as they advanced the edge of their empire, Tawantinsuyu, into the southern Andes during the fifteenth century. The Collasuyu also encompassed the more forbidding southern stretches of the *altiplano*, where in certain seasons the

Antarctic winds scour the high plains and where vast salt lakes play mind games of optical illusion. Yet even there, the eastern slopes of the Andes offered ecological relief, thanks to their temperate climate and fertile river valleys. From north to south, the Amazon side of the Andes provides a rich complement of ecological zones to be tapped for its extraordinary biodiversity.

This condor's view of Andean landscapes reveals a magnificent alpine complex of climatic, topographic, and ecological diversity. Indeed, nineteenth-century European explorers and naturalists were awestruck by its spectacular mountains, jungles, and coasts – this land of such dramatic contrasts in climate and vegetation almost defied the European imagination. In the early 1800s, the German naturalist Alexander von Humboldt produced spectacular images of South America as nature – wild, abundant, dwarfing, and defying human powers of perception. He drew most of his literary and visual images from the mountains, jungles, and interior plains of the North Andes.[3] In contemporary scholarly literature, by contrast, some anthropologists have deemphasized ecological and ethnographic diversity in favor of a more unifying concept of the Andes as a "culture zone." They point to Andean civilizations that harnessed the resources of geographically dispersed ecological tiers to support highly dense settlements. Indeed, this uniquely Andean solution to the problem of subsistence in a territory broken up by altitude, aridity, and extreme temperature variations represented a major "human achievement," in the words of anthropologist John Murra, which permitted the florescence of a long line of civilizations, culminating with the empire of the Inca.[4]

---

[3] Alexander von Humboldt, *Vues des cordilleres et monumens des peoples indigenes de l'Amerique* (Paris, 1810).

[4] John V. Murra, *Formaciones económicas y políticas del mundo andino* (Lima, 1975). For a concise overview of Andean ethnology, which tended to approach the "Andean world" for its singular and unifying principles of social organization in the context of ecological adaptation, see Frank Salomon,

More recent ethnohistorical scholarship, including the work of John Murra himself, has shied away from grand homologies to probe the variety and complexity of ethnic polities flourishing in different parts of the Andean world before the Spanish arrival. These ethnohistorical studies revealed that highland Andean civilizations seemed to thrive on their ability to harness "the vertical landscape" and to turn it to their collective advantage. They did so, however, under different ecological, social, and political conditions, which in turn produced distinctive ethnic polities and political cultures under the successive empires of the Inca and Spanish.[5] From this perspective, it is possible to perceive ecological and cultural patterns that differentiated the small-scale ethnic polities of the North Highlands from the sprawling ethnic kingdoms of the South Highlands. In the North Andes, the relatively benign microclimates, insular highland basins, regular rainfall, and year-round maize agriculture gave rise to relatively small-scale chiefdoms in the highlands of, what are today, the nations of Ecuador and Colombia. In the South Andes, the cold dry climate and high-altitude ecology (together with its rich pasture and crop lands surrounding the vast inland sea Lake Titicaca, its southern salt pans, eastern flank of temperate river valleys, and far-flung tropical lowlands)

"Andean Ethnology in the 1970s: A Retrospective," *Latin American Research Review* 17 (1982), 75–182. A fine older example of an ecologically driven approach to Andean anthropology may be found in S. Masuda, I. Shimada, and C. Morris, eds., *Andean Ecology and Civilization: An Interdisciplinary Perspective on Andean Ecological Complementarity* (Tokyo, 1985).

[5] Spalding, *Huarochirí*; Steve Stern, *Peru's Indian Peoples and the Challenge of Spanish Conquest: Huamanga to 1640* (Madison, 1982); Frank Salomon, *Native Lords of Quito in the Age of the Incas* (Cambridge, 1986); John V. Murra, "An Aymara Kingdom in 1567," *Ethnohistory* 15 (1968), 115–186; Susan Ramírez, *The World Turned Upside Down* (Stanford, 1996); and J. Murra, N. Wachtel, and J. Revel, eds., *Anthropological History of Andean Polities* (Cambridge, 1986).

cradled expansive and powerful Aymara kingdoms. They posted settlement colonies (*mitimaq*) in distant places to take advantage of the rich variety of altitudes, climates, and ecologies up and down the vertical landscape. Even under Inca and later Spanish rule, these magnificent mountain polities (the Canas, Collas, Lupaqas, Pacajes, Soras, Carangas, Quillacas, etc.) continued to distribute maize, potatoes, coca leaves, hot chili peppers *(ají)*, wool, textiles, salt, and other precious goods, emanating from different ecological zones across this rugged land, through noncommercial means. Under Spanish colonial rule, Aymara-speaking people of the *altiplano* were located at a strategic crossroads, where the overland traffic in silver, salt, coca leaf, llama herds, wool, textiles, and the potato (the basic staple of the Andean highlands) all converged on route to various destinations both in the Andes and overseas. A few Aymara lords used their "comparative advantage" to establish trading cartels in coca and pack driving in response to the great silver mining boom of the early colonial Andes.[6]

By contrast, the Pastos, Caras Puruha, Canaris, and other indigenous peoples of the North Highlands did not spin expansive webs of exchange or send "islands of colonists" into distant ecological zones. Those ethnic groups enjoyed relatively easy access to high pastures, valley cropland, and tropical slopes amidst the tightly packed jumble of mountains and gorges. Furthermore, they remained out of the reach of the Inca for a longer period of time. The Inca ruler, Huayna Cápac, brought them into the empire in the

---

[6] See the relevant essays in Brooke Larson and Olivia Harris with Enrique Tandeter, eds., *Ethnicity, Markets and Migration in the Andes: At the Crossroads of History and Anthropology* (Durham, 1995); and in Kenneth Andrien and Rolena Adorno, eds., *Transatlantic Encounters: Europeans and Andeans in the Sixteenth Century* (Berkeley, 1991); John Murra, "Aymara Lords and their European Agents at Potosí," *Nova Americana* 1 (1978), 231–44; and Carlos Sempat Assadourian, *El sistema de la economía colonial. Mercados internos, regions, y espacio económico* (Lima, 1982).

early 1500s, toward the very end of the Inca reign. In fact, Huayna Cápac himself was struck down by smallpox in 1525, just as he was advancing the northern edge of Tawantinsuyu into territory that is, today, Ecuador and southern Colombia. Even under Spanish rule, the northern Andes remained on the political and territorial periphery of the new Viceroyalty of Peru. The Spanish colonial project was anchored in the emerging geo-political triangle of the South Andes – the capital of the Viceroyalty, Lima; the conquered Inca capital of Cuzco; and the booming silver mines of Potosí. Not only did the northern zone fall outside the Inca heartlands, but their lack of mineral riches discouraged Spanish entrepreneurs in the mid-sixteenth century. If the North Andes paled in comparison to the spectacular silver mines of the south, it eventually drew Spanish settlers eager to carve *haciendas* out of its fertile valleys and set up workshops to supply textiles to Lima, Potosí, and other southern Andean cities.[7]

In the nineteenth century, these north-south regional contrasts were still significant because they set preexisting social and cultural contexts within which the terms of specific nation-building projects got worked out. For example, Andean peasants throughout the northern highlands of Colombia and Ecuador remained more fragmented, scattered, and assimilated into Hispanized society than did the indigenous peoples of the southern highlands of Peru and Bolivia. In the meantime, the African slave population had continued to expand in Colombia's tropical coastal economies and in the cities during the colonial period. By the early nineteenth century, the Colombian elites tended to worry more about their black slave

---

[7] See Kenneth Andrien, *The Kingdom of Quito, 1690–1830: The State and Regional Development* (Cambridge, 1995); Karen Powers, *Andean Journeys. Migration, Ethnogenesis and the State in Colonial Quito* (Albuquerque, 1995); and Susanne Alchon, *Native Society and Disease in Colonial Ecuador* (Cambridge, 1991).

populations than they did about the "vanishing" Indians scattered across the mountains and tucked away in isolated areas of the vast Amazonian zone. Until tropical commodities burst onto the economic scene in the second half of the nineteenth century, Colombian policy makers studiously neglected the forest peoples in Chocó or the Putumayo. When they did think about Indians, they usually had in mind the peasant populations in the eastern *cordillera*, near highland Hispanic settlements, and land issues were usually involved. Colombia's Chibcha peoples retained *resguardos* (political and territorial units owned communally and guaranteed by the crown), but by the early nineteenth century, *resguardo* lands were melting into amorphous smallholding and *latifundista* regimes. Still, Colombian liberals pushed aggressively for land reform in the 1830s and 1840s.[8] Highland ethnic enclaves – the Páez and Pasto Indians for example – were by the nineteenth century confined to the isolated mountains of the southern Cauca department, well out of the range of most Hispanic settlements. Overall, Colombia's highland native people composed a relatively small portion of the population (less than a quarter of the total population). Colombia's highland Indian peasants seemed to meld into the richly variegated population of Creoles, *mestizos*, mulattos, and Africans who made up the early republic (see Chapter 2).

By contrast, Ecuador's Indian peasantries constituted the majority of the republic's total population. The last colonial census of 1785 estimated the Indian population to compose two-thirds of Ecuador's total population. (The republic of Ecuador was carved out of the colonial territorial and juridical unit known as the Audiencia de Quito, named after its largest city, which housed the high court, or *audiencia*.) Ecuador's unique political economy of colonialism – with its landed estates, textile mills (*obrajes*), relations

---

[8] Frank Safford and Marco Palacios, *Colombia: Fragmented Land, Divided Society* (Oxford, 2002), 184–5.

of peonage, and heavy migratory streams – had taken its toll so that by the nineteenth century most Indians no longer inhabited independent communities. A majority of the native peasantry had been converted into tenant laborers, attached to Creole estates or inhabiting freeholds.[9] Thus the territorial dimension of indigenous society never loomed as large in nineteenth-century republican politics as it did in the South Andes, since traditions of communal landholding had fragmented and disintegrated. Processes of Indian community dispersion continued in the nineteenth century, producing migratory and cultural streams of *mestizaje* in the towns, cities, and coasts across the North Andes.

Demographics in the South Andes (particularly in the central and southern highlands of Peru and throughout the *altiplano* of Bolivia) was heavily weighted in favor of highland indigenous peasantries. Native Quechua- and Aymara-speaking peoples composed large majorities in both Peru and Bolivia (see Map 4). Furthermore, a large portion of the native peasantry, if not the majority in certain regions, was still attached in significant ways to freeholding communities, or *ayllus*, around the mid-nineteenth century. The term *ayllu* refers to Andean kinship groups, which based their claim to specific territories on their descent from a mythical ancestor who defined their lineage. Andean *ayllus* also depended on acquired, Spanish colonial titles to legitimate their collective and customary claims to communal land rights. Inside the *ayllu*, the allocation of usufruct rights to land was governed by the ideal of reciprocal labor exchanges among families of the *ayllu* and by communal labor efforts under the authority of ethnic lords *(kurakas)* or local Indian councils. (In general, I tend to use the term interchangeably with "Indian community." In the Bolivian case, however, the notion of

---

[9] Alchon, *Native Society and Disease*, 123; Kenneth Andrien, *The Kingdom of Quito, 1690–1830*, 121–8.

PAEZ &
GUAMBIANO

INGANO

COLOMBIA

Quito

ECUADOR

Putumayo River

Napo River

Tigre River

Iquitos

SHUAR,
ACHUAR
AGUARUNA

LAMAS
CHACHAPOYAS
CAÑARISO

CAJAMARCA

Marañón R.

Ucayali R.

OTHER AMAZONIAN ETHNIC GROUPS

BRAZIL

Mamoré River

Trujillo

PERU

Huallaga River

Huaraz

SHIPIBO &
ASHÁNINKA

Urubamba R.

Huancayo

Lima

Ayacucho

Abancay

Cusco

Ica

BOLIVIA

MOXOS

Lake Titicaca

Arequipa

La Paz

Cochabamba

PACIFIC OCEAN

Moquegua

AYMARA

Oruro

Arica

Lake Poopó

Sucre

Potosí

Tarija

GUARANÍ

N

CHILE

Antofagasta

CHACO
ETHNIC
GROUPS

0   300 mi

0   300 km

ARGENTINA

Santiago del Estero

Quechua and Other Ethnic Areas

	Southern Cusqueño		Yungay
Central		Chinchay Northern
	Main Non-Quechua Ethnic Groups

Map 4. Quechua areas

ayllu is widely used in local and political parlance to this day. As a result, I tend to use it frequently in the Bolivian case study in Chapter 5.) After 1860 or so, state and market expansion in the South Andes began to run up against the mobilizing action of *ayllu* or *comunidad* peasants. There, in the highlands of Peru and Bolivia, Creole national projects would possess a particularly violent edge, as would Indian politics of defense and retribution. And during episodes of military invasion, civil war, and rebellion in the 1880s and 1890s, militarized peasants would force their way into the national theater of war, politics, and discourse to press their varied claims, concerns, and visions.

Against this backdrop, we can anticipate different regional patterns of Andean nation building. Each process involved a complex alchemy of new politics and political cultures acting upon deeper social and demographic structures that seemed to be permanent fixtures of the landscape. For instance, Colombia's drive to modernize by absorbing Indians into a Europeanizing majority may have had more affinity with Brazil's "whitening" project than it did with the neocolonial policies implemented by Ecuador, Peru, and Bolivia. But ethnic militarization and warfare in the southern mountains of Cauca ultimately forced Colombian elites to reinstate partial paternal protection of some Indian minorities. Across the border, conservative Ecuador delivered the task of "civilizing" Indians to the Church, and used the state to coerce the flow of Indian labor into the nation's road-building program. But the state could not control the human hemorrhage of Indian communities, as many peasants moved into the orbit of cities, estates, and rural mestizo towns.

In Peru and Bolivia, indigenous-state relations proved to be potentially more dangerous, since political liberalism and market expansion necessarily confronted Andean colonial heritages of landholding and community that had persisted under Spanish absolutism. Bolivia stands out among the Andean republics for

sustaining its colonial institutions (tribute, corporate landholding, forced labor practices, etc.) longer than the other republics.
This situation put the Bolivian state on a direct collision course
with Aymara- and Quechua-speaking communities across much of
Bolivia's northern *altiplano* and southern highlands. Overall, these
projects and conflicts destroyed any semblance of state legitimacy
and instead prepared the ground for violent encounters in the late
nineteenth century.

REPUBLICAN FANTASIES, RACIAL FEARS

If we are to understand how many Andean peasants came to experience and perceive late-nineteenth-century liberalism and its discon-
tents in different national contexts, we need to root this comparative
synthesis in the broader arena of Spanish American history during
the transition from empire to nation in the early 1800s. The peculiarities of Andean nation building stand out against the transatlantic tides that swept Spanish America into the era of independence
and early republicanism.

Certainly from the viewpoint of most Spanish American elites,
the emancipation from Spain represented a political revolution
promising (or threatening) unlimited and unforeseen possibilities
of change after three centuries of Spanish rule. After the Catholic
monarchy was shattered, Creole fantasies of liberalism, prosperity, and political consensus served as vague guidelines to political
self-rule. Many Creole leaders of independence denounced Indian
tribute, the *mita* (the colonial system of coerced Indian labor in the
silver Potosí mines), and other colonial practices as crimes against
nature and liberty, which had inflicted moral degradation on the
Indians. Both great liberators, Simón Bolívar and José de San
Martín, for example, proclaimed the abolition of tribute and envisioned the creation of an industrious class of yeoman smallholders,
endowed with property rights to small parcels of land.

Such republican fantasies confronted a stubborn reality, since the new republics of Latin America were unwilling to wage a comparable revolution in the economy or in society. Bolivarian dreams of egalitarian peasant homesteaders evaporated, for example, as soon as the liberators retired from the scene. One by one, the Andean republics reinstituted Indian tribute during the late 1820s in order to raise fresh revenues for cash-starved state bureaucracies under depressed economic conditions. Abolition of servitude on manorial estates was another disappointment of early liberal reformism. As historian Nils Jacobsen argues, the privately held Andean *hacienda* was "largely excluded from agrarian reform legislation" for the first century after independence. In fact, it was not until the mid-twentieth century that the Andean nations began to break up manorial estates, abolish feudal-like servitude, and redistribute plots of land to peasant families.[10] Thus the Andean republics entered the new political era, dragging behind them the detritus of colonial attitudes, habits, and institutions. In particular, the Andes continued to host rigid hierarchical societies of Creole "whites" extracting labor from African, Indian, mestizo, and other nonwhite populations in agrarian or mining economies. Even after two decades of popular mobilization, war, Spanish emigration, and massive physical destruction, and notwithstanding republican discourses proclaiming universal principles, Creole elites still managed to cling to their racial, economic, and political privileges that underwrote the *ancien regime*.

Yet the reversion to colonial forms of power and social control was neither the logical nor inevitable outcome of the independence wars. As Latin America's Creole elites appreciated all too well, the passage to independence had to be navigated with caution

---

[10] Nils Jacobsen, "Liberalism and Indian Communities in Peru, 1821–1920," in Robert Jackson, ed., *Liberals, the Church, and Indian Peasants* (Albuquerque, 1997), 128.

and concern about the dangerous dislocations that would ensue. Surrounded by coerced, nonwhite laborers, the Creole elites of those societies were motivated more often by their *fear* of local political disorder and social unrest than by their *desire* for political freedom and free trade. Historians John Lynch, David Brading, and others have noted this peculiarly Creole dilemma – to be "forever caught between the intrusive authority of the European metropolis and the explosive discontent of the [African slave or] native masses."[11] This "postcolonial Creole predicament," to borrow Mark Thurner's phrase, assumed its starkest dimensions in those regions where century-long traditions and memories of peasant or slave resistance were most deeply entrenched.[12] Whereas Spanish America's bustling Atlantic port cities of Buenos Aires and Caracas were locales of Creole liberal hopes and aspirations, its Amerindian highlands and African plantation belt configured a moral topography of Creole royalism, fear, and defensiveness. One such enclave of Creole conservatism was the Spanish Caribbean, where the horrors of the 1791 slave rebellion in the French colony of St. Domingue had shocked planter elites in the neighboring colonies of Cuba and Santo Domingo. The unfolding Haitian revolution and its violent road to Independence (1804) convinced those panicky planter elites to fend off the patriotic forces of independence, tighten social controls over their slave populations, and stay loyal to Spain until well into the nineteenth century.

In the Andes, too, recurring nightmares of "race war" stalked the subconscious terrain of Creole landowners, priests, labor

---

[11] David Brading, *The First America: The Spanish Monarchy, Creole Patriots, and the Liberal State, 1492–1867* (Cambridge, 1991), 484; quoted in Mark Thurner, *From Two Republics to One Divided: Contradictions of Postcolonial Nationmaking in Andean Peru* (Durham, 1997), 3. See also John Lynch, *The Spanish American Revolutions, 1808–1826* (New York, 1986).

[12] Thurner, *From Two Republics to One Divided*, 3–4.

contractors, tax collectors, and others who lived in close geo-cultural proximity to the rural peasant masses. Fresh memories of the 1781 peasant insurrections, which had swept across the South Andes and broken out almost simultaneously in several northern Andean regions, still haunted Creole landowners and officials in the 1810s and 1820s. For them, barely a generation had passed since Andean peasant insurrection had threatened their lives and landed estates. Furthermore, the Bourbons' apparatus of cultural repression, put into place after the peasant insurgencies of the 1780s, had long since disintegrated, along with the colonial state. Indeed, the collapse of the monarchy in 1810 provoked a spectacular series of crises and responses ricocheting across the Atlantic, and eventually triggering the onset of South America's continental campaign for independence in the 1820s. But the brief flurry of liberal reforms, under the renegade constitutional movement in the Spanish port city of Cádiz between 1811 and 1812, also had repercussions in remote Indian villages and parishes throughout the Andean highlands. Historians Christine Hunefeldt and Charles Walker chronicle the extraordinary intensity and range of peasant political responses to the burst of Spanish constitutional rhetoric and reform at the beginning of the independence era – a subject to which I will return. Suffice it to say here that the Spanish constitutional assault on the colonial policy of legal-political segregation, caste, and Indian tribute in 1811 and 1812 unleashed a whole series of peasant political activities, which constituted in the Creole mind a fundamental threat to the established social order.[13] By the time the Spanish monarch was restored to the throne in early 1814, Creole elites in Lima and elsewhere in the Andes

---

[13] Christine Hunefeldt, *Luchas por la tierra y protesta indígena: Las comunidades indígenas del Perú entre colonia y república* (Bonn, 1982); and Charles Walker, *Smoldering Ashes: Cuzco and the Creation of Republican Peru, 1780–1840* (Durham, 1999), 93–108.

"could be persuaded to support the decrepit Bourbon monarchy, not least because they feared the consequences of widespread Indian unrest more than they reviled Spanish tutelage."[14] It is no accident of history that political emancipation, when it finally came to the Andean regions in the mid-1820s, was imposed from outside, by the invading patriotic forces of San Martín and Bolívar.

By then the great liberator, Simón Bolívar, though unwavering in his republican convictions, feared that his dream of an Andean confederation (composed of Gran Colombia, Peru, and Bolivia) was doomed to disintegrate before the onslaught of political chaos and partisan conflict. The more pessimistic Bolívar became, the more he moved toward ever more authoritarian constitutions for the Andean territories he liberated. By the time he liberated the region of Alto Peru, renamed "Bolivia" in 1826, Bolívar had perfected an authoritarian form of constitutional rule. He did away with the principle of free elections – "the greatest scourge of republics" and a deep well of anarchy. His Bolivian constitution, he noted with pride, would have "all the strength of centralized government, all the stability of monarchical regimes."[15] On his deathbed, Bolívar gave up the last of his political illusions, predicting that political stability, unity, and fraternity would remain mere figments of the liberal imagination.

Simón Bolívar's bitter disappointment illuminated the structural problem of political authority created by the collapse of Spanish absolutism. Early on, Bolívar had anticipated the crisis of political legitimacy that was bound to follow the end of three centuries of absolutist rule. Having achieved the freedom to rule in their own right and to engage in overseas trade, the Creole elites suddenly

---

[14] Thurner, *From Two Republics to One Divided*, 4.
[15] Circular Letter to Colombia, 3 August 1826; quoted in Edwin Williamson, *The Penguin History of Latin America* (London, 1992), 231.

had to come up with an apparatus of government and new cultural blueprints of nationhood. Furthermore, there was an urgent need to establish new political rules and procedures for settling disputes and mapping the boundaries of national sovereignty and belonging. All this was to be achieved in a political vacuum because, in spite of their fertile nationalist imaginings, Creole political factions could call upon no unifying myth, no accepted rule of law, no deep well of political experience, and no converging class interest in universalist ideals that might guide them in their efforts to navigate postcolonial transitions.[16]

This political crisis was exacerbated in the Andean region because the independence struggle itself had irreparably divided the Creole ruling classes into patriots and royalists, thereby destroying any semblance of political consensus around which those republics might be assembled. Internal divisions sprang from many sources – economic, regional, political, and ideological. At base, the Creole ruling elites faced two options: to restore the basic architecture of aristocratic, hierarchical rule based on the colonial precept of caste so as to secure their authority over the indigenous and plebian masses, or to create modern liberal states vested in individual rights to property, equal protection under law, and other political liberties. Creole elites were plunged into factional struggles between the conservatives, who fought to maintain all the trappings of a hierarchical society and Hispanist values, and the liberals, who hoped to reshape their societies in the mold of England, France, and North America. Thus, as historian Edwin Williamson notes, the early republican period in the Andes, and in Spanish America more generally, may be characterized as an ongoing struggle between Creole liberal and conservative factions to reshape society in accord with their mutually incompatible views on how to achieve the same ends – the reproduction of the wealth, power, and privilege of their own class.

---

[16] Ibid., 232–6.

Neither faction wanted to see its economic interests threatened by radical reform, popular mobilization, or endemic instability in what was becoming a virtually stateless countryside.[17]

The beleaguered liberal vanguard of the Andes went to work fashioning a political architecture that might fit their own "backward" societies, composed of despotic landowners and unruly nonwhite populations. As time went on, the liberal-conservative gap began to close around the Bolivarian ideal of authoritarian republicanism. Only Colombian liberals managed to prevail into the mid-nineteenth century. In the other Andean republics, liberals beat a hasty retreat from imported ideals of egalitarianism, laissez-faire capitalism, and citizenship democracy. As power dispersed among powerful landed elites, or regional strongmen (*caudillos*), whole regions came to resemble small decapitated kingdoms, ruled by rural despots or provincial oligarchies, still under the sway of Hispanist values. Of course, there were important variations and permutations in the pattern of these intraelite conflicts, as well as in the unfolding dynamics of Indian–state relations, which molded distinctive contours of Andean republicanism during the late nineteenth century. These varied national and regional patterns, mentioned earlier, are explored in detail in the remainder of this book. But it is also important to capture the broader political drift toward neocolonial and authoritarian forms of power and discourse that characterized the postindependence Andean republics. Creole architects of Andean republicanism demonstrated their ability to adapt to change, but also to keep it within strict bounds, so as to contain popular mobilizations and political expectations. Yet one of the great ironies of this period is the crude disjuncture between the Creole quest for political authority and social control, on the one hand, and the endemic political factionalism and rural instability that thwarted their ongoing quest, on the other.

[17] Ibid., 233–9.

THE VEXING ISSUE OF INDIAN TRIBUTE

In Ecuador, Peru, and Bolivia, this ongoing turmoil had much to do with the contentious issue of Indian tribute. Since early colonial times, tribute was a pillar of Spanish colonial rule. Not only was it a head tax on the colonized sedentary peasants, but tribute was also the juridical keystone of Spanish policy of racial hierarchy and segregation. In the late sixteenth century, the crown elevated the Amerindians to the legal, albeit subordinated, status of native vassals and endowed them with a separate corpus of rights and responsibilities under the *"república de indios."* This colonized "republic of Indians," with its separate laws and tribunals, juxtaposed to the dominant "republic of Spaniards," became the juridical basis of caste. The Indian-Spanish divide was quickly complicated, however, by the explosion of interstitialized people of mixed races (mestizos, *cholos, castas*, etc.), African slaves, and free persons of color. But, as Peter Wade points out, Indians continued to occupy a special institutionalized location in the Spanish colonial order vis-à-vis the body of rights and obligations granted them under the colonial republic of Indians.[18] Despite the demographic and social explosion of "mixed races" and amalgamated cultures in seventeenth-century Spanish America, and despite the constant incursion of regional landed elites into putatively separate Indian lands and jurisdictions, the colonial policy of legal-political segregation created a dominant "language of contention." It provided a legal-discursive medium through which Indians might negotiate or contest colonial policy or local transgressions. *Indio* carried multiple meanings and functions under Spanish rule: legal, administrative, fiscal, and racial. But bundled together, these manifold meanings and uses of Andean Indianness defined what anthropologist Tristan Platt has called a "tributary pact," which was imposed by the Spanish crown to

---

[18] Wade, *Race and Ethnicity in Latin America* (London, 1997), 27–30.

regulate the extraction of Indian tribute and labor in exchange for
Christian evangelization, usufruct rights to communal lands, local
self-governance, and royal protection.[19] In the late sixteenth century, this tributary arrangement of indirect rule was stamped onto
the Andes by Viceroy Toledo's machinery of Indian resettlement,
extraction, local self-governance, cultural regulation, religious discipline, and surveillance. Toledo's draconian measures did violence
to local indigenous traditions and settlement patterns; at the same
time they created certain parameters of Indian self-rule and legal defense under the imperial order. As historians of the colonial
Andes have shown, the dialectic of Toledan protection and discipline imposed strict limits on the forms and content of native
Andean contestation that ultimately added up to extraction, subju-
gation, and loss.[20]

With independence, the former Spanish colonies inherited this
juridical system of racial-caste differentiation. Blacks were still enslaved in many parts of Spanish America; the various groups of
castas still suffered from legal and social restriction in education,
government, and taxation; and Indian communities still belonged
to a separate "republic" under their own body of law and local government, in exchange for the ethnic head tax (now often dubbed
contribución) they paid to the state. Although most ruling elites
still adhered to Hispanist values and hierarchies, some liberal legislators viewed the corporate rights and status of Indians as a civic
aberration, similar to the colonial privileges inherited by the clergy.
Theoretically, of course, liberalism was predicated on the ideals of

---

[19] Tristan Platt, *Estado boliviano y ayllu andino. Tierra y tributo en el norte de Potosí* (Lima, 1982).

[20] See, for example, Kenneth Andrien, *Andean Worlds: Indigenous History, Culture, and Consciousness under Spanish Rule, 1532–1825* (Albuquerque, 2001), 49–56; Stern, *Peru's Indian Peoples and the Challenge of Spanish Conquest*, 76–9; and Nicolás Sánchez-Albornoz, *Indios y tributos en el Alto Perú* (Lima, 1978).

universal equality and individual property rights under one unifying body of law. Pragmatically, it called for the abolition of African slavery and Indian tribute (and associated coerced labor obligations), as well as the end to other anachronisms like communal land rights and legal protections embodied by the tributary compact. Thus under the ideological influences of liberalism, the status of Indianness – and specifically the status of communal land rights – eventually came under attack.

On the ground, the decrees abolishing Indian tribute and caste provoked all sorts of conflicts and contestation in the Andes. Not only did the new republican governments of Ecuador, Peru, and Bolivia quickly turn their backs on the tenets of liberalism in order to secure colonial forms of power and tribute monies in the aftermath of the devastating independence wars, but local peasant leaders themselves struggled to interpret the possible implications of "citizenship" and "equality" so as to try to protect their local interests. And in many cases, indigenous authorities fought to retain, or reassemble, some semblance of their inherited colonial lands, rights, and protections – even if it meant restoring their tribute obligations to the republican state.

Such indigenous movements of defense sprang, not from a congenital peasant conservatism or nostalgia for times past, but from the very real, lived experiences and memories of early liberalism. With the sudden burst of Spanish liberal reforms in 1811 and 1812, indigenous communities had to weigh liberal promises of tax relief, direct political representation, and equality against the possibilities of heavier extraction and land divestiture by local elites. To make matters worse, indigenous leaders and their local councils (*cabildos de indios*) had to navigate these stormy political waters in the midst of Spain's crisis and collapse. With Spain occupied by French troops and the monarch under arrest in 1812, the brash Spanish liberals in the port city of Cádiz were redrawing the political rules of colonialism and empire. Many Andean peasant communities quickly grew skeptical of the promise of tribute and *mita* abolition, especially when news of land redistribution and taxation began to circulate.[21] In 1812, peasants in the highlands of Ecuador and Peru petitioned the Spanish authorities to reinstate the Indian tribute because, in the words of one Peruvian villager from Pupuja (Province of Puno), they thought it was "better to renounce the honor of equality with Spaniards" than to face the pressures and uncertainties of the new political regime.[22]

Small wonder that indigenous responses to the news of abolition in 1811 and 1812 were ambiguous, varied, and reversible. While indigenous leaders in some regions mounted petitions to restore it, others used the news to riot against the mine owners of Huancavelica or to refuse to serve on the silver mining *mita* of Potosí. Still others in the southern Peruvian region of Puno, for example, took over the town council to demand that the new Spanish constitutional government end Indian "humiliation and degradation" and allow the Indian majority to keep vigil over the public order and collect rents in the parish.[23] Tristan Platt's work on the Quechua communities of Chayanta in the southern Bolivian highlands offers a vivid case of indigenous authorities petitioning for the right to continue paying tribute, and even serving on the colonial mining *mita,* in exchange for state protection of their *ayllu* lands, as well as access to the cultural accoutrements of "civilization" – Spanish-language schools and literacy! Their 1828 petition for a local village school was couched in a hybrid mix of tributary and liberal entitlements – another clue as to how peasant intellectuals were beginning to fashion popular meanings of *republicanismo* in

---

[21] Andrien, *Andean Worlds*, 49–56; Stern, *Peru's Indian Peoples*, 71–79.

[22] Hunefeldt, *Lucha por la tierra y protesta indígena*, 167; and Mark Van Aken, "The Lingering Death of Indian Tribute in Ecuador," *Hispanic American Historical Review* 61: 3 (1981), 436.

[23] Hunefeldt, *Lucha por la tierra y protesta indígena*, 162.

particularly Andean ways. As Mark Thurner has studied so insightfully for the Huaylas region of Peru, indigenous renderings of the
meaning and materiality of tribute, and more broadly the parameters of postcolonial *republicanismo,* could cut several ways.[24]

Given such intense local politics of tribute, many Creole politicians were averse to the idea of abolition, which, in any event, had
been thrust upon them by the Cádiz liberals and later by the patriotic liberators. Nicolás Sánchez-Albornoz notes this halting retro-
gression in Bolivian state policy: "marches and countermarches, in
one general direction – [toward] the contribution [i.e., tribute] of
the Indians."[25] In the late 1820s, the tribute system was restored in
Ecuador, Peru, and Bolivia. Here and there, an authority might note
the calamities that tribute abolition had wreaked on the Indians, but
most politicians were more driven by economic expedience. Without thriving export economies or sustained overseas trade providing
customs revenues for insolvent governments, tribute monies filled
the bill, by providing almost half of all state revenues in Bolivia, for
example, until the mid-1800s.

A sad irony of this neotributary era is that tribute, the most uni-
versally onerous symbol of Spanish colonialism in the Amerindian
highlands, probably represented a certain measure of reprieve for
many peasant communities under the early republic. First, it partially restored the legal-discursive framework within which indigenous authorities could defend their communities from commercial incursions. Second, restoration itself was a symptom of sluggish economic growth and agrarian decompression, which post-
poned aggressive liberal policies of communal divestiture. Historian
Tulio Halperín Donghi notes the persistence of indigenous forms of

---

[24] Tristan Platt, "Liberalism and Ethnocide in the Southern Andes," *History
Workshop Journal* 17 (1984), 6–7; Thurner, *From Two Republics to One
Divided,* 20–53.

[25] Sánchez-Albornoz, *Indios y tributos en el Alto Perú,* 192, note 10.

livelihood, community, and politics in the Andes during the first half of the nineteenth century. Neither the region's flaccid state bureaucracies nor its floundering export economies was yet capable of regulating indigenous labor or cultural practices.[26] To be sure, this transitory period of republican tribute and "reindianization" was bleak in many ways: peasant penury, the dispersion of power to regional elites and despotic landlords, and endemic political instability were hardly the stuff of pastoral quiescence. Yet in hindsight, we may also appreciate this postindependence period as a sort of institutional and economic interim – bridging experimental Spanish liberalism and the wars of independence in the 1810s and 1820s, on one end, and the advent of aggressive liberalism after 1850, on the other. For it opened ambiguous political spaces for Andean peoples to renegotiate tributary pacts; recover lost lands; restore ethnic authorities; rearrange translocal networks of patronage, kinship, barter, and trade; and practice religious rituals away from the watchful eye of would-be "civilizers" and nation-builders. If indeed there was such a moment of relative political reprieve under the early Andean republics, however, it only intensified the forces of liberalism and capitalism that gathered on the temporal horizon after midcentury.

1850s – A BENCHMARK

Around the middle of the nineteenth century, European and North American demand for raw materials, markets, and knowledge began to pull the Andes out of its state of stagnation, neglect, and obscurity. From the late 1850s on, foreign capital poured into South

---

[26] Tulio Halperín-Donghi, "Economy and Society," in Leslie Bethell, ed., *Spanish America after Independence, c. 1820–1870* (Cambridge, 1987), 26–7. See also Magnus Morner, *The Andean Past: Land, Societies, and Conflicts* (New York, 1985), 124–34.

America in the form of loans to build railways and roads, modernize ports and mines, and develop new industries. Foreign investors also eyed opportunities in the Andes, in spite of daunting logistical and political obstacles. British investors apparently had overcome their earlier reluctance to invest in the feeble Andean nations, which had led to massive British commercial losses in the 1810s and 1820s. The English were beginning to return to Andean South America in the 1860s, driven by imperial ambitions and more favorable economic conditions.

Incipient export-driven capitalism penetrated the Andes slowly and unevenly. British capital investment spread along the Peruvian coast during the 1840s, when Peru's miraculous islands of *guano* (bird dung) began to attract European merchants and steamships to the deep, cold Pacific waters. By the 1860s and 1870s, European and American vessels were shipping that "black gold" to use as fertilizer throughout Europe's depleted wheat fields, so as to boost food production to feed the laboring masses.[27] Other Andean export products followed: nitrates, wool, silver, and other minerals plugged many parts of the Andean coast and highlands into the swirling currents of the North Atlantic's industrializing economy. By the 1870s and 1880s, commercial agriculture was starting to find overseas markets, as well. Modernizing oases of sugar, wine, and cotton plantations flourished along the arid coastline of Peru, and cacao trees grew in the subtropical vicinity of Ecuador's main port city of Guayaquil. Without recourse to African slavery, which was abolished everywhere in the Andes by the 1850s, many coastal plantation owners arranged to import cargoes of Chinese laborers, while other planters devised labor recruitment strategies to induce highland Indians to serve as seasonal migrant laborers. Finally, a third wave of European capitalism flowed into the jungle interior

---

[27] Paul Gootenberg, *Between Silver and Guano: Commercial Policy and the State in Postindependence Peru* (Princeton, 1989).

of the Andean republics. Exotic commodities like rubber and quinine drew intrepid European capitalists and naturalists into the Amazonian headwater regions of Putumayo and other areas on the far side of the *Cordillera Oriental* (see Map 3).

Compared to the extractive economies of the coast, the logistical and technological difficulties of trade and industry in the mountain interior proved far greater. To compound the problem, labor-hungry capitalists had to break Andean subsistent economies if they had any hope of securing the flow of peasant labor into the export sector. Consequently, economic change came more slowly, haltingly, and violently to the Andean highlands. Furthermore, this uneven regional pattern widened the perceived gulf between the Creole world of bustling coasts and Europeanizing cities, on the one hand, and the somnolent, antiquated Indian sierra, on the other. But by the 1870s, tangible signs of economic modernization were found in many regions of the sierra. British-owned railroads lurched their way up over the *cordillera*, connecting remote interior mines and towns to the cities and seaports on the Pacific coast. A steamship ferried across the deep blue waters of Lake Titicaca, in full view of llama caravans lumbering along ancient lakeshore trails en route to distant pastures and markets. Miners of southern Bolivia pumped out the flooded shafts of old silver mines and were busily extracting ore again. About the same time, Colombian merchants discovered a rich source of quinine bark in the subtropical forests shading the eastern slopes of the Páez territory in the southern department of Cauca. Coffee plantations were spreading along the northeastern slopes of Colombia. Perhaps most dramatic of all was the violent enclosure movement that rapidly displaced traditional herding communities and peasant markets across the *altiplano* of southern Peru and northern Bolivia, as the world market began to absorb an increasing quantity of Peru's raw wool exports and as the new railroads began shipping Chilean wheat and other products into the interior regions.

As elsewhere in Latin America, the imperatives of export-driven capitalism revived Creole interest in liberal free-trade doctrines. In particular, the emerging export oligarchies pushed forward agendas to dismantle protectionist barriers, develop their nation's infrastructure, promote export trade, and encourage foreign investment. Beyond these mercantile goals, however, rising oligarchies demanded the fundamental reordering of political, institutional, and discursive relations with the indigenous and mestizo peasants and laborers, whose tribute and labor power once sustained the fledgling republics. Indian tribute – the symbolic and material mainstay of the dual-republic regime partially restored after independence – was fast becoming a minor source of state revenue by midcentury. For the first time since the 1820s, Ecuador, Peru, and Bolivia signaled their readiness to revoke Indian tribute: Peru led the way in 1854, followed by Ecuador in 1857 and, much later, by Bolivia in 1874. At the same time, the new export-driven prosperity demanded, and made possible, some degree of political consolidation and stability under limited forms of constitutional politics and the rule of law.

Creole entrepreneurs and politicians thus began to place a premium on Indian land and labor in their quest for economic modernization. As capitalism entered a new territorial phase of expansion, it turned Indian lands into a scarce, valuable, and conflict-ridden commodity. Liberalism, postulating its ideals of equality and liberty, was invoked against any restriction or privilege, particularly the inherited corporate privileges of indigenous communities and the Church. As discussed earlier, state-driven liberal land reforms, even when they included protective clauses, threatened dispossession to indigenous peasants who still cultivated communal village lands. Processes of divestiture were particularly dramatic in the South Andes, where thousands of communal peasants were often pushed into the rural proletariat and their lands swallowed up by the spreading *latifundia* system (the vast estates held by Creole landowners, who were usually liberal or conservative actors on the national political stage). In brief, the uneasy peace gave way to powerful economic and ideological forces of change after 1850.

Modernization's material mandates thus required the ideological work of nation making – the essentializing work that went beyond the limits of law and policy to reorder internal ethno-racial hierarchies and map the boundaries of civil society and citizenship. Overriding oligarchic aims to eradicate rural anachronisms and contain unrest led many politicians to advocate strong state action and to imagine a sort of enlightened despotism that would finally solve the putative "Indian problem." But *how, and with what social consequences*, those modernizing states tried to manage their indigenous populations would become one of the great dramas of Andean nation making. What would be the ideological mainstay of the "imagined political community" in Ecuador, Peru, and Bolivia, where *one-half to two-thirds* of the registered population still spoke indigenous languages, were bound to rural subsistent economies, asserted folk-legal claims to land and justice, and remained stubbornly at the core of their nation's social and economic geography?[28] How

---

[28] Benedict Anderson, *Imagined Communities: Reflections on the Origin and Spread of Nationalism* (London, 1983). Anderson's provocative study of the cultural forms of nation building emphasized the rise of print technology, which broadened the circulation of political ideas and identities during the late eighteenth and early nineteenth centuries. He points particularly to the novel and the newspaper, two late-eighteenth-century venues for "'representing' the kind of imagined community that is [or became] the nation" (30). Anderson's novel approach also pointed to proindependence Spanish American Creoles as revolutionary pilgrims, who transported liberal and republican ideals across the Atlantic, in both directions. Anderson's study produced a lively debate among scholars of postcolonial and subaltern politics, where the imagining of nationhood took place among largely nonliterate subordinate populations, and/or where emerging nation-states had to be constructed out of the multiethnic, religious, and regional "fragments" of a former European colony. See, for example, Partha Chatterjee, *The Nation and Its Fragments: Colonial and Postcolonial Histories* (Princeton, 1993). For the Andes, see Thurner, *From Two Republics to One Divided*, esp.

would Creole liberals advance their "whitening project" against the entrenched enclaves of blacks, mulattoes, and Indians in these fragmented lands? In short, how would the white ruling elites try to envision a unifying national culture (white, Spanish-speaking, "civilized") refracted through the lens of colonial-racial difference?

Toward that end, Creole political leaders often looked to other "civilizing projects," perhaps to an earlier era of Bourbon cultural regulation following the Andean peasant insurrections of the 1780s, or to other nations engaged in parallel projects of Indian population management. In the 1880s and 1890s, Chile, Argentina, Mexico, and the United States themselves were launching military and assimilative policies to deal with their nomadic *indios bárbaros* on the territorial margins of those nations. But Argentina's "Conquest of the Desert" campaign to exterminate the Araucanian peoples of the southwestern pampas, or Mexico's forced resettlement of the Yaqui tribes in the northern Province of Sonora, were not viable models for dealing with the peculiarities of the Andean "Indian problem." Only Colombia seemed capable of anchoring its unruly Indians on reservation (*resguardo*) lands in the isolated interior of the Province of Cauca. It was hardly tenable for Ecuador, Peru, and Bolivia to entertain such fantasies while indigenous peasants still constituted the overwhelming demographic majority, supplied the labor force to expanding rural haciendas, and performed all sorts of unpaid, "customary" labor services in provincial towns and, later, on modernizing states. Finally, too, we must remember that the Andean republics never replicated the kind of strong man rule that Mexico experienced under President Porfirio Díaz (1877–1911) or created

chaps. 1 and 2; Florencia Mallon, *Peasant and Nation: The Making of Postcolonial Mexico and Peru* (Berkeley, 1995); Walker, *Smoldering Ashes*, esp. chap. 6 on urban political and popular culture; and Joanne Rappaport, *The Politics of Memory: Native Historical Interpretation in the Colombian Andes* (Cambridge, 1990).

a stabilizing system of parliamentary democracy similar to the one that bolstered the Chilean oligarchy at the end of the nineteenth century. Thus, in the Andes, Creole modernizers continued to push their liberal and disciplinary schemes against debilitating forces of internecine strife, partisan warfare, civil war, foreign invasion, and territorial loss.

Thus, despite tangible signs of economic modernization, the ideal of national sovereignty still seemed more theory than reality to many Peruvian and Bolivian state builders in the last years of the nineteenth century. And as many dangers seemed to lurk *within* their own societies and national borders as outside them. Here, then, was the critical national question still confronting the Andean nation-states at the end of the nineteenth century: how finally to solve the Indian problem – interpreted by Creole discourses as the main impediment to order, progress, civilization, and modernity.

The case studies that follow do not intend to find any definitive answer to that question, since the question itself is soaked in racist premises. My aim instead is to explore the complex historical processes by which the Andean republics came to naturalize the Indian problem and turn it into the political and rhetorical centerpiece of their varied nation-building projects during the second half of the nineteenth century. It might be argued that Creole nation-builders constructed their national narratives simply by borrowing from European ideologies and institutions. But as historians recognize, nation-building projects are not plucked from the heavens of pure ideas or political imaginaries but are rooted in the earth of social history. And this was never truer than in the Andes. It was not just the rugged Hispanized *caudillos* (leaders of factional armies) who rode across the nineteenth-century landscape, creating endemic political instability and perpetual crises of authority but also the more hidden counternarratives of native Andean nationalist imaginings, ethnic resurgence, and everyday forms of resistance that went into the unmaking, or reordering, of postcolonial political formations. Once we emphasize the interactions, understandings, and practices of rural Andean peoples, we can begin to appreciate the powerful material and cultural forces that Creole oligarchies came up against. By looking at postcolonial nation-making from the margins, we may also grasp the manifold ways that capitalism and modernity insinuated themselves into the material and cultural lives of rural people.

PATHWAYS INTO THE RURAL ANDEAN WORLD

How is it possible to excavate native Andean social experiences, understandings, and actions through the opaque lenses and distorting discourses of Creole writers, reformers, and politicians? Certainly the intrinsic limitations of official sources and Eurocentric subjectivities burden historical research on the nineteenth-century Andes. To begin with, there may be fewer historical traces of Andean peoples in the nineteenth century than in any other time period. The collapse of the colonial bureaucracy, two decades of warfare, and Spanish emigration destroyed the great edifice of imperial record keeping, and the floundering new republics were slow to rebuild centralized states capable of counting, inspecting, or cataloguing their own indigenous populations. Part of that postindependence neglect stemmed from liberal or anticolonial denial of all things Indian. Beginning with Simón Bolívar, many Creole patriots preferred to look to Europe, and to the future, for their ideals of modern "white" nationhood. This climate of administrative neglect was strongest in Colombia and Ecuador, where state officials managed to efface Indians from their population census records in the second half of the nineteenth century, even as they debated the Indian question in other venues. Thus Indians entered into republican sources only intermittently during the nineteenth century.

For many years, the relative invisibility of Andean peasants from nineteenth-century historiography also may have had to do with historians' implicit assumptions about native Andean societies and cultures. Stereotypes of Indian poverty, ignorance, and isolation in the "dark age" of the nineteenth century have helped to reinforce the elision of Andean agency and subjectivity in the older historiography. This book seeks to destroy any such myths about the "quiescent" rural Andean world of the nineteenth century. I draw my inspiration from those Andean historians who have delved into the local archives of small town notaries, judges, scribes, and indigenous communities, who have parsed Creole newspaper, trial, and government reports on the Indian hinterland, or who have sifted ethnographic nuggets from Creole literary and scientific writings on the great themes of the late nineteenth century – history, nature, and race. I am also indebted to anthropologists who began their fieldwork in contemporary Andean peasant societies but eventually found their way into the archives and oral testimonies of the past (see the Bibliographic Essay).

For heuristic purposes, it is perhaps useful to chart three methodological pathways of study into the rural Andean world. Depending on the specific historical context, I follow one or another of these "pathways" into the rural Andes in the four case studies that follow. First, as we saw earlier, the intensifying struggles over the Andean colonial heritage after 1860 throws into bold relief indigenous peasant politics revolving around issues of authority, tribute, and land. This, in turn, opened the floodgates to indigenous law suits, petition campaigns, notarized boundary disputes, pilgrimages to the archive, the scramble for peasant literacy, and so on. As some peasant leaders entered the Hispanic world of "print capitalism," they or their scribes mastered literacy in order to make their collective views known to Creole politicians, judges, lawyers, scribes, and even journalists.[29] Because liberal assaults challenged Andean

[29] Ethnohistorians have long noted the importance of colonial documents for constituted ethnic identities under the colonial *república de indios*, so it

claims to a collective existence, peasant authorities also tapped into deep customary and legal traditions, *ayllu* history and memory, and sacred meanings of their contested territories in order to defend themselves against the new land reforms.[30] Andean strategies of defense took diverse forms, and sometimes the advent of aggressive liberalism precipitated intense intra-Andean conflicts and readjustments in which some peasants seized new legal, cultural, and commercial opportunities to advance their individual interests. For them, the export-driven economy might offer escape from the tyranny of rural routines, grinding poverty, a despotic landlord, or the stigma of Indianness on the margins of a Creole world. But insofar as diverse communities of Andean peasants experienced assaults on their collective legitimacy, those struggles frequently crystallized into broader ethnic mobilizations. Indeed, defensive peasant movements were commonplace all across the Amerindian highlands during the era of liberal state formation. Who among us can forget the symbolic power of Emiliano Zapata's wooden box of ancient land titles and other communal documents, which contained the textual

comes as no great surprise that indigenous communities continued to guard their precious colonial land titles, or else rallied their authorities to find and make copies of such documents in the event of a land conflict. Historians of Bolivia have been especially creative in tracing legal and documentary strategies of *ayllus* and, at a theoretical level, challenging narrow conceptions of what constitutes a literate community. See, for example, Carlos Mamani Condori, *Taraqu, 1866–1935: Massacre, Guerra y 'Renovación' en la biografía de Eduardo L. Nina Qhispi* (La Paz, 1991); and Tristan Platt, "Writing, Shamanism, and Identity, or Voices from Abya-Yala," *History Workshop Journal* 34 (1992), 132–47. See also, Joanne Rappaport's pathbreaking *The Politics of Memory.*

[30] For a sample of the scholarly literature on Andean "moral memory" in the context of struggle over rights to land, community, self-rule, and representation, see Alberto Flores Galindo, *Buscando un Inca. Identidad y utopía en los Andes (Lima, 1988)*; Rappaport, *The Politics of Memory*; and Thomas Abercrombie, *Pathways of Memory and Power. Ethnography and History among an Andean People* (Madison, 1998).

artifacts of collective struggle, territorial justice, and identity during the peasant uprisings in Morelos around 1910? In the rural Andean world, as one might expect, indigenous uses of the colonial past for purposes of *ayllu* mobilization and defense are particularly salient – especially for many areas of the South Andes, where propertied communalism was still entrenched in the late nineteenth century. Confronted by threats of dispossession, Andean peasant leaders quickly learned how to articulate colonial history, ethnic descent, and land claims into discourses and lawsuits leveled against the precepts of the liberalizing state and its divestiture policies. Thus the colonial past, refracted through the political imperatives of the moment, was forged into a discursive weapon and wielded by threatened peasant subcultures throughout the Andes, from the Páez of southern Colombia to the Chayanta *ayllus* of southern Bolivia.

A second methodological pathway into the domain of peasant politics seizes the conjunctural moment. Long periods of official neglect were sometimes punctuated by a frenzy of reports on the "barbarian hoards" waging "race war" in the hinterlands, which threatened to alter the course of regional or national history. Such moments are the stuff of social history, and since the late 1970s historians have written a good deal about Andean peasant politics, popular discourses, and cross-cultural diplomacy in moments of war, and repression.[31] The first breakpoint came with the Spanish

---

[31] Besides Steve Stern's edited volume, *Resistance, Rebellion, and Consciousness in the Andean Peasant World, 18th to 19th Centuries* (Madison, 1987), several monographs on peasant politics in nineteenth-century Peru also stand out: Nelson Manrique, *Campesinado y nación: Las guerrillas indígenas en la Guerra con Chile* (Lima, 1981); Mallon, *Peasant and Nation*; Walker, *Smoldering Ashes*; and Thurner, *From Two Republics to One Divided*. On the participation of peasants and other popular sectors in clientelist and electoral politics in Bolivia, see Marta Irurozqui Victoriano, *"A Bala, Piedra y Palo": La construcción de la ciudadanía política en Bolivia, 1826–1952* (Sevilla, 2000); compare the work of Bolivian historians on Aymara resurgence and the struggle to revitalize ethnic solidarities and

American movement of independence, discussed earlier. In the second half of the nineteenth century, there was a comparable conjuncture: the Chilean-Peruvian War of the Pacific (1879–1883) and its aftershocks. Those years saw the territorial invasion and occupation of Peru and Bolivia by its neighboring aggressor, Chile. The war caused enormous territorial loss for both Andean republics, leaving Bolivia totally landlocked to this day. It also sent shock waves through the countryside, eventually heightening class and racial tensions throughout rural Peru and Bolivia. The central highlands of Peru were breeding grounds of oppositional peasant cultures and even distinctive *patrias chicas* (local homelands).

In such moments, Andean peasantries were compelled as never before to question and critique the authority and morality of their overlords who, in the midst of war, were quick to mobilize the Indians under the banner of patriotism and citizenship only to denigrate them later as "bandits." Peasant leaders had a chance to thrust themselves into national political life, as they spun their own rhetorical and political strategies of representation and social critique. Andean deployment of popular political "isms" (monarchism, republicanism, federalism, republicanism, nationalism, racism) intersected with local cultural values, interests, and identities, which were preserved in oral, written, pictographic, and ritual forms.[32]

claim a place in the Bolivian nation, for example: Silvia Rivera Cusicanqui, *Oprimidos pero no vencidos. Luchas del campesinado aymara y qhechwa, 1900–1980* (La Paz, 1986) and Carlos Mamani Condori, *Taraqu, 1866–1935.*

[32] In a recent retrospective look at the scholarly literature on peasant politics, Steve Stern writes that by the 1990s, "the empirical findings of Andean historians and anthropologists had uncovered a dizzying variety of political expressions by native Andean peoples since the times of Spanish conquest. These phenomena were not easily reducible to explanatory visions based on peasant moral economy. The combination of millenarian movements, local peasant rebellions, Indianist supraregional insurrection, peasant nationalism, peasant pacts with radicals and populists, and periods of apparent

It is in this protean intersection that historians sometimes catch glimpses of Andean political aspirations, as well as the social and political forces that shaped, or altered, them.

Third, popular religion (and other modes of cultural expression) was a crucial site of "everyday state formation" in the Andes (and elsewhere), as nineteenth-century secular state builders sought to suppress or regulate religious festivities in Indian and mestizo towns.[33] Although independence had weakened the Church in much of the Andes, muting Church-state conflicts that so troubled nineteenth-century Mexico, ecclesiastical authorities were still charged with carrying out "civilizing missions" under the auspices of modernizing states. Crushing popular expressions of Catholicism turned into an instrument of cultural control across the Andes. In the 1830s, for example, Bolivia got papal dispensation to reduce the number of religious feast days in order to limit Indian "vice" and "laziness." In Peru during the early 1880s, while the War of the Pacific still raged, provincial town councils in the central *sierra* banned Indian fiestas out of fear of insurgent threats and uprisings. And both Colombia and Ecuador, in their separate ways, launched "anti-idolatry" campaigns against local ritual practices. In

political quiescence had shaped the political contours of rural history in Peru and Bolivia and seemed to present a conceptual challenge to [Marxist] theory-derived visions of consciousness.... The newer [historiographical] approach would problematize peasant politics and consciousness in its own right rather than have the theme spin off as a by-product or epiphenomena of resistance and adaptation to regional regimes of political economy" ("Between Tragedy and Promise: the Politics of Writing Latin American History in the Late Twentieth Century," in Gilbert Joseph, ed., *Reclaiming the Political in Latin American History. Essays from the North* (Durham, 2001), 32–77, quotation on 43).

[33] The term, "everyday state formation," is adapted from the influential volume on the Mexican revolution: Gil Joseph and Daniel Nugent, eds., *Everyday Forms of State Formation: Revolution and the Negotiation of Rule in Modern Mexico* (Durham, 1994).

the meantime, the four Andean republics invented civic traditions, replete with Bolivarian statues, patriotic processions and songs, bull runs, and the heraldry appropriate to newly liberated countries. In spite of the republics' repressive measures and invented traditions, however, popular religiosity flourished in Indians towns and *ayllus*. "Civilizing" vanguards condemned such practices as signs of backwardness and barbarity, an utter anathema to European norms of civil society. Republican church hierarchies felt more ambivalence, depending on the political position and authority they held in their respective nations.

For many *ayllus*, on the other hand, the religious-ritual calendar played a crucial function in the organization of seasonal rhythms of agriculture, labor sharing, treks, and other aspects of communal life. For centuries, Andean peoples had appropriated and transmuted Christian symbols and institutions so that, by the late colonial era, Christian and indigenous deities commingled in dynamic cultural-religious syntheses.[34] Andean interpretive uses of Christian deities and devils were as much a part of Andean religious repertories as were their specific local gods, sacred genealogies and landscapes, and pastoral-sacrificial rites. Religious fiestas also were vital occasions drawing together people from the *parcialidades* ("halves," or moieties) of their dualistic communities to perform acts of ritualized solidarity and rivalry. They were moments to release pressures, renew communal bonds, redraw boundaries, conduct trade, collect

---

[34] See Sabine MacCormack, *Religion in the Andes: Vision and Imagination in Early Colonial Peru* (Princeton, 1991); Kenneth Mills, *Idolatry and Its Enemies: Colonial Andean Religion and Extirpation, 1640–1750* (Princeton, 1997); and Carolyn Dean, *Inka Bodies and the Body of Christ: Corpus Christi in Colonial Cuzco* (Durham, 1999). On the mixture of religions and civic iconography in the Bolivian Andes, see the provocative essay by Tristan Platt, "Simón Bolívar, the Sun of Justice, and the Amerindian Virgin: Andean Conceptions of the Patria in Nineteenth Century Bolivia," *Journal of Latin American Studies* 25 (1993), 159–189.

tribute, mobilize communal workforces, redistribute communal responsibilities and resources, install new officers of rotating civil-religious hierarchies, settle disputes, and/or reinvigorate communal efforts to recover stolen lands. On occasion, "folk" and "pagan" expressions of Catholicism could even be invoked to legitimate popular rebellion against constituted official authorities, although radical peasant religiosity was more common in highland Mexico than in the Andes. In any event, everyday forms of popular religiosity can often provide a barometer for registering social-moral issues and tensions at play in local indigenous societies. In the late nineteenth century, those tensions intensified in response to growing Church intrusions. Indeed, the Church performed the sort of bodily discipline to which later positivist discourses and social reformers would resort in their efforts to mold "dark bodies" and "dim minds" into pious and productive peasants. Like Europe's cotemporaneous civilizing missions in Africa, certain ruling factions were eager to direct the Jesuits, or other men of the cloth, in new state-driven integrative and disciplinary projects mandated by Catholic-Hispanism and its version of modernity.

REWORKING RACE

Fired up by metropolitan theories of race, environment, and evolution, Creole intellectuals produced a profusion of literary, scientific, and political writings on the Indian problem and other urgent racial matters. More than ever before, the imperatives of market capitalism and modernity called for state-driven efforts to extend the arm of the centralizing state and dominant Hispanic culture into the mountainous interior, especially in those regions where rural populations continued to claim territorial sovereignty and were willing to defend it. Most urban *letrados* (i.e., men of letters and/or the law) still put enormous faith in the power of reason, civilization, science, technology, contract law, the market, and other accoutrements of

Western modernity to steamroll over stubborn Andean anachronisms of the indigenous and colonial past. But the devastating War of the Pacific (1879–1883) had sundered any assumption about territorial sovereignty in Peru and Bolivia. So, too, the general penury of the countryside and the persistence of rural violence were exposing the limits of economic progress and state power in the interior provinces. Not least, almost a century of endemic political violence had made a mockery of the ideal of participatory democracy. This convergence of metropolitan race doctrines and domestic doubts created a compelling need for Creole intellectuals to diagnose their own internal geographies, races, and traditions. Most such exploratory projects in the Andes eventually came to fix their gaze on the Indian race.

Yet they sprang from different narrative traditions. Some race theorists worried about the "barbarous races" of blacks and Indians and their absorption by the supposed superiority of the white race (the trope of progressive evolutionary, Social Darwinian, and modernization narratives). For them, racial improvement would be best accomplished by breeding whiteness, helped along by state-directed programs of European immigration and eugenic reforms.[35] More

---

[35] Latin America's foundational narrative in this mode, Domingo Faustino Sarmiento's allegorical epic, *Civilization and Barbarism: Life of Juan Facundo Quiroga* [1845] (Buenos Aires, 1958), pits the triumphal forces of cities, civilization, and civil society against the counterforces of wild nature (the *pampa*), brute force (the *gauchos*), and provincial anarchy (embodied by the *caudillo*, Facundo). Taking a more prosaic tone, Colombian and Peruvian elites at midcentury took the lead in promoting narratives of economic and racial progress. They dreamed of throwing open their interior backlands to the modernizing forces of European civilization, capitalism, immigration, and railroads thanks to free-trade liberal policies and improving world market conditions (see Frank Safford and Marco Palacios, *Colombia: Fragmented Land, Divided Society* [Oxford, 2002], chap. 10; and *Paul* Gootenberg, *Imagining Development: Economic Ideas in Peru's "Fictitious Prosperity" of Guano, 1840–1880* [Berkeley, 1993], chap. 4).

pessimistic race thinkers drew on the notorious French race theorist, Count Arthur de Gobineau, and prevailing European strictures against miscegenation to diagnose social illness and to warn against the degenerative effects of racial-mixing in national contexts of racial diversity.[36] Still other writers engaged in nostalgic pastoralism by decrying the loss of their nation's authentic rural folk heritage or by collecting the artifacts of those vanishing cultures in order to fashion an originary national culture. But in the Andean heartlands, the Quechua and Aymara peasantries were hardly about to vanish into the mists of modernity, so the romantic and redemptive impulse of dissident writers there tended to assume reformist or radical implications. Most notably, postwar Peruvian writers, the vanguard of the *indigenista* movement that would flourish in the 1920s and later, turned their critical essays and redemptive

More generally, see Nancy Stepan, *The "Hour of Eugenics." Race, Gender, and Nation in Latin America* (Ithaca, 1991).

[36] Count Arthur de Gobineau's treatise, *Essay on the Inequality of Races* (Paris, 1853–5), held enormous sway over many leading positivist intellectuals and literary nationalists in Latin America until well into the twentieth century. (See Aline Helg, "Race in Argentina and Cuba, 1880–1930: Theory, Policies, and Popular Reaction," in *The Idea of Race in Latin America, 1870–1940* [Austin, 1990], 37–70; and Charles A. Hale, "Political and Social Ideas," in Leslie Bethell, ed., *Latin America: Economy and Society, 1870–1930* [Cambridge, 1986], 254–267.) One of his most famous disciples was the expatriate Bolivian intellectual, Alcides Arguedas, who wrote *Pueblo enfermo* [1909] (La Paz, 1936, 3rd ed.). Metaphorical uses of disease to condemn miscegenation, dark bodies, the sexuality of nonwhite women were commonplace in both European and Latin American writings on colonialism, gender, and race. See, for example, Sander Gilman, *Difference and Pathology: Stereotypes of Sexuality, Race, and Madness* (Ithaca, 1985); Anne McClintock, *Imperial Leather: Race, Gender, and Sexuality in the Colonial Contest* (New York, 1995); Robert Young, *Colonial Desire: Hybridity in Theory, Culture, and Race* (London, 1995); and Benigno Trigo, *Subjects of Crisis: Race and Gender as Disease in Latin America* (Hanover, 2000).

allegories against the "feudal" landlords of the *sierra* and their local accomplices.[37] A later generation of Peruvian writers would take on the whole *latifundista* heritage by invoking Inca socialism as a radical alternative to racial and class oppression.[38]

---

[37] Mid-nineteenth-century European Romanticism inspired some Latin American writers to the idea of originality in writing, culture, nationality, and nature, spurring a turning inwards toward genuinely American landscapes, which in turn lent themselves to incipient patriotic or regionalist themes. Romantic and folkloric genres achieved literary greatness in Argentina's celebrated *"gauchesque"* tradition, with the publication of José Hernández's epic poem, *Martín Fierro* [1872] (Buenos Aires, 1953). Although no Andean analogue emerged, many writers began to express nostalgia for quaint popular cultures, traditions and customs, pastoral order, and lush landscapes of the provinces. This emerging interest on the part of the urban *letrados* in contemporary provincial society and rural life was significant because, while the Indian of the past and especially the glories of the Incas figured prominently in nineteenth-century writings (especially in European travelogues), the contemporary Indian occupied little place in national literatures except in its function as the inherited dead weight of the past, obstructing the forces of enlightenment, progress, and civility. But when the Indian subject finally did assume its new place in emerging, dissident literary movements, it was almost invariably positioned as a passive victim, frequently spurred to spasmodic savagery by a corrupt and barbaric landowning elite, itself an anachronism of the colonial past. Cruelty and violence in Peru's feudal countryside was vividly depicted, for example, in the famous novel, *Aves sin Nido* (Buenos Aires, 1889) by Clorinda Matto de Turner, and in the short stories of Ventura García Calderón, published in his *La verguenza del cóndor* (Madrid, 1924). Bolivian race theorist, historian, and novelist, Alcides Arguedas sharpened his attack on the corrupt and "sick" elite in his *Pueblo enfermo* by indicting the landowning class in his debut novel, *Wata-Wara* (1904), later revised and published as *Raza de bronce* [1919] (La Paz, 1988).

[38] Peru's dissident literary-political tradition, which flowered in the 1920s and 1930s, is rooted in the diverse writings of Manuel González Prada, anarchist and founder of the political party, *La Unión Nacional*; José Carlos Mariátegui, founder of the Peruvian Communist Party; Victor Raúl Haya de la Torre, founder of *Alianza Popular Revolucionaria Americana* (APRA); and Luís Valcarcel, founder of Peruvian ethnology.

The variety of these racial-evolutionary discourses, briefly mentioned here, cautions against the temptation to view racial discourse as a finely hewed instrument of biopower in the hands of a monolithic modernizing state. Countering Michel Foucault's limited interpretation of racial genealogies, Ann Stoler has insisted on the polysemic nature of race thought, and its multiple interconnections with discourses of colonialism, gender, sexuality, and sentiment – particularly in contexts of European colonialism.[39] Clearly, there was no unifying vision of the Indian Other that shaped, or guided, state policy making in the Andes. In fact, official race thinking often became a battle site for liberal, conservative, and dissident factions of the oligarchy to argue over the parameters of the Indian problem and the sorts of legal, social, and therapeutic reforms that were needed to solve it. The race theme also lent itself to ideological debate over broader social issues like immigration, education, citizenship, poverty, morality, criminality, and public hygiene. Indeed, it was by applying the new diagnostic disciplines (racial social-psychology, criminology, pedagogy, etc.) to the Indian population that progressive reformers began to experiment with new policies of social control. These early experiments in fashioning the modern subject out of the subjugated Indian

---

[39] Ann Laura Stoler, *Race and the Education of Desire: Foucault's History of Sexuality and the Colonial Order of Things* (Durham, 1995); and her *Carnal Knowledge and Imperial Power: Race and the Intimate in Colonial Rule* (Berkeley, 2002). Her source of critical inspiration is Michel Foucault's *History of Sexuality* (New York, 1985), among his other works. Exciting new work in Andean anthropology is taking up Stoler's challenge to explore the interplay between gender, race, and culture in the making, or unmaking, of Indian, *cholo(a)*, and *mestizo(a)* identities; see, for example, Marisol De La Cadena, *Indigenous Mestizos: The Politics of Race and Culture in Cuzco, Peru, 1919–1991*; Deborah Poole, *Vision, Race, and Modernity: A Visual Economy of the Andean Image World* (Princeton, 1997); and Mary Weismantel, *Cholas and Pishtacos: Stories of Race and Sex in the Andes* (Chicago, 2001).

were taken up in earnest by state bureaucracies in the 1930s and 1940s.[40]

Out of the explosive politics of race came two broad impulses, however. One impulse, identified in broad political terms by historian Charles Hale, was the Latin American elites' turn away from the precepts of liberal-universalism toward positivism, with its strong proclivity for practical, disciplinary, and authoritarian reform.[41] In the 1890s, the ideals of literacy, suffrage, and citizenship were in full retreat before the advance of vogue schemes of racial order, industrial instruction, and restricted suffrage. As mentioned previously, the advent of new diagnostic sciences also permitted social reformers to use that normalizing knowledge to assess the congenital or cultural capacity of Indians to improve themselves and their race for the greater good of the nation. Out of this turn toward modern disciplinary projects sprang the second clarifying impulse of race discourse – to use more pliant notions of cultural difference as a surrogate for hard-wired biological determinism. For, as several scholars have illuminated, turn-of-the-century race doctrines in Latin America tended to discard imported theories of genetic determinism because they condemned their nations' subaltern racial groups to a permanent state of biological barbarity.[42] By contrast,

---

[40] See Deborah Poole's critical Foucauldian approach to the visual production of race in postcolonial Peru: *Vision, Race, and Modernity*; and her pointed study of positivist knowledge and biopower in "Ciencia, peligrosidad y repression en la criminología indigenista peruana," in Carlos Aguirre and Charles Walker, eds., *Bandoleros, abigeos y montoneros. Criminalidad y violencia en el Perú, siglos XVII–XX* (Lima, 1990), 335–93.

[41] Charles Hale, "Political and Social Ideas," 231–5, 240–86. See his pathbreaking work, *The Transformation of Liberalism in Late Nineteenth-Century Mexico* (Princeton, 1989).

[42] Nancy Stepan, *The "Hour of Eugenics,"* 11–14; Peter Wade, *Race and Ethnicity in Latin America*, 31–2; and Marisol De La Cadena, *Indigenous Mestizos*, 12–20.

theories of cultural and moral difference (incipient models of "ethnic ascription") left open the possibility of purposive action aimed at uplifting and improving racial-cultural character. Latin American race thinkers, including a handful of progressive scholars in the Andes, preferred to play with several "causative agents" (history, environment, biology, culture, and morality) to explain, categorize, and rank race. This cultural turn in the Andes later flowered into modern *indigenista* projects of redemption and reform, which targeted the "pristine" Indian races of the highlands. And in some regions like Cuzco and Otavalo, Creole regionalist writers invested their redeemed Indians with enormous symbolic capital, as they became icons of regional, or national, identity.[43]

Variations of racial discourse also reflect the diversity of historical, social, and political contexts that shaped and mediated racial idioms. This point will become clearer in the case studies that follow. But for now it is possible to identify an overriding purpose that informed most taxonomic exercises: to determine the fitness, or not, of nonwhite subalterns for national inclusion. On a broader scale, race theorists worried about the fitness, or not, of their own pluriethnic societies for modernity. Even before the notorious Bolivian writer and critic, Alcides Arguedas, published his devastating 1909 diagnostic of social illness in Bolivia (and by extension of other national polyglots), Creole elites harbored anxieties about their own "contaminated" racial heritages. How "white" were they? And where did the boundary lie, anyway? If they derived these racial anxieties from their own reflections in the eyes of European travelers,

---

[43] See Blanca Muratorio, "Nación, identidad y etnicidad: imágenes de los indios ecuatorianos y sus imagineros a fines del siglo XIX," in her edited volume, *Imágenes e imagineros. Representaciones de los indígenas ecuatorianos, siglos XIX y XX* (Quito, 1994), 132–8; and De La Cadena, *Indigenous Mestizos*, chap. 1.

they most surely would have had cause to worry. As Mary Louise Pratt has so insightfully shown, South American elites often saw themselves reflected through a glass darkly in the writings of European travelers and naturalists.[44] English writers, in particular, made a specialty of criticizing the indolence and backwardness of the Creole elites who lived off servile Indian or black labor. In an exquisite expression of imperial contempt and hypocrisy, British travelers were quite ready to hire Indian porters to carry cargo or cart their pampered bodies in chairs over treacherous mountain paths while they penned their contemptuous remarks about the lazy Creole upper classes who lived off the toil and sweat of their Indian servants (Figures 1 and 2).

It comes as little surprise that Creole race thinking in the Andes eventually focused on the boundaries of whiteness and civilization, especially as those boundaries were ever more breached by migrants and "mestizos," those who were slowly pushing their way into the restricted domain of urban, lettered white society. For we find among many race thinkers in the Andes a singularly hostile stance toward the ideal of racial fusion, or even the idea of progressive cross-breeding as an intermediate step in the Indian population's upward evolution toward whiteness. The idea of *mestizaje* did not provide the dominant or unifying theme of Andean cultural nationalism, either before or after the Mexican revolutionary state forged its famous "mestizo" national identity. On the contrary, Andean cultural nationalisms tended toward redemptive renderings of racial purity in the form of the "authentic Indian" – ideally, one well versed in the niceties of civilization, piety, and hard work. The

[44] Mary Louise Pratt, *Imperial Eyes: Travel Writing and Transculturation* (New York, 1992), 150–3. For a pointed example of a North American traveler's view of "Caucasian debasement" among Spanish Americans, see H. Willis Baxley, *What I Saw on the West Coast of South and North America* (New York, 1865), 378–91.

Figure 1. The Burden of Race, ca. 1960. Nineteenth-century European and South American artists crystallized the image of the generic Indian as "beast of burden" in their various picturesque, exotic, and documentary renderings of the Andean human landscape (see also Figure 2). Later photographic compositions sometimes turned this human symbol of social backwardness into a critique of modernity, such as in this visual juxtaposition of a Quechua man hauling his cargo along railroad tracks in southern Bolivia. (Photograph courtesy of the Archivo de la Paz, Bolivia.)

"Otavalan race" of the Ecuadorian highlands provided one example of redeemed Indianness in a nationalist discourse. But it was the *negativity of mestizaje* that infused most theories and sentiments of race in the late nineteenth- and early twentieth-century Andes. Both at the level of ideology and practice, the mestizo was forged into a negative icon, much as the colonial state had done in the late sixteenth century. For the symbolic value of the mestizo was its ambiguous interstitial positionality in a colonial society still theoretically organized along the binary – Indian and white, Quechua and Spanish, oral and literate, country and city, subsistent and monied. Modern racial-colonial discourses thus located the classic colonial triad (white, mestizo, Indian) at the center of debates about national identity and racial destiny. Blackness in turn was relegated to the margins of this dynamic triad of racial hierarchy.

These nested binaries were, of course, constitutive elements in the organization of material life in the Andean republics. Racial schemes reworked colonial binaries because, as anthropologist Olivia Harris points out, "there were strong local vested interests in maintaining a distinctive category of Indians." Not only did great white landowners have a stake in maintaining colonial-racial divisions, but so did whole provinces of petty officialdom and merchants. For the reproduction of Indianness propped up enduring institutions of labor extraction, thereby short-circuiting wage labor in the incipient capitalist economy. Harris takes this point further by exploring the interplay between shifting power and mercantile relations in the Andean countryside and the transfiguration of folk Indian-mestizo dichotomies in everyday practice. She argues that, by 1900, the Indian-mestizo gap was becoming a quasi-class relationship owing to the rise of "mestizo monopolies" over local channels of trade, usury, petty landownership, and officialdom in many regions. Emerging economic elites often asserted mestizo identities as part of their strategy to distance themselves from their rural impoverished roots, just as the urban white elite expressed its own collective contempt for these "racial-class hybrids." Thus, through ideology and practice, the normality of turn-of-the-century Indianness was pegged to class, as well as to biocultural attributes.[45]

Equally important to this analysis is the proactive role that Creole modernizers played in the reconstitution of racial binaries within the parameters of liberalism and nation building. For, as I have argued, most progressive state-builders who wanted to promote liberal-integrative projects (wage labor, civilization, military conscription, and even citizenship, eventually) forged modern race categories into instruments of social regulation and control. Elite discourses of Indianness inevitably proved to be treacherous business, however, because peasant leaders themselves used Indianness to assert their right to lands and *ayllu* sovereignty. As we have already seen, elite and popular mobilizations of racial-ethnic discourses could cut both ways. As land conflicts spread, liberalizing elites needed to dismantle the discursive-legal structures of Indian communalism in order to bring Indians under a unifying regime of contract law and individual property. But an equally powerful motive behind late nineteenth-century Creole racial discourse and policy was to restrict the spatial, political, and social mobility of transgressive Indians (dubbed *cholos*). Creole nationalist and civilizing discourses thus sprang from the contradictory psychosocial forces of national need (to remake Indians into disciplined modern subjects) and racial anxiety (inherent in the tensions and transformations of pluriethnic postcolonial societies). Given the volatility

---

[45] Olivia Harris, "Ethnic identity and market relations: Indians and mestizos in the Andes," in Brooke Larson and Olivia Harris with Enrique Tandeter, eds., *Ethnicity, Markets, and Migration in the Andes: At the Crossroads of History and Anthropology* (Durham, 1995), 363; 363–7.

of rural Andean society around the turn of the twentieth century, it is not surprising to see the axis of Creole race discourse tip toward racial exclusion. As the various case studies will suggest, modern Andean racial-cultural hierarchies were built to shore up the exclusive domain of whiteness in the face of erosive market forces, threats of "race war," and subaltern social practice.

2

▪▪▪▪▪▪▪▪▪▪▪▪▪▪▪▪▪▪▪▪▪▪▪▪▪▪▪▪▪▪▪▪▪▪▪▪▪▪

Colombia

Assimilation or Marginalization of the Indians?

On the northern periphery of the Andes, Colombia (known as New Granada, the name of the old colonial viceroyalty, until 1863) entered the mid-nineteenth century poised on the threshold of a liberal experiment in nation building. After two decades of robust liberal rhetoric and halting reforms, although tempered by protectionist measures, Colombian elites coalesced around the orthodoxies of economic liberalism. The 1849 election of General José Hilario López, a veteran of independence and a wealthy landowner, inaugurated Colombia's heyday of liberalism. For the next several years, there was a frenzy of reform activity, ranging from a precocious experiment in universal male suffrage (later suppressed) to the expulsion of the Jesuits in 1850. The culmination of liberalism's social reforms was the swift abolition of African slavery in 1851. Wedded to the ideal of free trade, the liberal vanguard wanted to end all restrictions on the free play of "natural economic laws," including the incipient labor market.[1]

---

[1] In general terms, economic liberalism refers to a corpus of ideology, theory, and policy that sought to relax institutional constraints on economic activity, allowing it to be governed by the free play of market forces. It also

This economic logic also governed Liberal Party thinking about the Indians. Unlike the other Andean countries, Colombian politicians did not look to Indian tribute as a viable source of government revenue in the 1830s and 1840s. Instead, Colombian policy makers hastened to liquidate colonial vestiges of Indian landholding and segregation, as well as to encourage overseas trade. New liberal policies mainly targeted Indian communities that held usufruct rights to common lands (*resguardos*) in Colombia's eastern Cordillera, the hinterlands of Bogotá. But the division of the *resguardos* proved to be more difficult than expected – there were legal complications, lack of surveyors, and considerable indigenous resistance. Some policy makers even tried to stall the land reforms by imposing a short-term policy of protection during the 1840s. But in 1850, this gesture of protection was reversed, when the Congress authorized provincial lawmakers to throw all *resguardo* lands on the market.[2]

Geography played a paradoxical role in Colombia's lurch toward liberalism. On the one hand, geography compelled Creole elites to look outward toward the Atlantic economy from early on. Having lived in economic isolation for decades, locked in the mountainous interior of the country, wealthy merchants and landowners harbored hopes that the country's tropical products (tobacco, cinchona bark, coffee, sugar, and cotton) would find markets in Europe and the United States. When the new generation of liberals swept into power in 1849, they moved quickly to tear down tariff

promoted the international division of labor through the alleged comparative advantages of each part of the world economy (given differing factor endowments). The precepts of economic liberalism underscore the strictures against governmental regulation of economic life and the international application of free trade policies. See Frank Safford, "The Emergence of Economic Liberalism in Colombia," in Joseph L. Love and Nils Jacobsen, eds., *Guiding the Invisible Hand: Economic Liberalism and the State in Latin American History* (New York, 1988), 35; and Frank Safford and Marco Palacios, *Colombia: Fragmented Land, Divided Society* (Oxford, 2002), chap. 10.

[2] Safford and Palacios, *Colombia*, 184–5.

walls and invite foreign investment into the nation. On the other hand, this fragmented land and inchoate set of regional economies soon dashed liberal expectations. Driven more by ideology than by real economic incentives, Colombia's nation builders had embraced liberal prescriptions long before the country possessed an integrated national market or expanding export economy. Indeed, free-trade liberalism sprouted in a comparatively hostile economic environment. In the 1850s, Colombia still depended on the sluggish export market in gold, an economic holdover of the colonial era. Tobacco, no longer a state monopoly, was beginning to spread along the upper Magdalena River Valley, thanks to the advent of steamboats on the river. But highland food production for the growing cities and the growth of potential export commodities, such as the coffee bean, suffered from tremendous logistical problems. Most regional markets were cut off from the seacoast and overseas markets by mountains and ravines, tropical climates, seasonal rainfalls, and enormous overland freight costs. Pack mules carried most cargo until the end of the nineteenth century, and transportation between the port of Cartagena and Europe was faster and cheaper, for example, than was the overland route connecting the port of Cartagena to the capital city of Bogotá.

These "primitive" conditions were not lost on the inquisitive European or North American traveler who ventured into the interior of early-nineteenth-century Colombia (or New Granada, as it was still called). Indeed, many foreign visitors hired Indian porters to carry them on their backs across the wretched mule paths, so they could see for themselves Colombia's quaint, isolated provinces and forlorn Indians, so long hidden from foreign eyes behind Spain's closed-door policy of colonialism (Figure 2). They left discouraging impressions about the natural and social impediments that stood in the way of scientific expeditions and economic progress.[3] But

---

[3] Mary Louise Pratt, *Imperial Eyes: Travel Writing and Transculturation* (London, 1992), 150–3.

Figure 2. *Cargueros* of the Quindio Pass in the Province of Popayán, ca. 1827. *Carguero* literally means "carrier." The porter of human cargo was also called *sillero*, in reference to the chair strapped onto the porter's back. Nineteenth-century European travelers to Colombia were fixated on its mountains, rugged terrain, and impassable roads, widely considered to be the worst in South America. Unlike the South Andes, where the upkeep of old Inca and colonial highways was still sustained by *corvée* labor, Colombia's nineteenth-century

Colombian elites did not need the vicarious experiences of European travelers to appreciate the appalling state of their roads, the decadence of internal commerce, and the growing regional economic autarchy. The yawning gap between utopian liberalism and stubborn realities around 1850 disquieted Creole politicians and writers, who began the task of diagnosing the root causes of Colombia's economic backwardness. And they fixed their gaze on the inescapable presence of Indians and Africans in their midst.

REINVENTING INDIANS AS ECONOMIC OBSTACLES

Among the four Andean republics, Colombia's Creole elite was the first to produce a rhetorical argument that pinned the country's economic backwardness squarely on the concept of racial inferiority. Although the content of their racisms varied, most midcentury social theorists did not deploy the orthodoxies of genetic determinism. Rather, writers like José María Samper, Manuel Ancízar, and Augustín Codazzi explored the effects of climate, culture, and history on the social characteristics of racial

[*caption to Figure 2 (cont.)*] roads had deteriorated badly, making mules almost worthless as transport animals. Indian backs became the preferred mode of overland transport for many foreign travelers. But as writers, they did not hesitate to turn the *sillero* into a visual symbol of South American barbarism and backwardness in their travel narratives. In his survey of Colombia for the British government in 1824, for example, Colonel J. P. Hamilton wrote of the human beasts of burden that carried cargo and people on their backs across the Quindío pass, the main east-west axis of the country. See, Michael Taussig, *Shamanism, Colonialism, and the Wild Man* (Chicago, 1987), 296–305, on Charles Cochrane's harrowing journey by Indian porter through Colombia; and Benigno Trigo, *Subjects of Crisis: Race and Gender as Disease in Latin America* (Hanover, 2000), 16–46, on perceptions of race, time, and landscape in European travel literature. Source: Col. J. P. Hamilton, *Travels Throughout the Interior Provinces of Columbia*, 2 vols. (London, 1827), 2: 211.

groups.[4] In particular, liberal writers were fond of invoking the Black Legend of Spanish colonial oppression to explain the degradation of Colombia's Indian and African races.[5] Even José María Samper, the most rigorous race theorist of the group, did not wholly accept the premise of biological descent as destiny. As we shall see shortly, he firmly believed in the possibility of cultural redemption if certain measures were taken to instill in the inferior groups the values appropriate to a modern civil society. But however much they nuanced their studies of Colombia's "racial types," they were beginning to produce a scientific and literary canon that associated "whiteness" with progress and civilization and its negative opposite, "nonwhiteness," with the obstacles that blocked the pathways to modernity.

The social construction of race occurred in two types of "scientific" literature. The first type was the modern variant of discovery and exploration narratives. They were written by geographers, ethnographers, and essayists, and often illustrated by artists, all of whom sought to unlock the secrets of the nation's forgotten or forbidding frontiers. A second genre was the geography of region and race, and Colombia's 1849 geographic study provided the canonical standard of all subsequent investigations. The *Comisión Corográfica* was produced by a team of foreign and

---

[4] José María Samper, *Ensayo sobre las revoluciones políticas y la condición social de las repúblicas colombianas* [1861] (Bogotá, 1984); Manuel Ancízar, *Peregrinaciones de Alpha por las provincias del Norte de la Nueva Granada* (Bogotá, 1956); Augustín Codazzi, "Descripción jeneral de los indios del Caquetá," in Felipe Pérez, ed., *Jeografía física i política de los Estados Unidos de Colombia*, 2 vols. (Bogotá, 1863), II.

[5] The "Black Legend" was invoked by Spain's imperial rivals and colonial critics, from the seventeenth-century British to nineteenth-century Spanish American patriots, to vilify the Spanish moral character and to attack its regime of colonialism, for its cruel and despotic rule over its Indian subjects. It has also permeated twentieth-century scholarly debate on Spain's empire in America.

national scientists, commissioned to record the country's demographic, economic, and sociocultural peculiarities (Figure 3). More
than a mere aggregation of facts, these studies charted the moral topography of race, which located Colombia's diverse "racial groups"
in geographic space and in hierarchical relationship to an economic
activity and to each other. Region and race served as the organizing
principles of knowledge. Thus, for example, scientists depicted the
innate characteristics of the Harvesters of Aniseed: Mestizo and Indian Types, Province of Ocana," and the "White Miners, Province
of Soto" (Figure 4). Of particular interest was the economic behavior of each racial group, implicitly measured against bourgeois
virtues of thrift and hard work. Taken together, these provincial surveys provided racial typologies, characterizations, and illustrations
of Colombia's diverse regions and races.[6]

The new geography bipolarized Colombia into the civilized highlands populated by "white and mestizo types" and its savage
hinterlands – the interior tropical forests of nomadic tribal peoples
and the southern Pacific littoral and the Caribbean coastal region
where large concentrations of black people lived. Afro-Colombians,
many recently emancipated, also inhabited inland pockets of rural
and urban territory. But what they putatively shared in common
was their affinity for the torpor of the tropics, whether coastal or
inland, and their "lamentable" indolence, superstition, and volatility. Highland Indians occupied an ambiguous middle ground in this
geo-cultural and racial order. Neither savage nor civilized, the highland Indians of the northeastern provinces near the city of Bogotá
were the best candidates for cultural improvement and eventual
assimilation, according to the prevailing wisdom. Samper described

---

[6] See Frank Safford's fascinating gloss on this set of surveys, "Race, Integration, and Progress: Elite Attitudes and the Indian in Colombia," *Hispanic
American Historical Review* 71: 1 (1991), 20–7; and Benigno Trigo, *Subjects
of Crisis. Race and Gender as Disease in Latin America* (Hanover, 2000),
Chapter 1.

Figure 3. Campsite of the *Comisión Corográfica* in the Province of Soto, ca. 1850. The commission took the first official geographic survey of an Andean country, following in the steps of earlier Enlightenment travel and discovery projects. In contrast to late colonial expeditions focusing on flora and fauna, this new geography provided the first exploratory synthesis of regional and racial identities making up the interior landscapes of Colombia in the mid-nineteenth century. Source: *En busca de un país. La comisión corográfica. Selección de dibujos ...* (Bogotá: Carlos Valencia Ed, 1984).

Figure 4. Harvesters of aniseed: Mestizo and Indian "types," Province of Ocaña, ca. 1850. This watercolor painted by one of the artists of the *Comisión Corográfica* synthesizes region, socioeconomic occupation, and "racial type" (marked dramatically by clothing and by the positioning of the Indian engaged in work and the mestizo [overseer?] at rest). Source: *En busca de un país: La comisión corográfica. Selección de dibujos*...(Bogotá: Carlos Valencia Editores, 1984).

the Chibcha of the eastern *cordillera* as "frugal but intemperate, patient but stupid," yet ultimately "civilizable." But if the northern Chibcha's failings were benign, his southern counterpart's were not. The Páez and Pasto Indians of the south were considered to be sedentary savages, not much farther up the evolutionary scale than the hunters and gatherers of the tropical forests. They were dangerous races: "resistant to civilization [and] unmoved by progress," according to Samper.[7] Indeed, the Páez and Pastos had a long history of ethnic mobilization to defend or advance their collective interests. Samper was only codifying in racial terms the images, memories, and fears that white nation-builders harbored toward the militant indigenous peoples of the far south.

As they peered into their nation's variegated "heart of darkness," the liberal vanguard busily produced a corpus of prescriptive economic thought that aspired to a modernity in which a culturally homogeneous nation attended to the prosaic needs of commerce and industry. Borrowing the precepts of political economy from Montesquieu and other Enlightenment thinkers, they associated the idea of civil society with commerce, money, and communication. The edges of market culture (ideally conceived) delineated the hierarchical division between civilization and barbarism. At best, Indians and Africans inhabited the frontiers of civilization because they seemed to lack everything the Creole liberals identified as civilized: money, commerce, comfort, hygiene, Christianity, and the cultural values associated with such things. Indeed, the new civilizing rhetoric defined the essence of Indianness and blackness as the antithesis of the *Homo economicus*, the rational economic actor endowed with bourgeois cultural norms. Armed with their pseudo-scientific regional-racial typologies, Creole authorities manufactured images of lazy, antimarket Indians and Africans content to live

---

[7] Samper, *Ensayo sobre las revoluciones políticas*, 87–9; quoted in Safford, "Race, Integration, and Progress," 26.

in poverty and sloth. Liberal merchants were concerned with judg-
ing the lower orders by their potential as laborers and consumers. By
midcentury, they had lost the earlier Bolivarian ideal of turning Indians into industrious yeoman farmers, simply by subdividing and pri-
vatizing *resguardo* lands. Instead they saw the "darker races" as taking their "natural place" among the laboring poor who might, over
time, form a mass domestic market for commodities. Thus there
was much debate over the intrinsic worth of Colombia's African and
Indian races as laborers and consumers, measured against the Caucasian ideal: "if we take a [black] Magdalena boatman or an Indian
from Cundinamarca and compare him with an educated Bostonian,
we will have before us both our starting point and our goal," wrote
a leading liberal reformer in 1896.[8] In the meantime, liberal intellectuals blamed Colombia's invertebrate national market on black
and Indian indolence and indifference to material comfort. Ethnographers often pointed to the "typical" thatched-roof windowless
hut of the highland Indian as tangible evidence of their subsistent
nature. Hence, poverty and misery could be blamed on the victim
and at the same time used to ascribe racial identity. Postcolonial
categories of race and class were converging.

Like other "civilizing" agents, Colombian liberals envisioned a
culturally homogeneous, market-driven society moving rapidly into
the company of cosmopolitan nations. Ideologically, they shared
more in common with the nation-building rhetoric and goals of their
Brazilian, Argentine, and Chilean counterparts than with the postcolonial ambivalence of Creole elites in Ecuador, Peru, and Bolivia.
Colombia's liberal counterparts in those countries continued to face
powerful conservative forces still wedded to colonial-paternalist

[8] Enrique Cortés, a leading liberal educator published these words in his work,
Escritos varios (Paris, 1896); quoted in Marco Palacios, *Coffee in Colombia,
1850–1970: An Economic, Social and Political History* (New York, 1980),
72.

traditions and vulnerable to tremors and eruptions from below. In contrast, Colombian elites had inherited a strong Bolivarian tradition,[9] which laid the groundwork for the "civilizing" project of the 1850s, 1860s, and 1870s. Although Colombian reformers may have failed at realizing their utopian liberalism in the immediate postindependence period, they succeeded in breaking up *resguardo* lands and crushing Indian opposition throughout much of the northern provinces. Only in the southern provinces did they still confront militant indigenous communities. But in sharp contrast to Peru and Bolivia, Colombian Indians composed a small minority of the total population (perhaps as little as 16 percent in the late colonial period) and in the northeastern *cordillera*, most had mixed into the mestizo majority. Fewer still occupied *resguardo* lands and those located in the colder climates were not suitable for cultivating export crops (coffee, tobacco, etc.). Indian integration was deemed important for the purposes of expanding the consumer and labor markets, but not for the conquest of land. Furthermore, tribute had long since withered away, removing any fiscal interest the state might have had in preserving caste distinctions. Instead Colombia was lurching toward an idea of nation based on linguistic, cultural, and racial homogeneity. Liberal and conservative elites were united in a common concern: how to create out of ethnic and cultural diversity a new and purified white population on which "true nationhood" could be built. The goal was set; only the means to reach it were in question.

---

[9] Under Bolívar's leadership, the Congress of Cúcuta in 1821 had declared that black slaves and Indians would be incorporated into the new republic as citizens. New Granada's elites intended to abolish legal distinctions among the "castes" in their euphoric embrace of egalitarian principles, but most planters soon resisted freeing their slaves, and Creole elites channeled their liberal idealism into land reform policies that aimed to divide communal lands and eventually integrate highland peasants into the expanding market economy and Hispanic society (Safford and Palacios, *Colombia: Fragmented Land, Divided Society*, 180).

Debates swirled around the potential for constructing a nation out of a patchwork of cultures and races. But most liberal thinkers imagined a nation emerging from several generations of biocultural regeneration, or in the parlance of the day, "whitening." Ultimately, they sought to de-Indianize (and de-Africanize) Colombia over several generations through genetic assimilation into a vigorously expanding white population. The new theories of evolution in the 1860s offered theoretical comfort to those who pushed the idea of genetic improvement through whitening. It was to be accomplished by both social and natural means. First, the state would import large numbers of European immigrants, attracted perhaps by a generous homesteading policy. Second, as the European stock increased, the inferior races would disappear through high mortality rates and intermarriage. The liberals had high hopes for the genetic assimilation of highland Indians, in particular. In fact, this policy represented an urgent national priority in the second half of the nineteenth century because they believed that only through the intermarriage of Indians and mestizos, and mestizos and whites, would the nation accomplish its genetic integration and counteract the ominous sense that Colombia's black population was "naturally" more prolific and unruly.

Here, then, we begin to understand the peculiar ways that Colombian nation-builders "privileged" highland Indians as readily assimilable, and therefore civilizable. In Colombia, the most intractable "problem of race" was affixed to blackness, not Indianness. The roots of this double standard of prejudice, of course, go back to the dawn of colonialism in the New World, when the crown and Church sanctioned African, but not Indian, slavery. During the late colonial and independence periods, Enlightenment and Creole patriot discourses had disparaged and feared blacks, even as Bolívar's armies recruited and liberated Afro-Colombian slaves. Fears of black insurrection, banditry, endemic crime, and "natural fecundity" continued to preoccupy the dominant class throughout the nineteenth century. And as liberals consolidated their project of national integration, they looked charitably upon the highland Indian (particularly of the northern regions), not the black, as more likely to be absorbed by the superior races. Even the most racist of authors, José María Samper, was relatively optimistic about the natural processes of Indian atrophy. The new official surveys seemed to add scientific support to his projection. Manuel Ancívar, who surveyed Colombia's eastern and northeastern provinces in 1850–1, proclaimed that Indians were rapidly disappearing into *mestizaje*, and by degrees, into whiteness. "Today one notes in the new generation the progressive improvement of the castes," he wrote about the Province of Tunja. Although the Indians are "still there . . . you cannot see them."[10]

It was a good observation. Chibcha descendants living in the departments of Cundinamarca, Boyacá, Santander, and Santander del Norte had all but "disappeared" in the eyes of colonial authorities, as early as the mid-eighteenth century. Even in the "Indian province" of Tunja (where native peoples composed two-fifths of the total population in the mid-eighteenth century), whites and mestizos already outnumbered Indians by more than ten to one in their own *resguardos*. Bourbon inspectors described a *ladino* countryside, where only a small percentage of the remaining Indians held legal rights to *resguardo* lands. As a consequence, the leaders of the new republic inherited a land opening up to the possibilities of private colonization on former Indian lands. In the 1830s, liberal policy makers saw the need to dismantle the *resguardos* and redistribute titled plots of land to Indians, before selling off the remaining tracts. But even before they could begin the process, they had to

---

[10] Ancívar, *Peregrinaciones de Alpha*, 214, 250; quoted in Safford, "Race, Integration and Progress," 28. See also Peter Wade, *Blackness and Race Mixture: The Dynamics of Racial Identity in Colombia* (Baltimore, 1993).

distinguish between "Indians" and "mestizos" in the highly integrated and densely populated *resguardos* in the northeastern highlands. Indeed, the republic had officially expunged Indians from the national census and parish records following independence. But priests and other people resorted to code words (such as, *vecinos* and *filegrises*) to distinguish between the "Indians" and "non-Indians" in their everyday social transactions.[11]

Thus Colombia's civilizing project charted the pathway toward nationhood through the process of cultural and biological *mestizaje* and, eventually, whiteness. This project would falter in the 1880s and 1890s, as the Conservative Party restored certain traditions of the colonial *sociedad de castas*. But Colombia's search for national identity through whitening eventually excited the political imagination of liberals in the other Andean nations, although they reconstructed and applied this project of genetic improvement under very different national and historical circumstances. As discussed, the mestizo often had powerful negative connotations in the dominant discourses on race and social evolution in the more deeply divided societies of Ecuador, Peru, and Bolivia. But in Colombia the mestizo sector was valued for its power to move race and culture toward a homogeneous white, Christian, Spanish-speaking, capitalist nationality. While *mestizaje* represented a relatively progressive force, it had not yet congealed into a symbol of racial synthesis or nonwhite national identity, as it would do in mid-twentieth-century populist rhetoric. (In the 1920s, 1930s, and 1940s, *mestizaje* would be reconfigured as a superior mix of races by some Latin American

---

[11] Safford, "Race, Integration, and Progress," 128; and personal communication. Recent historical scholarship has begun to examine the regional dimensions of race making—for example, the construction of Antioquia as the nation's "whitest" province. See Nancy Appelbaum, "Whitening the Region: Caucano Mediation and 'Antioqueño Colonization' in Nineteenth-Century Colombia," *Hispanic American Historical Review* 79: 4 (1999), 631–67.

nationalists eager to construct new legitimacies on more inclusive racial and class grounds. Even then, however, *mestizaje* remained a vexed metaphor for many cultural nationalists in Ecuador, Peru, and Bolivia.) Nineteenth-century meanings of *mestizaje* were embedded in the ideology and policies of whitening, which aimed to import European immigrants, eradicate racial-cultural diversity, and construct a monolingual nation and bourgeois market culture under a unitary rule of law. Such definitions of nationhood implicitly indicted the democratic or autonomist claims, as well as the local cultural practices, of the diverse amalgams of mestizo, African, indigenous peoples.

This liberal vision of Indian integration propelled policy makers to hammer out the specifics of economic and cultural reform. One set of reforms was designed to redefine the relationship of Indians to the larger economy and polity. Anxious to stimulate commerce, the new liberals wanted to hasten the subdivision and privatization of *resguardo* lands by removing the last restrictions on their sale. Yet, they also sought to federalize land reform policies, allowing provincial governments to enact their own legislation. Thus, the very federalist system the liberals put into place undermined their goals of agrarian integration, leaving extremely haphazard patterns of land reform. In the southern regions of Popayán and Pasto, regional elites were more reluctant to break up *resguardos*, whereas Bogotá called for the immediate division of all remaining *resguardo* properties in its own Department of Cundinamarca. In general, however, elite consensus turned against earlier protectionist policies and, in particular, removed the literacy clause that had forbidden illiterate Indians from selling their lands. After 1850, Indians were more vulnerable to litigants, merchants, and creditors who coveted their communal or family plots of land. Yet they also discovered how selective the application of civil equality could be when the liberals imposed a literacy clause for the right to vote. Hurled into the market but shut out of the political system, Colombia's indigenous poor were beginning to experience the double standards of citizenship.

But the road to civilization and prosperity also required the moral "redemption" of the "Indian race." We still have very little knowledge about nineteenth-century experiments in cultural suppression and reform, but the very idea of converting subsistent peasants into disciplined workers and acquisitive materialists called for a massive "civilizing mission" and European immigration scheme beyond anything the federalist, laissez-faire government was capable of. The Liberal Party had more vision than muscle in this regard. Even so, through its own rhetoric, the civilizing mission assumed a legitmacy of its own. Piecemeal measures were proposed and sometimes implemented. Moralizing the Indian character would require resocialization through education and religious indoctrination. Heathenism, drunkenness, fiestas, and other barbarian practices would have to be rooted out. Vagrancy and vagabondage needed to be controlled, the latter especially targeted to destitute women who were seen to be migrating to Bogotá and turning to prostitution in alarming numbers. In later years, reformers would turn to problems of epidemic, disease, and hygiene. But for most of the nineteenth century, concern centered around moral discipline, crime, and punishment. The civilizing mission was to penetrate the intimate cultural spaces of local Indian lifeways.

INDIAN DISPOSSESSION, DEFENSE, OR DEFIANCE?
NORTH-SOUTH CONTRASTS

Beyond the cultural aggression such projects sanctioned, the experiences and responses of indigenous groups varied sharply during the late nineteenth century. The weak, uneven, and contradictory application of liberalism and, after 1880, the counterreforms of the conservatives certainly contributed to patchwork patterns of social change. Moreover national land, labor, and export markets only began to expand in the 1870s. Thereafter the very nature and intensity of commodity markets were extremely uneven and acted upon distinctive regional, class, and ethnic heritages. Without delving into specific regional variations, we can appreciate starkly different north-south highland patterns of social and cultural change under the converging pressures of market expansion and nation building. The official geography and ethnography of midcentury Colombia provides important clues about the nature of these regional contrasts: market pressures and Indian strategies of social reproduction were far more explosive in the south, among the Indians of Popayán and Pasto than elsewhere. Indian *caudillos* and *cabildos* in those provinces carried on militant traditions of *resguardo* land defense and recuperation, both inside and outside the bounds of civil law. Chibcha peoples farther north felt the pressures of poverty and dislocation no less intensely in the years after 1870, but their own long history of communal erosion, peasantization, and integration in local and regional markets (notwithstanding elite stereotypes to the contrary) foreclosed the possibility of insurgent ethnic responses to growing subsistent threats.

Late-nineteenth-century expansion in commercial agriculture quickened the pace of change for most peasant communities in the highland areas of Cundinamarca, Boyacá, and Antioquia. Coffee spread rapidly along the western slopes of Cundinamarca and on the hills sloping down to the *llanos* in the east. Coffee flourished in warmer climates and was cultivated on private estates in pioneering zones. Established on foundations of the traditional *latifundia*, coffee cultivation often did not take place at the expense of communal lands or peasant smallholding, as it did in other parts of Latin America. Problems of peasant landlessness and dislocation in the eastern highlands did not stem directly from the rise of commercial coffee. In contrast, the spread of cattle ranching across the grasslands surrounding the city of Bogotá gobbled up lands of the abolished *resguardos* and dislocated small-scale farmers and medium-sized landowners who had engaged in intensive cultivation of cereals, fruits, and vegetables. These ranches cleared the plains for extensive cattle grazing. But even in these hinterlands of Bogotá, where stock ranching had a potentially violent edge, there was no direct assault on *resguardo* lands. Communal lands had long since withered, and the territorial question, so terribly explosive in other parts of the Andes in this period, no longer held primacy in this changing landscape of power.[12]

Consequently, the roots of economic and cultural change must be sought in the subtle everyday forms of peasant initiative and survival, often under deteriorating circumstances. After 1870, the twin processes of hacienda growth and peasant dispossession gave rise to a floating labor force that eventually swelled the categories of tenant farmers, sharecroppers, and indentured servants (*concertados*). The convergence of overseas market incentives and liberal orthodoxies rapidly advanced the edge of coffee and cattle haciendas into highland areas of Cundinamarca, Boyacá, and Antioquia, zones already well connected to urban markets and overseas trade. But to explain the shift toward large landholding in Colombia simply in terms of external pressures is to overlook the complex internal dynamics of *minifundismo* (the tendency toward increasingly fragmented smallholds). Partible inheritance, land disputes, and mounting population pressures on smallholding regimes did their part to prepare the way for estate expansion and peasant landlessness in many regions of Colombia. By the 1880s in parts of Cundinamarca and Boyacá, smallholding peasants were being transformed into servile laborers and sharecroppers living on hacienda lands that once belonged to the *resguardo* of their own grandparents. Within three

---

[12] On Colombia's nineteenth-century political and economic history of coffee production, see Charles Bergquist, *Coffee and Conflict in Colombia, 1886–1910* (Durham, 1968); and Marco Palacios, *Coffee in Colombia, 1850–1970: An Economic, Social and Political History* (New York, 1980).

generations, small-scale farmers had seen the status of their lands change from *resguardo* into *minifundia* and eventually become swallowed up by a *latifundium*. As Orlando Fals Borda describes it, "white [land]owners simply watched over fences and boundary ditches with [the community of] Saucío, while the old resguardo started to look like a mouse-hole – hundreds of beings kept busy in Lilliputian pockets next to these estates."[13]

In more isolated eastern regions of Boyacá, land-starved peasants migrated into the lower temperate zones of coffee cultivation. Little is known about the process of labor expulsion from highland *minifundio* regions. To what extent did the grinding poverty of highland agriculture push surplus laborers into the expanding coffee zones? Did labor contractors (*enganchadores*) employ mechanisms of debt and coercion to draft seasonal pickers for the coffee plantations? Few clues are left to us by contemporary chroniclers, who generally described seasonal workers as drifting down from the mountains into the coffee zones and happily settling on the plantations with their families. These migratory workers were often categorized in regional-racial terms, which naturalized them as servile workers suited for the degradations of tropical field work. "The *indio* of Boyacá and Cundinamarca," wrote the conservative intellectual, Vergara y Velasco, in 1901, "is a machine, for he serves all causes with equal passiveness and duty.... He obeys the bidding of the whites... whom he both fears and respects."[14] Many seasonal workers apparently did attach themselves to the new plantations, but popular stories and songs more often recount the injustices inflicted on migrants by infamous *enganchadores*,

---

[13] Orlando Fals Borda, *Peasant Society in the Colombian Andes: A Sociological Study of Saucío* (Gainesville, 1955), 105. See also, Juan Friede, *El indio en la lucha por la tierra. Historia de los resguardos del macizo central columbiano* (Bogotá, 1944).

[14] F. J. Vergara y Velasco, *Nueva geografía de Colombia* [1901], 3 vols. (Bogotá 1974), 3: 666; quoted in Palacios, *Coffee in Colombia*, 72–3.

some of whom continued to operate well into the twentieth century.[15]

Communal disintegration and cultural *mestizaje* were already hallmarks of Colombia's northeastern highlands in the early nineteenth century. But after the 1870s, further fragmentation of property, impoverishment, and transience eroded the bonds of traditional agricultural and artisanal communities. Population pressures, grinding poverty, and deteriorating market conditions were far more disruptive forces for traditional artisans and farmers than the grandiose civilizing missions, which were supposed to create industrious laborers and consumers out of slothful Indians. But even as the deepening subsistence crisis of the highlands created a casual labor force for the lowland coffee estates, some highland Indians found ways to prosper as small coffee producers, mule drivers, itinerant traders, labor contractors, and country lawyers. Indeed, in the north, where smallholding pressures were acute and where the structures of communal action and defense had crumbled, peasant family economies had to diversify into nonagricultural activities. A small minority of peasant families were, indeed, well positioned to prosper from the expanding market. For them, the pathways out of poverty and Indianness often converged, as they slipped into the amorphous mestizo majority, which putatively shared with whites the positive attributes of acquisitiveness and enterprise.

The distinctive native groups of the southern provinces of Popayán and Pasto met the challenges of modernity under very different historical and regional circumstances. The south was a crucible of mercantile and political violence. *Resguardo* Indians clashed with hostile, then paternalist, republican policies; experienced successive civil wars; and saw the quinine industry ravage

---

[15] Palacios, *Coffee in Colombia*, 69–70. See also, Silvia Broadbent, "The Formation of Peasant Society in Central Colombia," *Ethnohistory* 28:3 (1981), 258–77.

the forests, drain the villages of workers, and ultimately open up interior Indian frontiers to white colonization. Through years of endemic war and economic extraction, the southern ethnic groups were plunged into the vortex of state building and economic modernization. It was in the isolated mountains and leafy quinine forests of Páez and Pasto territories that liberal Creole dreams of Indian assimilation died an early death.

Against the violence of modernity, many indigenous communities could call upon their own ethnic traditions, memories, and identities to confront the threats to their existence. At the core of ethnic politics lay the communal lands of the *resguardo*, now a smaller and weaker unit than in the eighteenth century but still the social and cultural basis of local community and identity. Although liberal legislation had abolished hereditary chiefdoms, some Páez communities had empowered their small, elected *cabildos* (councils) to litigate and negotiate deals to shield themselves against threatening land claims. The communities of Pitayó and Jambaló, for example, lived on the western slopes of the *cordillera*, where they were openly exposed to land-hungry hacendados who shared their borders. Their councils became the rallying points of defense against land encroachments. In the 1850s, white entrepreneurs in search of quinine were astonished to meet "the Indian governor of Pitayó...[who] presented himself before us, armed and accompanied by many other Indians, in order to prevent us continuing our work and to embargo what quinine we had already harvested."[16] Other *cabildos*, especially those representing the remote interior hamlets of Tierradentro, had less experience dealing with republican policies, white land-grabbers, and the invasion of quinine entrepreneurs. As we shall see shortly, those Páez

---

[16] *El Tiempo*, 4 May 1858; quoted in Joanne Rappaport, *The Politics of Memory: Native Historical Interpretation in the Colombian Andes* (Cambridge, 1990), 87.

communities often fell victim to the forces of extractive agriculture. But whether strong or weak, the institution of Indian *cabildo* exercised limited power over municipal units. And as such it paled in comparison to the new breed of Páez political-military leader, who emerged from the din and dust of the independence struggle and successive civil wars to become self-styled, de facto *caciques* commanding the loyalty of far-flung Páez communities and their local *cabildos*.

PÁEZ CHIEFTAINS AND THE TREACHERY OF WAR

Páez territory became the hearth of Indian *caudillismo* in Colombia during the independence wars, when the Páez collaborated with patriotic armies as their porters, spies, messengers, and trailblazers. Later, during nine civil wars fought at various times throughout the century, the Indians were recruited to civil war armies, often forcibly on festival days, to advance the cause of the Conservative or Liberal Parties. Civilizing rhetoric aside, the white elites feared as much as they needed the "warrior tribes" of the Páez. Where liberal civilizers saw "sedentary savages," partisan military leaders saw "savage soldiers" who might be recruited to their cause, often under their own native commanders. A *caudillo* was not just an officer but a military chief with a following of his own. Most native *caudillos* rose to prominence among their own people in the heat of military action and used the battleground to acquire prestige and loyalty among widely dispersed communities.

These shadowy figures still elude the historian's eye, but the contemporary press provides glimpses of their contradictory influences and actions. Some *caudillos* assimilated into Colombian society, wielding their influence on behalf of partisan politics, military recruitment, or land and mining investors. Others maintained their independence and used their guerrilla firepower to cement alliances among Páez communities, protect or reclaim *resguardo* lands, or retaliate against outside encroachers. Joanne Rappaport shows that Páez *caudillos* did not rely upon their military virtues alone to build their base of support, but "cemented their dominion over broad expanses of territory, reproducing colonial *cacicazgos* by forging [strategic] marital ties."[17] Aspiring Páez chiefs consolidated their legitimacy across disparate communities by marrying the daughters of colonial *caciques* or by claiming noble descent. In this way, the rise of guerrilla leaders among the Páez replicated the institution of hereditary *cacicazgo*, although the latter was abolished at the time of independence.

But postcolonial *cacicazgos* did not signal simply the symbolic defiance of republican law. They laid the groundwork for perpetual guerrilla warfare throughout the century, keeping the southern mountains of Cauca a dangerous place for white people. During the various civil wars, Páez forces were repeatedly used in military operations by Liberal and Conservative armies, and inevitably official news reports followed with stories of armed bands of Indians invading farm houses, stealing cattle, and terrorizing the white citizenry. Mobilized for military action, Páez warriors quickly turned insurgent or criminal, more savage than soldier, in the eyes of most Colombian politicians and writers. They had long been associated with the most violent opposition to the liberal land reforms of mid-century, and they continued to be feared and hated for their bellicose ways. It is hardly surprising that the Caucan provincial elite rejected the liberal ideal of Indian assimilation. Instead, their Indian policies lurched between appeasement and repression.

That Páez *caudillismo* never escalated into a cohesive, militant ethnic movement had less to do with republican policies, however, than with the intrinsic weakness of nineteenth-century Páez politics. Native *caudillos* could wield their influence over dispersed Páez communities, but they also participated in the Colombian political

---

[17] Rappaport, *The Politics of Memory*, 90.

party system. In Joanne Rappaport words, "on the ground, a broad range of *caudillos* with conflicting party allegiances organized military units independently of one another."[18] Partisan divisions, as well as ethnic rivalries, ultimately fragmented the Páez into competing bands. At times, native *caudillos* used the pretext of war to launch raids on rival territories. In various military operations, Páez guerrilla bands waged war against each other on opposite sides of the partisan divide. This was the case, for example, during the War of the Thousand Days, which raged between 1899 and 1902. The war broke out between Conservative and Liberal factions of the political elite in a moment of severe commercial depression. After six months of conventional warfare and partisan bloodletting, the war fragmented into a series of guerrilla skirmishes. In 1902, as war subsided, the Colombian province of Panamá split off from the nation, to become a strategic economic and transport colony of the United States. In the meantime, however, the southern highlands of Cauca were thrown into turmoil. Páez soldiers from different regions fought pitched battles against each other, while autonomist guerrilla bands roamed the mountains in pursuit of their own ends during the War of a Thousand Days. Páez practices of partisan politics and warfare probably served the interests of individual native *caudillos* and their communities in myriad ways. And they certainly revitalized translocal ethnic bonds and loyalties, which flew in the face of liberal laws abolishing colonial *resguardos* and *cacicazgos*. But ultimately, the relentless cycles of warfare, pillage, rape, and dislocation that rode roughshod over Páez communities and often pitted Páez against Páez left them more vulnerable than ever before to white invaders looking for easy conquests and quick profits.

---

[18] Ibid., 93. See also María Teresa Findji and José María Rojas, *Territorio, economía, y sociedad páez* (Cali, 1985).

BETWEEN FOREST AND WORLD MARKET

Around midcentury, a major source of quinine was discovered in the forests of Cauca, turning Páez territory into the newest economic frontier of the world market. Europe and North America demanded quinine to treat malaria, and Colombia became their major supplier. Cinchona bark was collected in many interior regions, but the finest quality came from the area around Pitayó. As with rubber and other wild products available for the taking, this extractive industry catalyzed ecological and cultural changes, already set in motion by the militarization of Páez society. The collection of quinine was an intense, short-lived extractive industry that pillaged forests and villages alike. Rappaport writes that "the quinine boom moved like a wave across the cinchona forests, leaving behind a wake of destroyed and dead plants."[19] It was Colombia's new gold rush, drawing thousands of white and mestizo merchants, entrepreneurs, and colonists to the region. The small town of Silvia exploded into a marketing center, populated by merchants, shopkeepers, muleteers, hacendados, and small farmers. They developed trading and credit relations with Páez bark collectors (*cascarilleros*), a new breed of Páez entrepreneur who sometimes earned good money in the bark trade. As the boom coincided with the civil wars of 1854, 1859–62, and 1876–7, trading activities were risky, fluctuating, and frequently coercive. It was not unusual for bands of armed Indians to enter the town of Silvia and press their dried cinchona bark on unwilling merchants at a fixed price. Militarism, extraction, and trade combined to create a small elite of entrepreneurs among the Páez, who shattered entrenched stereotypes of slothful savages resistant to enterprise and hard work.

But it came at a terrible cost. There is no doubt that the quinine boom weakened the bonds of communal solidarity and

[19] Rappaport, *The Politics of Memory*, 97.

territoriality. Like war, the quinine industry drained off men and boys into the outer frontier of the industry. As the quinine frontier advanced into the interior, so did the *cascarilleros*, leaving behind their families, lands, and communal responsibilities for weeks or months at a time. Sometimes Páez households migrated and resettled in distant lowlands, closer to the quinine frontier. This pattern of dispersion and transience must have radically disrupted subsistence agriculture and eroded the institutions of communal life. Increasingly, Páez traders and cutters negotiated their own mercantile deals with the monied world of the white export merchant. Not only were they vulnerable to raw commercial exploitation under radically unequal power relations, but such relationships chipped away at the Indian *cabildo* and *cacique* as the sources of communal authority and mediation with outsiders.

This situation proved devastating to the *resguardos*, suddenly under the twin threats of liberal land reforms and the invasion of entrepreneurs eager to annex lowland forests for their exportable treasures (quinine, and later sugar cane, coffee, and cattle). As we noted earlier, land reforms had an uneven impact on the southern *resguardos* over the first half of the nineteenth century. Indian protest, the noncompliance of Caucan elites, and the federalist political system itself had all undermined the Liberal Party's offensive against the *resguardo* in the Caucan provinces of Popayán and Pasto. But in the hands of the venture quinine capitalists, anti-*resguardo* legislation opened a new era of territorial conquest. Liberal laws dealt a double blow. On the one hand, the privatization of *resguardos* hastened the transfer of Indian lands to merchants, entrepreneurs, and foreign companies capitalizing on the quinine boom. On the other hand, Colombian policy aggressively promoted colonization of putatively "empty lands" (*los baldíos*) that composed Colombia's vast interior tropical forests.

After the 1860s, the *baldío* system posed the worst threat to indigenous territorial and political autonomy. On ideological grounds, it challenged *resguardo* rights and imposed borders where none had existed before. Where Páez territory ended and public land began was subject to conflicting, often violent, interpretation. The government acknowledged the problem in 1869: "few *resguardos* have written title; instead actual possession gives indefinite extension to the imagined properties of Indians in the high regions of the *cordillera.*"[20] In material terms, procolonization schemes quickened the pace of land alienation, migration, and deforestation. These search-and-destroy operations continued until world demand for Colombian quinine subsided around the turn of the twentieth century. But massive internal colonization of Indian lands continued during the first three decades of the new century, as new commodities (sugar, coffee, and cattle) turned interior regions of Cauca into agro-export economies. By then, white encroachment on Indian land was preparing the groundwork for violent confrontation between dispossessed peasants and the Caucan elite.

Throughout the late nineteenth century, the threat to indigenous landholdings produced a counterforce of resistance and protest against the expansion of estates onto their communal properties. The Indians of Popayán and Pasto were famous for the legal and military skills they deployed to preserve, recuperate, or reconstitute what remained of their patrimonies. As *baldío* claims and other threats of land loss grew more menacing, Indian communities intensified their search for colonial *resguardo* titles in local, provincial, and government archives; Indian *cabildos* schooled themselves in the fine points of the law to revalidate existing land titles or draft new ones; and through song, dance, verse, and stories, whole communities refreshed and reconstructed historical memories and

---

[20] *Diario Oficial*, 13 December, 1869; quoted in Rappaport, *The Politics of Memory*, 100–1. On Colombia's ambitious homesteading policy, internal colonization, *latifundismo*, and peasant protest, see the important study by Catherine Legrand, *Frontier Expansion and Peasant Protest, 1850–1936* (Albuquerque, 1986).

topographical knowledge. As happened in other native Andean societies, liberal policies of divestiture – ultimately designed to reinvent Indians as individual laborers and consumers in an expanding
capitalist, export-driven economy – provoked powerful backlash
effects of ethnic and communal action and consciousness that often spearheaded Indian campaigns to defend or recover the rights to
land and local self-government. The rise of Páez *caciques* – who positioned themselves as military chiefs of noble lineage and translocal
authority in spite of liberal laws liquidating hereditary *cacicazgos* –
is only the most dramatic instance of Páez resistance to civilizing
projects. But the Indian *cabildo*, perhaps more than the military
cacique, continued to be a principal site of resistance to invasive
land threats.

Curiously, in the last years of the nineteenth century amidst the
rush to colonize the interior tropical slopes of Cauca, the Conservative Party came to power. Led by Rafael Núñez, a former doctrinaire
liberal now turned ultra-centralist and pro-Church, the Conservatives brought a small measure of relief to some Indian *cabildos* in the
southern highlands. While the Conservative Party shared the overarching goals of civilizing and modernizing Colombia through the
process of whitening, it advocated a slower, more mediated route to
modernity. First, the Conservative Party aimed to replace the federalist system with a more centralized state capable of correcting
for the "excesses" of laissez-faire capitalism and secular liberalism.
Second, the Conservatives favored a more gradualist approach to
the civilizing project, one which would give the Catholic Church
a larger, multifaceted role to play. And with respect to the southern highland tribes, the new Conservative regime wanted to bring a
pragmatic balance to its Indian policies. So, for example, "to reduce
savage Indians to civilized life," they were to be disciplined and socialized properly and also set apart as legal minors in need of state
protection and tutelage. To slow down processes of land divestiture,
the Conservatives granted legal protection to *resguardos* for a period of fifty years. Thereafter, they could be subdivided and sold.

Although provincial governments rarely had the means or will to enforce these paternal protections, the Conservatives' protectionist land reform galvanized Indian communities almost overnight. As rumors spread across the southern *cordilleras*, the "Law 89" unleashed a torrent of land claims, litigations, title searches, surveys, inspections, and land invasions and counterinvasions. In some areas, peasants brandished colonial land titles to press their legal claims, which later escalated into long-term campaigns of "recuperation" aimed to recover stolen *resguardo* lands and to revitalize communal myths and memories. As anthropologist Joanne Rappaport shows, these land struggles not only pushed Pasto and Páez authorities into the notary offices, archives, and courts in order to make strategic use of colonial documents and the new law, but they intensified oral and ritual traditions, which might provide a framework for remembering the past as well as a source of inspiration for pursuing the struggle itself. In her ethnographic and archival work, Rappaport depicts the complexly articulated images and narratives that native intellectuals elaborated on the basis of colonial documents (mainly *resguardo* land titles). Through their stories, they constructed a colonial past, the proverbial "golden age," of powerful eighteenth-century *caciques*, fierce warriors, and vast territorial domains – all of which disappeared into deep mountain lakes with the onset of nineteenth-century liberalism. Within the matrix of the community, indigenous authorities also deployed colonial documents and oral traditions to mark the boundaries of the *resguardo* and to encode the sacred sites of communal geography.[21] In short, they interpreted the significance of legal land titles

---

[21] Rappaport, *The Politics of Memory*, 139–53; Diana Digges and Joanne Rappaport, "Literacy, Orality, and Ritual Practice in Highland Colombia," in Jonathan Boyarin, ed., *The Ethnography of Reading* (Berkeley, 1992), 139–55; and María Teresa Findji, "From Resistance to Social Movements: The Indigenous Authorities Movement in Colombia," in A. Escobar and S. Alvaréz, eds., *The Making of Social Movements in Latin America* (Boulder, 1992), 112–33.

through layers of oral and ritual expression. Thus native historical memory and sacred geography were continually renegotiated
in the community, as well as in the public arena, through political
struggle.

On a more pragmatic note, we may wonder how many of these
judicial battles were resolved in favor of Indian *cabildos*. It is not
known. But we may assume that Conservative's tutelary impulse
emboldened many landless and smallholding peasants, as well as
shrunken *resguardo* communities, to advance their land claims on
the basis of the new legal criteria of Indianness. The upshot was to
catalyze a movement of legal "reindianization" as a necessary step
toward land recovery. This, in turn, led to curious conflicts over the
phenotypical, genetic, and cultural definitions of Indian identity in
many local land struggles.[22]

Still, resurgent Indianness during the last years of the nineteenth
century remained atomized at the local level and geographically
confined to Colombia's southern highlands, a safe distance from
the main urban centers of power and progress. Colombia's ruling
oligarchs remained wedded to the project of modernity and civilization, but for the time being they could afford to pass paternalist laws
patronizing (and, hopefully, pacifying) unruly Indians. Indeed, as
they cast their eyes toward the "whitening" provinces surrounding
the capital of Bogotá, they probably still felt somewhat optimistic.
In the heartlands of coffee and commerce, the Indian race had all
but vanished. And reducing the rest to civilization seemed to be a
question of Indian regulation and discipline. Meanwhile, the government would look to European immigration to hasten Colombia's
march forward into the sunshine of modernity. Eventually Indians
would disappear into cultural *mestizaje*, and *mestizos* in turn would

---

[22] Not surprisingly, white authorities anxious to deny the legitimacy of Indian
land claims now began to narrow and carefully stipulate the racial parameters of Indianness! See Joanne Rappaport, *Cumbe Reborn: An Andean
Ethnography of History* (Chicago, 1994), chap. 1.

absorb the superior traits of European immigrants, taking their place in history as the bearers of economic progress in the Colombian backlands. Not even the bellicose Páez peoples had managed to destroy those liberal *illusions* – not yet anyway.

But the new century would open a new chapter in Indian-state relations. In the 1910s and 1920s, the Páez mounted a militant ethnic campaign to recover lands and autonomy under a more protectionist state. Faced with new subsistence threats – as the regional Caucan elites expanded their coffee, sugar, and cattle estates onto the western slopes of the shrunken *resguardo* – the Páez reinvigorated and expanded their opposition to land grabbing under their leader, Manuel Quintín Lame. Several scholars have documented this extraordinary pan-Indian movement in which literate Spanish-speaking leaders, who had come of age as Colombian soldiers and laborers in places far from their ancestral homelands, returned home to forge a militant indigenous movement and to influence government policy in the early twentieth century.[23] The rise of modern ethnic movements in the southern highlands would spread and reverberate across the twentieth century, until Colombia's indigenous people forced their way into the center of the nation's constitutional politics in the 1980s and early 1990s.

---

[23] Rappaport, *The Politics of Memory*, chaps. 5 and 6; Gonzálo Castillo Cárdenas, "Manuel Quintín Lame: luchador e intellectual indígena del siglo XX," in Manuel Quintín Lame, *En defense de mi raza* (Bogotá, 1971), xi–xlv, which was translated and republished in the volume, *Liberation Theology from Below* (Maryknoll, 1987). See also the direct testimony of Quintín Lame in his *En defense de mi raza* and *Las luchas del indio que bajó de la montaña al valle de la 'civilización'* (Bogotá, 1973). For a broader historical treatment and indictment of Colombia's Indian policy, see Nina de Friedemann, Juan Friede, and Darío Fajardo, *Indianismo y aniquilamiento de indígenas en Colombia* (Bogotá, 1981), 2nd ed.

3

Ecuador

Modernizing Indian Servitude as the Road to Progress

The breakup of Gran Colombia in 1830, Simón Bolívar's short-lived dream, dissected the northern highlands of South America into three republics (Ecuador, Colombia, and Venezuela). Across Colombia's southern border, Ecuadorian elites, heirs to the old *audiencia* of Quito, set out to construct a distinctly different nation-building project – one more deeply grounded in the country's colonial past and responsive to its peculiar set of regional power balances and dynamics that set Ecuador apart from its northern neighbor. Ecuador had emerged from the independence wars with a fairly cohesive aristocratic ruling class – badly damaged by the chaos of the wars and regionally fragmented but still largely in tact. Ecuador's conservative Creole elites were extremely skeptical about Colombian schemes of free trade, slave and tribute abolition, secular education, and even republicanism itself. Indeed, monarchism continued to hold a powerful grip on the political imaginings of many an Ecuadorian politician well into the nineteenth century.

Although Creoles never took the drastic step of inviting Napoleon III to send one of his nephews to rule its unruly lands (as did Mexican Conservatives in the 1860s), they eventually found a strong, authoritarian leader in President Gabriel García Moreno, who quickly enlisted the Catholic hierarchy in his "civilizing mission." The capital of Quito remained the site of conservative rule, a city famous for its cacophony of church bells and plethora of black-robed curates.[1] There, too, lived Creole landlords in close proximity to government ministries, military barracks, and a few literary salons but also convenient enough to their outlying estates and to densely populated Indian hamlets and mestizo towns throughout Ecuador's north-central highlands. After 1870, Liberal Party opposition grew more powerful, but it remained largely confined to the Guayaquil ("cacao") coast until the "liberal revolution" of 1895 catapulted a free-trade reformer into the presidency. In short the compass of political and ideological reform remained much narrower in nineteenth-century Ecuador than in Colombia. Rather than inventing a nation out of the liberal ideals of the Enlightenment, complemented by racial schemes of "whitening" as the Colombian liberals tried to do, Ecuadorian Creoles fashioned a conservative nationalism out of the shards of colonialism.

As everywhere in the Andes, Ecuador's nation-building experiments were conditioned and limited by the diverse interactions, experiences, and understandings of a cultural mosaic of peoples of whom the overwhelming majority was poor, nonwhite, and peasant. But ethnic balances and dynamics varied widely among the four Andean nations, as did the institutional and political legacies of specific colonial formations and the fallout from the independence wars. Even among the northern Andean nations of Colombia and Ecuador, ethnic balances were almost inversed at the end of the

---

[1] This is not to deny the existence of Church-state tensions in republican Ecuador, however. Because the Church had such a powerful presence after independence, jurisdictional and power struggles raged. Some of those conflicts revolved around the Church's paternal control over Indians; for example, in the 1830s ecclesiastics protested republican decrees removing the right of priests to use corporal punishment to discipline Indians. However, Church-state alliances were cemented by the papal Concordat of 1863.

colonial era. In 1770 the *audiencia* of Quito (composed of what later became the republic of Ecuador and the southern provinces of Colombia) registered Indians as 50 percent of its population, while *libres* (free people of African or mixed descent) composed only 10 percent. By contrast, in the *audiencia* of Santa Fé (northern Colombia), Indians constituted 20 percent, and *libres*, 50 percent.[2] A more rigorous census, compiled under the Bourbon reformers in 1785, estimated that Indians of colonial Ecuador composed 65 percent of the total population.[3] Long lapses in republican population counts defy attempts to trace Indian demographic change over the nineteenth century, although provincial censuses in the north-central provinces of the 1840s suggest that Indians still made up almost 50 percent of their total population.[4] But the predominance of *indios* (as they were officially defined) created the social and demographic basis for adapting colonial practices and ideologies to the republican (dis)order.

Indian tribute, for example, made up one-third of tax revenues collected in the *audiencia* of Quito on the eve of independence, and it was quickly restored once Bolivarian liberalism faded in the late 1820s.[5] State finances continued to rely on Indian tribute until

---

[2] Peter Wade, *Blackness and Race Mixture: The Dynamics of Racial Identity in Colombia* (Baltimore, 1993), 54.

[3] Suzanne Austin Alchon, *Native Society and Disease in Colonial Ecuador* (Cambridge, 1991), 123.

[4] Galo Valarego Ramón, "El Ecuador en el espacio andino: idea, proceso, e utopía," *Allpanchis* (Cusco) 35/36: 2 (1991), 517–77, 548. On the absence of nineteenth-century demographic records on Ecuador's indigenous population, see Hernán Ibarra, "La identidad devaluada de los 'Modern Indians,'" in I. Almeida et al., eds., *Indios. Una reflexión sobre el levantimiento indígena de 1990* (Quito, 1991), 319–49, 326–7. Twentieth-century census materials are nearly as impoverished as nineteenth-century records regarding ethnic and racial categories.

[5] In addition to heavy tribute burdens on the indigenous communities in the *audiencia* of Quito, the Bourbons imposed new commercial monopolies and

1857 – not just for reasons of fiscal expedience but also for fear of indigenous reprisals against more onerous schemes of taxation and military conscription.[6] In its thrust to restore elements of the colonial system of caste, symbolized by Indian tribute, Ecuadorian elites shared much in common with their southern counterparts in Peru and Bolivia. And like Peru, Ecuador restored tribute without granting the package of juridical rights and jurisdictions to Indian communities that accompanied tribute obligations under the colonial system of dual republics. Indians owed tribute (now called the *contribución personal de indígenas*) but were denied legal rights to corporate landholding or hereditary chiefdoms. On the tangible issues surrounding the ambiguous, fluid, and contested meanings of *"república"* – whether the new Ecuadorian republic should honor colonial legal codes or customary rights claimed by disparate groups of Indian tributaries – Creole leaders maintained a calculated, and prudent, indifference. They were neither willing nor able to impose a uniform land reform policy nor flatten the traditional Indian hierarchy. And certain indigenous communities used the postindependence period of political fragmentation and uncertainty, as well as its judicial flux, to press their claims to territory, protection, and a certain measure of autonomy.

By midcentury, however, the signs of economic and ideological change were beginning to prod Ecuador's conservatives into a more aggressively reformist frame of mind. Regional balances between

---

regressive taxes in order to support the expanded royal bureaucracy. These state policies did a great deal of harm to Quito's colonial textile industry and internal trade in the northern and central highlands. Thus, the new republic tried to reimpose tribute on an indigenous population already suffering from the long-term effects of disease, market fragmentation, and economic decline (Kenneth Andrien, *The Kingdom of Quito, 1690–1830: The State and Regional Development* [Cambridge, 1995], 210–15).

[6] Mark J. Van Aken, "The Lingering Death of Indian Tribute in Ecuador," *Hispanic American Historical Review* 61: 3 (1981), 429–59.

the *sierra* and coast were beginning to tip in favor of the latter, as overseas markets opened up for tropical agro-exports. Highland *haciendas* did not share in the growing prosperity of cacao plantations on the coast, for example, and this regional economic disparity only widened with time. Nonetheless, the resurgent export economy permitted the government to shift its tax base from tribute to commercial and propertied wealth. Tribute revenues had already dwindled by the late 1840s, and by 1857 tribute was officially terminated. Ecuador's native highland peasants (still designated as "Indian") were redefined in civil law as *contribuyentes* – contributors to the nation, still, but putatively on the same legal footing as everyone else. They were now registered as property holders, taxpayers, and potential military recruits in the *catastros* and subject to the same laws, obligations, and authorities as non-Indians. Official statistics effaced ethnic categories from the written record after 1857; Ecuador's first national census of 1876 cleansed "Indians" from the record. But in a revealing note to census takers, the government instructed them to collect information about Indians to facilitate tax collection and labor conscription.[7] This innocuous note in the margin, more than any ethnic-blind statistic, provides an important clue as to how Indians were going to fit into the posttributary republic bumping along the road to modernity and progress. As we will see, state-run labor drafts – a colonial institution in modern guise – were to staff state projects of modernization in the 1850s, 1860s, and 1870s.

COERCING INDIANS INTO "CIVILIZATION" AND CHRISTIANITY

To mount such a project, Ecuador's reformers first had to overcome structural and demographic obstacles – partly of their own making.

[7] Ibarra, "La identidad devaluada de los 'Modern Indians,'" 326–7.

Ecuador's strong *latifundista* tradition, the very font of conservative ideology, stood fast against the currents of reform. For one thing the skewed ratio between communal and estate-bound Indians worked against Creole plans for state-controlled labor schemes. At the end of the colonial period, almost half of all registered Indians were landless laborers bound in one way or another to estates.[8] *Latifundismo* was more entrenched in the southern highlands around Cuenca. But even in Ecuador's north-central "Indian zone," economic and demographic forces since the seventeenth century had boosted Spanish and mestizo control over Indian land and labor, shrinking the legal pool of tributaries and labor drafts to a much smaller scale than that inherited by the republics of Peru and Bolivia. What distinguished patterns of Indian labor in colonial Ecuador was not the existence of servile relations in the private domain but their increasing importance in colonial agricultural and industrial production. Early waves of *hacienda* expansion, heavy taxation, and the pervasive practice of labor drafts for colonial enterprises and cities set in motion migratory streams of Indians, thus removing Indians from their kin groups and villages. By the late seventeenth century, evolving relations of dependence and retainership tied growing numbers of Indians into the dynamic and expanding production of food, textiles, and craft goods destined for cities, towns, and mines throughout the Viceroyalty of Peru. Partly because of these severe social and demographic dislocations, seventeenth-century Ecuador emerged with considerable "comparative advantages" as the premier textile workshop of the Andean colonies. For over a century, Creole elites in the northern highlands thrived from the export trade in manufactured woolen cloth (*paños, bayeta,* and *jergas*) to Lima, Potosí, and New Granada. Its sweatshops (*obrajes*) flourished mainly from the cheap skilled

[8] Magnus Märner, *The Andean Past: Lands, Society, and Conflict* (New York, 1985), 77.

Figure 5. *Obraje* workers, Province of Imbabura, ca. 1890. Although the heyday of Ecuadorian *hacienda-obraje* complexes was long passed, primitive textile workshops like this one continued to thrive on the labor of contracted
laborers (*conciertos*) and peons well into the twentieth century. This 1890
photograph offers a rare glimpse into indigenous working conditions, in contrast to the prevailing aesthetic tendency to decontextualize and typologize
Indians (see Figure 14). Source: Lucía Chiriboga and Silvana Caparrini, eds.,
Identidades Desnudas. Ecuador, 1860–1920 (Quito: Abya-Yala, 1994), 53.
(Photograph reproduced with permission from Editorial Abya-Yala.)

labor of Indian retainers, supplemented by Indian labor drafts
(Figure 5).

Quito's highland textile manufactures served as the foundation
of the regional economy until "epidemics, natural disasters, and the
introduction of large amounts of European cloth combined to erode
the prosperity of the *obraje* sector by the early eighteenth century,"
writes historian Kenneth Andrien.[9] Thereafter Bourbon taxation reforms only aggravated the economic situation, plunging the whole

---

[9] Andrien, *The Kingdom of Quito*, 217.

region into a prolonged recession and prompting large numbers of indigenous people to seek work on Spanish estates. This exodus from indigenous communities to Spanish estates was commonplace in the provinces of Quito and Riobamba, where subsistence had become a daily struggle for many peasants. Other Indian migrants (*forasteros*) headed to the more prosperous provinces of the south, where a new cottage industry of cotton textiles was beginning to emerge. Other rural Indians sought seasonal labor in tropical lowland or coastal plantations. But whatever their destiny, these migratory waves often facilitated the gradual loss of indigenous lands to encroaching estates. Regional economic decline and Indian landlessness therefore were to become critical issues in nineteenth-century Creole projects of economic recovery and political integration.

It is not surprising therefore that midcentury debates over the morality of Indian tribute also addressed the more fundamental question of Indian bondage on private estates. It was the beginning of a century-long exercise in ideological equivocation over the necessity and morality of indentured Indian labor. The debate finally subsided in 1964 when the agrarian reform law of that year officially terminated the institution of *huasipungaje*.[10] Already by the

---

[10] Conditions and terminologies of bondage varied considerably among regions, over time, and even within one enterprise. Very broadly, however, bondage normally implied that resident Indians owed certain labor services to their masters, who also expected Indians to demonstrate steadfast loyalty and obedience to their personage. In return, the master was to provide for the subsistent needs of dependent Indians, usually by granting them usufruct rights, access to woods and pastures, token wage payments, and occasional gifts and favors. In Ecuador, nineteenth- and twentieth-century ideas and images of estate paternalism congealed under the labels of *concertaje* and *huasipungaje*. Static notions of peonage depicted families of resident laborers who were permitted to have huts and garden plots, as well as pasture and water rights in return for their labor services and a small cash wage. Obviously, the negotiation and contestation of paternal power relations was a constant dynamic – continually subject to everyday practices of sabotage,

mid-1850s, however, parliamentary debates implicated the practices of labor recruitment and retention on highland *haciendas*. Inspired by the polemics surrounding slave and tribute abolition, Liberal and Conservative legislators clashed over the status of unfreedom that adhered to *conciertos* (Indians subject to long-term labor contracts). Whatever the specious conditions under which Indians were "hooked" into labor service, the lawmakers questioned the terms of Indian indenture. Should Indians who redeemed their debt be "emancipated" and allowed to break their bondage before their stipulated term of years was up? Or, was indenture binding until the end of their contractual term? Should debt be inheritable generation after generation?

That the absolutism of landlord power, a fixture of rural Ecuador for centuries, became the subject of vigorous national debate signaled the beginning of a subtle ideological shift in Creole thinking. These arguments tested the legitimate limits of power that Ecuador's landlords exercised over the nation's landless Indians. More profoundly, they began to refocus national discourses on the "Indian problem." And once Creole elites began to nationalize the Indian problem, relocating it from the exclusive and narrow domain of private landlord concerns to the broad arena of public discourse, it became the trope of an aggressive civilizing project under the "perpetual dictator" of Gabriel García Moreno. It is perhaps ironic, then, that these muckraking debates of the 1850s also gave implicit confirmation to the practices of landlord paternalism and Indian servitude. Not only did those midcentury liberal legislators fail to enact laws limiting the power of labor contractors and landlords,

---

resistance, and neglect, and occasionally to insurgent actions from below. For a detailed, contemporary description of living and labor conditions on haciendas, see Friedrich Hassaurek, *Four Years among the Ecuadorians* [1867] (Carbondale, 1967), 169–72. See also the classic *indigenista* novel and exposé on Indian servitude, Jorge Icaza, *Huasipungo* (Quito, 1934).

but the very terms and language of those parliamentary debates worked to consolidate the image of the Ecuadorian highland Indian as a "poor, ignorant, and helpless" creature in need of paternal protection by benign landlords.[11] Conveniently, in this emerging discourse, hacienda paternalism granted moral agency to Ecuador's Conservative landed elites and implicitly legitimated the status of indentured servitude.

Indeed, the ideological sway of conservative landlordism in the late nineteenth century cast long shadows across Ecuadorian ruling class rhetoric and policy until well into the twentieth century. It had a curious impact on national amnesia, for example. Liberal and nationalist historiography virtually buried indigenous histories under apologetic (or sometimes critical) accounts of Ecuador's highland estates and their inert Indian serfs. Almost no indigenous events "of significance" are recorded in mainstream histories of Ecuadorian modernization between 1870 and 1930. The rhetorical defense of the paternal estate also underwrote later Liberal Party policies, aimed at consolidating the hacienda. After Eloy Alfaro's turn-of-the-century "liberal revolution," the Liberal government accelerated the privatization of Indian communities, with its 1908 Law of Disentailment of Lands. The Liberal Party pushed forward other reforms, such as its assault on the power of the Church and its decriminalization of debt servitude, yet – shockingly – the institution of debt servitude (*huasipungaje*) persisted until massive rural mobilizations demanded abolition in 1964.

Ecuador's peculiar conservative-authoritarian project of nation building crystallized under the repressive regime of Gabriel García Moreno, which lasted from his political ascendance in 1859 to

---

[11] Andrés Guerrero, "Una imágen ventrilocua: El discurso liberal de la 'desgraciada raza indígena' a fines del siglo XIX," in Blanca Muratorio, ed., *Imágenes e imagineros. Representaciones de los indígenas ecuatorianos, siglos XIX y XX* (Quito, 1994), 197–252.

his assassination in 1875. García Moreno's ironclad rule reversed decades of regional militarism, weak central governments, and innumerable constitutions. He sought inspiration for his own developmental model of state making not in Colombia's experiment in liberal federalism but in French authoritarianism under Napoleon III. García Moreno was pragmatic enough to realize, however, that European models of militarist centralism had to be revamped to overcome the obstacles facing a republic as economically fragmented, impoverished, and undercapitalized as Ecuador. In its full scope, the dictator's project rested on three main propositions: the need to modernize the bureaucratic and repressive apparatus of the state; the importance of bringing the Catholic Church back into the nation as the advance guard of civilization among the "backward" and "heathen" races; and, the moral imperative of redeeming the "Indian race" (*la raza india*) and harnessing it to the engines of economic modernization.

From the vantage point of peasants living outside the domain of paternal estates, perhaps the most visible sign of change was the thickening web of provincial bureaucracy that drew them more tightly into the state's net. With tributary protections gone, including the jurisdictional space granted (at least informally) to translocal hereditary *caciques*, local sites of ethnic authority devolved to Indian *cabildos*, whose members were elected to serve for a year over shrunken rural hamlets. At the micropolitical level, power was fragmented and distributed among a pool of small village leaders and council members (*pequeños curagas, cabecillas,* and *mandones*) who answered not only to their own kin and communities, but also to municipal, parish, and provincial authorities. This localization of indigenous authority ran counter to the centralization of white-mestizo officialdom, as García Moreno worked to roll back decades of indigenous, provincial, and paternal autonomies. His army of bureaucrats began to infiltrate rural towns and villages, performing the routines and rituals of rule: collecting taxes;

recruiting soldiers and laborers; adjudicating disputes; disciplining vagrants, debtors, and other "criminal" sorts; and generally keeping the social peace. Proliferating mestizo and white towns became links in a lengthening chain of command connecting Quito to dispersed Indian villages. As we will see, new occupational and cultural spaces opened in the interstices of society for upwardly mobile, bilingual, and transculturated people who no longer fit into bipolar categories of Indian or Creole (i.e., white). This motley group of spatial and cultural transients – whatever they were called in local parlance – constituted a rapidly growing sector of the rural population in nineteenth-century Ecuador. In the emerging public sector, they often served as agents of the dictator, but many mestizos thrived from their mercantile activities as traders, muleteers, and labor contractors, who funneled peasant laborers into labor-starved export economies of the coast.

From the perspective of white urban Ecuador, though, García Moreno's greatest (or, to the beleaguered liberals, his most infamous) feat was to remake the Church into a powerful agent of cultural change. The potential was already there because the Catholic Church had emerged almost unscathed from the chaos of the independence wars and had escaped the sorry fate of other anticlerical movements in postindependence Latin America. The Catholic hierarchy never lost its political footing in the new republic. But until the regime of García Moreno, it had symbolized the Hispanist past of paternalism and piety. García Moreno was a modern-day mix of Machiavelli and Erasmus: he wanted to cleanse the clergy of its corrupt ways and deploy the redeemed Church to educate and moralize the Indian peasantry in order to prepare it for gradual entry into the lower ranks of civilized society. This modern spiritual conquest was the dictator's route to nationhood, and in 1863 he went to the Vatican for papal blessings. For the "salvation of the fatherland," the president charged the Church with Christianizing the heathen Indians and of creating political order out of civil discord. These momentous tasks were to be entrusted mainly to the Jesuit order, the only group endowed with the self-discipline, ambition, and militancy García Moreno believed necessary for the job. Indeed, he had in mind an imperialist venture of French Jesuits piercing Ecuador's "heart of darkness" to civilize the heathens through religion, education, and discipline (Figure 6). In 1861, the first battery of friars arrived from France to establish primary schools for poor boys; the education of girls was left to chance or private charity.

According to observers of the day, the clerics had a herculean task before them. Even the more charitable commentators, who had nothing positive to say about Quito's polite society, heaped scorn on Indians for their filth, servility, superstition, drunkenness, and indolence. To religious and secular authorities, Indians were not only poor, degraded, and suffering laborers, but worse they were a fallen race without culture or reason. The frequency of their debauched fiestas seemed proof enough. While missionaries denounced Indian idolatries, hypocrisies, and licentiousness, secular authorities worried about rowdy, belligerent Indians converging on mestizo towns during week-long festivals. Political rhetoric was also colored by economic concerns, which blamed Indian misery and poverty on the victims and pointed to their cultural deficiencies as the fundamental cause of the nation's economic backwardness.

A minor point of contention between Church and state was the issue of alcohol and who was to blame for the problem of chronic Indian drunkenness. The Church pointed to corrupt merchants, judges, and police who monopolized the sale of cane liquor and *chicha* (corn beer) in cities and towns Indians frequented. Civil authorities denounced greedy priests who profited from Indian debauchery during religious festivals. At the local level, such debates often reflected raw power struggles between religious and civil authorities over their privileged access to Indian labor and commerce. But at the national level, consensus gathered around the need for

Figure 6. A Jesuit priest with his flock of Indian students, Pinchincha Province, ca. 1890. The Reverend Father Luís Calcagno poses with his students from the village of Zámbiza before the artificial backdrop of an elegant parlor. The portrait reflects the singularly prominent role that the Catholic Church, particularly the Jesuit Order, played in Ecuador's mid-nineteenth-century "civilizing projects." Source: Lucía Chiriboga and Silvana Caparrini, eds., *Identidades Desnudas. Ecuador, 1860–1920* (Quito: Abya-Yala, 1994), 66. (Photograph reproduced with permission from Editorial Abya-Yala.)

a harsher regime of moral and social discipline over unruly Indian infidels. Although they addressed the issues somewhat differently, both Church and state officials wanted to stamp out popular religious rituals and expressions.[12]

If a strong authoritarian government was to keep order and a reformed Church was to advance the edge of Christendom and civilization, it was the Indian majority that was to serve the nation in its arduous journey toward economic progress. In this respect as in others, García Moreno grounded his modernizing project in the shallow sands of coercive colonial practices. This became increasingly clear in the 1860s, when he began to nationalize the use of conscript laborers, rounded up from Indian communities, to build the nation's infrastructure. Although the abolition of tribute in 1857 had demolished the legal basis of colonial forms of racial discrimination, an earlier decree offered a mechanism for restoring compulsory Indian labor, now redirected to serve the nation's developmental goals. The old Bolivarian law of universal "voluntary contributions" was revived in 1854. It decreed that every citizen owed the state four days of labor, or its monetary equivalent, to promote the nation's public works projects. Without a committed and strong state to enforce the tax levy fairly, it soon evolved into a discriminatory tax on Indians, which merely reinforced local customs of coercing Indians into providing gratuitous services. By the 1860s, the labor tax fell most heavily on Indian communities and smallholders, while estate-bound peons frequently found protection through their paternal landlords.

---

[12] See Derek Williams, "Assembling the 'Empire of Morality': State Building Strategies in Catholic Ecuador, 1861–1875," *Journal of Historical Sociology* 14 (2001), 149–74; and Rosemary and Robert Bromley, "The Debate on Sunday Markets in Nineteenth-Century Ecuador," *Journal of Latin American Studies* 7 (1975), 85–108.

García Moreno constructed a modernized version of the colonial *mita* (the institution of compulsory, rotational labor to which most tribute-paying Indian males were subject in the South Andes) to realize his ambitious economic dreams. More than anything else he accomplished, he was remembered for his modern cart roads that scaled the *cordilleras* and finally brought Quito closer to the sea. Far more than a feat of modern engineering, it was a testimony to the coercive machinery he built and the sheer labor power that massive numbers of highland Indians were forced to invest. The dictator dispatched military men to round up Indian ditchdiggers, and in 1862 some 1,700 people began cutting the cart road through the *cordillera*, from mountainous Quito down to coastal Guayaquil. The sight of it was chilling even to García Moreno's admirers. In the early 1860s, the North American diplomat, Friedrich Hausseruk, watched Indians building a section of the wagon road to Guayaquil.

It was a lamentable sight to see how it had to be carried on. Heavy excavations had to be made through the high hills on both sides of the old mule path. There were no instruments except crowbars and shovels. There were no spades and pickaxes to dig with, nor carts or wheelbarrows to haul away the earth. It had to be filled in sheepskins and ponchos, which the Indians carried on their backs, and with which they climbed the hills where they deposited their scanty contents.... Paving stones, lime, and bricks for the construction of bridges ... were carried in the same manner on human backs. Sometimes beasts of burden were used; but the simplest and cheapest beast of burden is the Indian.[13]

A few years later, the villages of Otavalo and other northern regions were sent to dig hundreds of miles of mountainous roadway

---

[13] Friedrich Hassaurek, *Four Years among the Ecuadorians*, 111. At another point in his travelogue, this astute observer said that Indians were often referred to in slang as *begajes menores* (small beasts of burdens): "that is to say, as a beast of burden, the Indian is considered below the horse and the mule, and on a level with the donkey" (105).

down to the northern port of Esmeraldas. They were also charged with repairing the treacherous northern roads to Colombia after heavy rains, staffing the inns, and carrying the mail. Through their participation in *corvée* labor, Indian gangs literally subsidized Ecuador's economic modernization, just as their ancestors had subsidized the development of colonial Ecuador's textile factories, cities, parishes, and grain *haciendas*. While liberal reformists in the coffee houses of Quito extolled the virtues of free enterprise, they watched Indian work parties lay the roads and rails of progress. For white city folks, Indians became fixtures in the real and imaginary landscape: that their station in life was to dig the roads and sink the telegraph poles became as inevitable and immutable as the earth and the sky. "The Indian does more work than all the other races together," observed Hassurek, "but his position in the social scale is in an inverse proportion to his usefulness."[14]

Throughout the remaining years of the century, these official labor drafts and other duties hit the north-central Indian villages most heavily, wrenching people from their villages, fields, and families for long periods of time. Hassaurek made no pretense about the putative voluntarism behind "Indian contributions" to the nation: "the Indian does not work voluntarily, not even when paid for his labor, but is pressed into the service of the government...and is kept to his task by the whip of the overseer."[15] García Moreno had laid the institutional groundwork for this operation: a centralizing bureaucracy and military that penetrated to the local village and a judiciary that continued to criminalize Indian "laziness" and debt. More than any other institution, the debtors' prison symbolized the republic's continuing reliance on coerced Indian labor.[16]

---

[14] Ibid., 107.   [15] Ibid., 111.

[16] My argument here is the importance of debt and forced labor in defining *ideological* components of imposed Indianness in mid- and late-nineteenth-century Ecuador. However, this is not to say that debt servitude served as

It is hardly surprising, then, to learn that for most of the century Ecuador's conservative modernizers eschewed liberal ideals of free labor. García Moreno himself felt ambivalent toward the institution of indentured servitude. On the one hand, Indians in retainership on private estates were not easily mobilized for public works. On the other, his allies were conservative landowners unwilling to change their antiquarian ways. Indeed, his very model of nation building embodied postcolonial contradictions of coercive and market forces. While he worked hard to centralize state power, modernize the military and bureaucracy, build roads and rails, and establish rural schools, García Moreno was not inspired by liberal schemes of economic or genetic assimilation, as were his Colombian counterparts. His stance toward economic progress and the whitening solution was more equivocal. This was apparent in the official position on race and development that surfaced in Ecuador's first national textbook, *Catecismo de geografía de la República del Ecuador*, published in the early 1870s under García Moreno's second administration. While generally optimistic about Ecuador's economic future, the book characterized Indians as "unalterable and suffering laborers." The white race, in contrast, was cast as a people capable of carrying the republic into the company of civilized nations thanks to the conservation of their Hispanic heritage. Whiteness was constructed around conservative values

a blanket mechanism of Indian labor control in highland Ecuador. As I indicated earlier, highland landlords did not exercise unlimited power over Indian peons. Sharply different regional histories, the postindependence period of economic sluggishness, and local tensions between servile and paternal institutions, on the one hand, and peasant strategies of resistance, on the other, all point toward an extremely variegated social landscape. In comparative perspective, however, Ecuador stands out for its strong colonial institutions of coerced labor and its relatively cohesive Catholic-conservative aristocracy based in Quito (in the north) and Cuenca (in the south), which continued to promote compulsory Indian labor schemes.

and rooted in the colonial past (yet still inspired by Enlightenment ideals). The text characterized whites as "religious, honorable, generous, and lovers of independence and freedom."[17] Such, too, was the imagined national identity.

This experiment in harnessing colonial labor institutions to modernization disrupted local rural societies throughout highland Ecuador. Southern regions surrounding the city of Cuenca had long traditions of *latifundismo* that shackled most Indians to their masters through varied forms of debt, dependence, and paternalism. But on the edges of those estates lived smallholding peasants, increasingly squeezed by the internal pressures of population and heavier labor quotas they owed the state. Threatened by an increasingly precarious subsistent base, many Indian farmers passed into the ranks of the service tenantry on large estates. Others abandoned the highlands for wage work on the booming cacao plantations along the coast. The opening of the trans-*cordillera* highway in the 1870s only increased this migratory stream.

But economic and cultural change came more abruptly to the Indian regions of the north. The northern Indian villages suffered most from the dictator's draconian work projects, while the network of white and mestizo towns tended to prosper from the growth of petty officialdom, a booming pack industry, and interregional commerce and trade in textiles and other goods. For Indian farmers and herders, the modernizing regime laid siege to their lands and labors, while removing the juridical and customary means of communal defense and redress. It threatened to recolonize shrunken and flattened Indian communities, now directly subordinate to agents of the state and Church. And it left little discursive room for collective maneuver by denying Indians the judicial use of their colonial or customary past to recover their lost lands or advance their democratic claims. By all rights, this transformation of ex-tributary Indians

[17] Ibarra, "La identidad devaluada de los 'Modern Indians,'" 319.

(once endowed with certain legal rights under an early ambivalent republic) to a seasonal, coerced labor force under a modernizing state must have been subject to subterraneous tremors and occasional eruptions (as in Chimborazo in 1874). Yet curiously, Indian unrest in northern Ecuador apparently remained small-scale, scattered, and contained – at least, in comparison to contemporaneous peasant mobilizations in southern Colombia, Peru, and Bolivia.

Such an assessment must remain cautious and tentative, however, at least for the moment. As mentioned earlier, the official historiography largely effaces indigenous social practice from narratives of nation making in late nineteenth- and early twentieth-century Ecuador, and the "new ethnohistory" of indigenous-state relations is still being written.[18] Until recently, historical studies of the Ecuadorian countryside were steeped in racial premises and imagery, which inevitably fixed on the "innate obedience and servility" of the Indian race. Diagnostic studies by charitable Ecuadorian *indigenistas* couched Indian docility in the contexts of Inca tyranny, colonial oppression, or the degradation of hacienda life. The more sensitive ethnographic observer sometimes saw beyond racial stereotypes and *indigenista* platitudes and yet continued to be blinded by them. For instance, the traveler and diplomat, Friedrich Hassaurek, essentialized the Indian's "stupid and beastly nature [which] never revolts." But he went on at great length to depict the

---

[18] Since the 1990 uprising of highland indigenous people, there has been an explosion of studies on indigenous politics and ethnic consciousness in twentieth-century Ecuador (see the Bibliographic Essay). By contrast, ethno-histories of nineteenth-century Ecuador are few. One notable exception is Hernán Ibarra's study of the 1871 rebellion led by Daquilema, '*Nos encontramos amenazados por todita la indiada*': *el levantimiento de Daquilema* [*Chimborazo, 1871*] (Quito, 1993). See also Aleezé Sattar, "An Unresolved Inheritance: Postcolonial State Formation and Indigenous Communities in Chimborazo, Ecuador, 1820–1875." (Ph.D. dissertation, New School University, 2001.)

stubborn disinclination of Indians to comply with the favors or services asked of them by white people, unless under threat of force. Behind an etiquette of politeness and servility lurked a recalcitrant, untrustworthy Indian who had to be watched, in the view of this traveler. Indeed, Hassurek's intuition about indigenous dissimulation before the white overlord was not altogether wrong.[19] Ecuadorian observers also molded stereotypes of inert Indians. Historian Andrés Guerrero notes how even Ecuador's free-trade liberals at the end of the century conjured up a brutish race of *indios infelices*, reduced by centuries of colonialism and *concertaje*, to an animal-like state and incapable even of participating in commercial relations.[20]

In short, any overall assessment of peasant political quietude in nineteenth-century Ecuador must be subject to careful review in light of new and forthcoming work in social and cultural history. For the time being, however, it is useful to think about the sorts of "structural obstacles" that might have thwarted, or contained, the forces of peasant mobilization in highland Ecuador during the second half of the nineteenth century. Several lines of argument seem plausible: Ecuador's dominant Church-state alliance; the entrenched, regional power base of the *hacendado* class; and the historic fragmentation of communal power and identity. First, as we discussed earlier, midcentury liberal reforms took an authoritarian turn for the worse – by reinforcing the institution of indentured

---

[19] Hassaurek, *Four Years among the Ecuadorians*, 70–3. Ever since the publication of Eugene Genovese's masterful cultural history of slave strategies of accommodation and resistance to the paternalism, brutalities, and humiliations of slavery in *Roll Jordan Roll. The World the Slaves Made* (New York, 1972), this theme has attracted historical and ethnographic attention. Two other inspiring studies include E. P. Thompson, "Patrician Society, Plebian Culture," *Journal of Social History* 7: 4 (1974), 382–405, and James Scott, *Domination and the Arts of Resistance: Hidden Transcripts* (New Haven, 1990).

[20] Andrés Guerrero, *La semántica de la dominación: El concertaje de indios* (Quito, 1991), 56–7.

servitude and by rebuilding the extractive machinery of state power. García Moreno's project created a network of client outposts (missions, haciendas, roadways, and colonial labor systems) that could be deployed not only for labor mobilization but also for purposes of state vigilance and social control. In sharp contrast to the Church-state tensions that weakened and sundered ruling class coalitions in Mexico and other regions of Latin America at certain moments and even opened partisan spaces for popular forces to manipulate intra-elite quarrels, Ecuador's landed plutocracy cemented alliances with the Catholic Church around midcentury. Indeed, President García Moreno practically delivered the nation's "civilizing project" to the Jesuits and other missionaries.

A second line of argument must focus on the symbolic and real violence that Ecuador's "paternal landlords" perpetrated against the perceived dangers of peasant mobilization or resistance at the level of everyday practice. Not only did landlords impose their own forms of oppression and vigilance, making collective action all the more risky, but they also tried to intensify peasant sentiments of loyalty, dependence, fear, and rivalry with Indians of neighboring haciendas. To point out the obvious dynamics of class oppression is not to deny the possibility, or indeed the prevalence, of everyday forms of resistance in which submerged peasantries and other subaltern groups continually engaged. But it is important to remind ourselves that whole generations of peasant laborers in Ecuador and elsewhere lived grim lives of grinding poverty and harsh labor routines, punctuated perhaps by occasional acts of petty resistance, without ever experiencing the opportunity to participate in collective mobilization or insurgent action.

Third, any analysis of indigenous peasant politics must take into account individual strategies of subsistence, resistance, or escape from rural poverty that might have offered alternatives to collective forms of struggle and mobilization. The growing mercantilization of the Ecuadorian economy in the late nineteenth century, especially in the cities and towns of the northern highlands, in the tropical enclave economies of the jungle, and along the cacao coast, did open up channels of labor migration and probably produced a new wave of Indian aspirants to the condition (and identity) of mestizos (referred to by a variety of local terms). On the other hand, the existence of such "safety-valve" options for landless or semibonded peasants was certainly not unique to late nineteenth-century Ecuador. And, in any event, mercantile capitalism was always double-edged: while it may have created opportunities for seasonal labor migration, it also tended to intensify extractive relations, coerced labor relations, and class tensions in the countryside.

More salient perhaps is the historic weakness and fragmentation of the land-based indigenous community. The rural peasant world of the Ecuadorian highlands remained riddled by ethnic divisions and tensions, land disputes, and jurisdictional confusions and conflicts. Social and cultural fragmentation among northern ethnic groups was certainly not peculiar to the nineteenth century, but centuries-long communal land divestiture policies and practices, as well as the gradual erosion of hereditary *caciques* as cultural brokers, ethnic adversaries, and local intellectuals, were powerful social forces that conspired against the possibility of ethnic resurgence, even in moments of acute political tension at the national level. Then again, Ecuador was never invaded by an imperial force, tearing open the heartland and opening spaces for insurgent peasant action. In this way, too, Ecuador escaped the devastation of foreign military occupation, civil war, and massive rural upheaval that tore apart Peru and Mexico in the mid-nineteenth century.

In all, Ecuador entered the twentieth century as the only Andean nation that did not experience a militant grassroots movement of community-based peasants challenging government policies of land divestiture. Here again, we come up against colonial legacies of the entrenched hacienda system and the fragmented peasant community. Yet that landscape of apparent pastoral calm could be shattered at any moment by a conspiracy of global, national, or local events. So it happened in the early 1920s, when cacao exports declined, labor conditions deteriorated, and government troops were unleashed on striking plantation workers. Following the massacre of cacao plantation workers in Guayaquil in 1922, indigenous uprisings broke out on several highland haciendas, forever shattering nineteenth-century stereotypes of the docile peon. Having escaped the ravages of rural warfare and peasant rebellion so characteristic of rural relations in other parts of the Andes in the late nineteenth century, Ecuador was suddenly rocked by spreading labor militancy, class strife, and military violence in the early twentieth century.

TRANSCULTURAL PATHWAYS OUT OF RURAL INDIANNESS

If we are to understand the dynamics of rural society in late-nineteenth-century northern Ecuador, we need to return to the issue of rural strategies of livelihood and resistance – which, under some circumstances, might have served as the proverbial safety valve.[21] In some areas of highland Ecuador, for example, Indian

---

[21] This brief consideration springs out of an abundant scholarly literature on the structural causes, strategies, and symbolic expressions of peasant protest and rebellions. But see especially James Scott's conceptual shift from structural analyses of collective action to a more culturally sensitive reading of peasant patterns of "resistance" and "quiescence" in his trio of books, *The Moral Economy of the Peasant: Rebellion and Subsistence in Southeast Asia* (New Haven, 1976); *Weapons of the Weak: Everyday Forms of Peasant Resistance* (New Haven, 1985); and *Domination and the Arts of Resistance: Hidden Transcripts* (New Haven, 1990). For an interesting conceptual experiment in "testing" explanatory arguments about the patterns of Andean peasant rebellion and nonrebellion in eighteenth-century Peru and Bolivia, see Steve Stern, "The Age of Andean Insurrection, 1742–1782: A Reappraisal," in his edited volume, *Resistance, Rebellion, and Consciousness*

farming families retreated upland before the advancing edge of valley mestizo towns. Their highland villages clung to steep hillsides and scratched out meager existences, sometimes serving as small pools of casual labor for distant enterprises, including compulsory road work. An even greater number of Quichua-speaking families moved into the orbit of Quito, following along the rutted tracks made by centuries of cityward migrants. Nineteenth-century travelers were invariably spellbound by the sight of so many Indians "of a hundred different villages in every variety of costume" surging through the noisy, crowded streets of the capital. Hawkers, pack drivers, farmers, adobe brick makers, tailors, furniture makers, stable boys, servants, saloon keepers, beggars, and day laborers – Indians and *cholos* performed the labor and services that whites would not do. But the sight that caught most commentary was that of Indian porters carrying heavy loads of stone, brick, sand, furniture, flour sacks, meat, or firewood on their backs secured by ropes slung around their chests or foreheads (Figure 1). Women's burdens invariably included a small child, whom they carried astride their bundles while spinning cotton threads in their spindles, often as they trotted along footpaths or roads. "Almost everything that moves in Quito rides on the backs of Indians," wrote one North American traveler.[22]

Without the familiarity and security of the kin group, community, or landlord, most Indians probably found urban life to be dangerous and degrading. And while some people managed to integrate themselves into paternal or kinship networks in the city, others began to embrace strategies and relationships drawn from the dominant

in the Andean Peasant World, 18th to 20th Centuries (Madison, 1987), 34–93.

[22] Harry A. Franck, *Vagabonding Down the Andes: Being the Narrative of a Journey, Chiefly Afoot, from Panama to Buenos Aires* (New York, 1917), 161.

society that could offer pathways out of poverty and Indianness. Quito was not the only escape valve for Indian social climbers. It was perhaps better for socially mobile, enterprising natives to seek refuge in the buoyant textile-producing towns and cities of Riobamba and Otavalo, or along the thriving pack-train routes that operated out of northern villages like Atuntaqui en route to Colombia. After 1870, the quickening pace of textile production and trade and the expansion of petty officialdom created a growing sector of *cholos* – people of Indian roots or parentage whose culture, demeanor, and lifeways took on a more mestizo cast. Many lived on the geographic and cultural edges of mestizo towns. These new migrants sought work in trade, industry, and petty bureaucracy in a fluid cultural setting, where almost everyone spoke Quichua laced with Spanish, or vice versa. Economic survival usually depended on their ability to serve as go-betweens, brokering economic, political, and cultural exchanges between the rural Indian world and the urban mestizo one, because it was precisely their knowledge and manipulation of the symbolic lexicon of Quichua-speaking villages that gave the migrants advantages over white competitors in dealing with Indian clients. On the other hand, social advancement usually required migrants to change their ethnic markers (language, dress, diet, place of residence, family name, etc.) in pursuit of status and prosperity in the urban milieu. To survive and thrive in the countryside, however, itinerant *cholos* donned their ponchos, "dusted off" their Quichua, and carried small tokens to their Indian clients. There, they served as crucial intermediaries, facilitating Indian access to mestizo officialdom, and they periodically renewed their village contacts by returning for local fiestas, births, and baptisms.

The most vivid example is the mestizo merchant and labor contractor – a roving figure who traveled the mule paths across the interior landscape. The least ethical ones preyed openly on the miseries and misfortunes of Indians – wielding the ubiquitous threat of debtors' prison before their Indian customers. For many of them, this was the pathway to prosperity, even if it entailed the certainty of social alienation. Yet it is also true that mestizos seeking to secure long-term trading partners among their "social inferiors" rarely conducted their affairs with the ruthlessness that Creole elites tended to impute to them. (Indeed, such stereotypes fed the anxiety and contempt that urban elites felt toward racial "hybrids" invading their cities.) In the countryside, quotidian expressions of ethnic, class, and gender inequalities between Indians and mestizos were more subtle. Throughout Ecuador and the rest of the Andes, regionally specific vernaculars and social practices captured the gendered, class, and local nuances and contingencies of racial and ethnic ascriptions among an increasingly amorphous mass of rural peasants and plebes. Local terminologies of ethnic identity and attributes created slippery, ambiguous, interstitial groupings (*cholos, castas, ladinos, mistis,* etc.) that bespoke the dynamics and vigor of transculturation processes at work in many regions.[23]

A lesser known but equally significant mestizo stereotype emerged in the interstices of the political machinery of modernization during the late nineteenth century. He was the back country

---

[23] Much interesting new work is focusing on discursive practices of ethnic identity as historically rooted cultural process. For a sweeping overview, see Olivia Harris, "Ethnic Identity and Market Relations: Indians and Mestizos in the Andes," in Brooke Larson and Olivia Harris, eds., *Ethnicity, Markets, and Migration in the Andes: At the Crossroads of Anthropology and History* (Durham, 1995), 351–90, as well as older but still salient essays in Fernando Fuenzalida et al., *El indio y el poder en el Perú* (Lima, 1970). On the engendering of *chola* and Indian identity in dynamic contemporary contexts, see Mary Weismantel, *Cholas and Pishtacos: Stories of Race and Sex in the Andes* (Chicago, 2001); and the important articles by Linda Seligman, "To Be in Between: The Cholas as Market Women," *Comparative Studies in Society and History* 31: 4 (1989), 694–721; and Marisol de la Cadena, "'Women Are More Indian': Ethnicity and Gender in a Community Near Cuzco," in B. Larson and O. Harris, eds., *Ethnicity, Markets and Migration in the Andes*, 329–50.

lawyer – typically a literate bilingual mestizo who knew the bureaucratic ropes and could fill small spaces left by the suppression
of indigenous leaders and the official Protector of Indians (abolished in 1854). Self-styled litigants of Indians appeared on the
provincial scene throughout the Andean highlands, and already by
midcentury *tinterillos* (country lawyers, notaries, and scribes) were
familiar figures in rural highland Ecuador. These shadowy souls
occupied a strategic position in rural society amidst extreme judicial and political flux. Many *tinterillos* practiced chicanery of all
sorts. But some individuals served as indispensable brokers helping
Indians negotiate the posttributary judicial system in the absence
of their own hereditary ethnic lords and separate legal code. As
such, they proved to be a major nuisance to white society, tying
up landlords in interminable lawsuits over land titles, debts, or labor or whipping up Indian resentment over debt contracts. Not
surprisingly, their reputation quickly soured. They became archetypal "outside agitators" who preyed upon Indian illiteracy for their
own scheming ends and, in the process, slowed the march of order
and progress. Even the more-optimistic textbook of 1874 found
the Ecuadorian mestizo wanting. He stood closer to the unwashed
Indian masses than to the civilized whites on the racial-evolutionary
scale.

RELIGION, MARKETS, INDUSTRY: FORGING
THE OTAVALAN COMMUNITY

There was one striking anomaly in this bleak ideological landscape
of "docile, indolent Indians" and "parasitic mestizos": the people
of Otavalo, who inhabited the fertile valleys and mountain slopes
two days' journey by mule to the northeast of Quito. Since early
colonial times, the Otavalans had attracted European admiration
and royal protection for their superb skills as weavers. "I never saw

a race of finer looking people than an assembly of Otavalans on a Sunday," wrote an English traveler in 1825.[24] And in recent times, the villages of Otavalo have drawn anthropologists seeking to understand the secrets of their success – how they have managed the "acculturation problem" (through centuries of coercion and adaptation) and flourished as ethnic enclaves in a hostile political world in spite of their long-standing participation in market economies.[25] Theirs is a long, contentious history of cultural coercion, change, recovery, and self-affirmation through successive periods of regional, colonial, and national integration.

[24] William Bennet Stevenson, *A Historical and Descriptive Narrative of Twenty Years' Residence in South America*, 2 vols. (London, 1825), 2: 347; quoted in Frank Salomon, "Weavers of Otavalo," in Norman E. Whitten, Jr., ed., *Cultural Transformations and Ethnicity in Modern Ecuador* (Urbana, 1981), 420–49, 420.

[25] This formulation of the paradoxes of Otavalan cultural resilience belongs to Frank Salomon, "Weavers of Otavalo." These paradoxes are all the more perplexing if placed in long-term historical context. Segundo Moreno Yánez and Kenneth Andrien have shown the devastating impact of regional economic decline on the Otavalo and other indigenous peasantries in the north-central *sierra* in the eighteenth century: loss of lands, regional economic decline, heavy labor and tribute obligations, rigorous tax collection, and other punitive measures all contributed to poverty and upheaval in that region after 1770. Indeed, one of the largest and bloodiest revolutions occurred in Otavalo in 1777, sparked by royal attempts to carry out a new census and increase tribute (Segundo Moreno Yánez, *Sublevaciones indígenas en la Audiencia de Quito, desde comienzos del siglo XVIII hasta fines de la colonial* [Quito, 1985]; and Andrien, *The Kingdom of Quito*, 128–32). Against that background, the partial recovery of Otavalan lands, livelihood, and communal identity is all the more puzzling and merits close historical study. For a fascinating state-centric study of Otavalo-state relations, see Derek Williams, "Negotiating the State: National Utopias and Local Politics in Andean Ecuador, 1845–1875," unpublished Ph.D. dissertation, Stony Brook University, 2001; and the forthcoming edited volume on Indians and Nation Making in Ecuador by Kim Clark.

For the Otavalans, the nineteenth century was punctuated by a postindependence period of cultural reprieve and relative autonomy, only to be followed by the authoritarian phase of forced modernization in later decades. They had withstood the corrosive effects of land reform and managed to reintegrate themselves at the moiety level under de facto *caciques*, who controlled the process of tribute collection and continued to exercise their colonial prerogatives as ethnic authorities and advocates. Like the a*yllus* of southern Peru and Bolivia, the Otavalans wielded their everyday knowledge of history, mythology, genealogy, and colonial precedence preserved in written, oral, and ritual forms, to defend communal interests and press their claims on the new republic.

The abolition of tribute broke the implicit colonial precedent for *cacique* authority. It opened the way to ethnic fragmentation, incursions, and subordination to the emerging authoritarian regime. *Caciques* could no longer function as the interlocutors of an adversarial community or caste. Ethnic authority structures were leveled, jurisdictions were fragmented, and power was diffused among local, rotating Indian functionaries, who were called on to serve as agents of the religious and secular branches of the state. This was no small burden to bear under an extractive republican state. The business of the Indian *alcalde de justicia*, for example, was to procure Indian laborers or carriers for the public service whenever demanded. Beginning in the 1860s, Otavalan leaders had to dispatch small armies of conscript laborers to build the nation's wagon roads to the coast, down dizzying mountain faces overgrown with rain forest. Such terrible tasks could only be performed if the *alcaldes* backed up their own despotic powers with threats of government force and imprisonment. Equally complicit was the *alcalde de doctrina* (beadle or church constable), charged with keeping the chapels in good repair, procuring labor for the parish priests, and meting out punishment for moral transgressions. Friedrich Hassaurek happened upon a Sunday mass in

Otavalo one day and bore witness to the moral policing of Indian women:

Standing on the open square in front of the church, my attention was attracted by about two dozen Indians, most of them women, brought up by a few Indian alcaldes, who led them tied to one another with a long rope. Their offense consisted in having failed to attend religious service, especially the doctrina (lesson), for which they are compelled to meet twice a week. They were driven up and cuffed by the alcaldes, who for this purpose are entrusted with a little despotic authority.[26]

This "little despotic authority" undermined the fragile basis of ethnic authority and collapsed communal-wide options of political negotiation and defense. It necessarily changed the way peasants did politics. The new logic forced peasants to bargain for individual truces, rights, or favors in exchange for the fulfillment of their labor duties as Indian "citizen-subjects." Otavalan villagers developed the politics of petty paternalism to wrest small favors or retributions from outside mestizo authorities. But the most bitter pill was the fact that the state had abolished most customary jurisdictions and rights associated with tribute at the same time that it reimposed extractive relations. Not only did Otavalans face new incursions, but they now had few legal or institutional means of redress. Cultural lifeways adjusted, too, as villages honed ideological traditions of localism. Incursions, racial animosity, class, and language barriers increased the social and political isolation of the Otavalo at the same time that they were plucked from their villages to dig the nation's highways. At the same time, Otavalan villages seemed to evolve their own defensive practices and norms of endogamy, bound together through customs of intermarriage, communal work parties, and reciprocal relations. Yet paradoxically their communalism

---

[26] Hassaurek, *Four Years among the Ecuadorians*, 174.

was fragmented and local in scope. The Otavalan villages were no longer beholden to a common ethnic lord.

What, then, sustained the basis of ethnic reorganization and identity in this alienating and hostile environment? How did the Otavalan peoples manage to survive the oppressive and atomizing conditions imposed upon them during the second half of the nineteenth century? These questions remain fascinating historical enigmas. Historians know more about colonial and contemporary Otavalan society than they do about the Otavalo during the nineteenth century (see the Bibliographic Essay). But pending future research, there are enough clues to intuit how everyday forms of popular religion and market culture may have tempered the threatening forces of fragmentation and extraction.

One set of clues comes from the pen of Hassaurek, who recorded his impressions of a religious festival in Otavalo during the winter solstice. As elsewhere in the Andes, the Otavalan peoples celebrated the feast of San Juan, just as they did for a host of local patron saints. Hassaurek was astonished to see "dancing saints," "quaint mummeries," and other "mixtures of Catholicism and heathenism." And he was scandalized by the "live sacrifices of cocks" and other "barbarous customs."[27] During this week-long festival of dance, song, stories, drink, games, masquerades, and mummeries, Otavalans came together to affirm their ethnic identity and, like subaltern revelers everywhere, to briefly "turn the world upside down" through ritual dances that mocked and mimicked their social superiors. But it would be a mistake to dismiss this burst of expressive culture as a cathartic release of accumulated class and ethnic hatreds, ultimately in the interest of the status quo. In the context of nineteenth-century nation-building projects, particularly Ecuador's theocratic-authoritarian model, this open display of popular Catholicism and communal solidarity itself mocked the very

----

[27] Ibid., 158–9.

cultural values that dominant white society was supposedly inculcating in the Indians. Such open acts of "barbarity" advanced alternative cultural values and legitimacies that added up to a symbolic counterassault on the repressive civilizing mission of the Church.

No less importantly the theatre of communal festivities renewed a shared sense of bounded ethnic self. At the festival, people hailing from different places identified their ethnic-regional affiliations by their dress, hats, music, and dances and by their position in stylized spacial arrangements during the festivities. Hassaurek noticed the Otavalan women who dressed in identical fashion, wrapped in rustic red shawls and adorned in glass beads (Figure 7). Otavalan men were distinguished by their long braids, blue woolen ponchos, and short white pants. These visual ethnic boundaries were maintained throughout the riotous color and chaos of the festival.

Festivals also served to reinforce ethnic identity, pride, and loyalty in the domain of the marketplace, and here we have another clue regarding the cultural and material counterforces pushing against atomization. For centuries, the Otavalans had privileged their own collective identity as specialized, superior weavers under the Incas and Spaniards. Before the Spanish conquest, the Otavalan people had already developed a strong regional pride, even chauvinism, as weavers and traders of cotton blankets and cloaks, which a brief period of Inca rule did little to change. Eventually the Quichua language supplanted Cara and the Inca-introduced wool-bearing camelids, but the Otavalans emerged with the skills and breadth of their textile trade stronger than ever. When the Spaniards overran the Andes, the Otavalans fared better than did most native peoples. They eventually became major suppliers of the colony's textiles, especially rustic shirt cloth, woolen blankets, and ponchos. The Spanish crown recognized these skilled workers and set aside the villages in a crown *encomienda*. Spanish-owned mills developed a parallel track of industry, concentrated mainly in the Riobamba region to the south of Otavalo. Several Otavalan textile

Figure 7. Otavalan women. With their distinctively elaborate ceremonial and market-day dress, composed of their own weavings, large brimmed hats, and multiple strands of gold and red beads, Otavalan women (as well as their menfolk) have drawn the ethnographic eye of foreign travelers and Ecuadorian nationalists alike, since the late nineteenth century. This portrait might well have served as a nineteenth century *carte-de-visite* for Europeans interested in the "exotic cultures" and "racial types" of South America, but it was published in the 1933 ethnographic study of Ecuador by the eminent Mexican anthropologist, Moisés Sáenz. See his *Sobre el Indio Ecuatoriano y su incorporación al medio nacional* (Mexico City, Secretariat of Public Education, 1933).

workshops sprang up, but they belonged to corporate communities or the crown. Neither private industries nor *haciendas* made many inroads into Otavalan territory until the late colonial era. Even then, when those communities were under growing pressure from creeping *latifundismo* and relentless labor drafts, the Otavalans were able to function as independent textile producers and traders of great repute. Their commodities found markets throughout the length of the Andes.[28]

Postindependence political transformations – the violence and high cost of the Independence wars, abolition of *cacicazgos*, state incursions, loss of traditional colonial markets, and influx of British textiles – conspired against Otavalan material and cultural autonomies. But by midcentury, the villages had rebounded as important textile suppliers of regional, national, and even international markets. They continued to face competition from Spanish-owned textile mills, now more capitalized than before. But unlike many of those precocious capitalist ventures, which could suddenly fall on hard times, the Otavalans' cottage industry seemed to have staying power. Although they could not undersell English factory-made clothing or even the products of old-style *obrajes*, they could often outlast them. Their secret lay in the flexibility and diversity of their peasant family economies, which combined craft and agricultural production and therefore boasted a considerable degree of self-sufficiency and adaptability as market and harvest conditions fluctuated over time. Second, it lay in their strong cultural traditions of selective innovation and initiative, which guided the choices people made about how they used their labor, capital, and cash. Such economic choices were mediated by cultural values and memories that placed a premium on communal strength, territoriality, and independence. Time and again, Otavalans adopted European tools, techniques, and consumer products to put to use within the bounds

---

[28] Salomon, "Weavers of Otavalo," 440–1.

of their own cultural matrix: to reinforce their subsistence security and cultural autonomy, to stave off poverty and servitude.

In short, they evolved an alternative mercantile culture, which reinforced the ethnic boundaries and identities of the whole group. The Sunday market at Otavalo was a weekly renewal of ethnic associations, norms, and identities at the same time that it served to integrate Otavalans into larger cash economies as both commodity producers and consumers. Like their rituals of folk Catholicism that indicted the dominant norms of white Catholic society, then, the marketplace served as the symbolic terrain of an alternative culture of commodity exchange – one that was integrally related to Otavalan histories and memories of struggle. Gradually, over the last years of the nineteenth century and the early years of the twentieth, new market and capital breakthroughs sustained the prosperity of many Otavalan families and allowed them to purchase parcels of fertile bottomland in their quest for territorial autonomy.

This remarkable case of ethnic resilience and adaptation was mostly lost to white nation builders, unwilling or unable to see small miracles in a vast landscape of poverty and misery. Most of them were blinded by frozen, homogenized stereotypes of the Indian race. Others, like Hassaurek, who took the trouble to explore the Indian hinterlands, dismissed the Otavalans as a more haughty version of the heathen Indian. But by the end of the century, the ascendance of liberal reformism produced social critics of conservative-Hispanism casting about for new real and symbolic models of nation building. The quest for national identity and authenticity became somewhat urgent in the 1890s, as Ecuador prepared for her national debut at the 1892 World's Fair on the occasion of the four-hundredth anniversary of Columbus's arrival. Ecuador was to offer an exhibit at the American Historical Exposition to promote a favorable image abroad and cultivate diplomatic and trading relations with Spain. Ecuador's propagandists searched for an exhibit of their country's "exotic cultures" that might excite European interest. After much debate, they settled on specimens of the "Otavalan race." Deemed safe, quaint, and picturesque, the Otavalan people were thought to display an industriousness consonant with the nation's modernizing mission. Decorative weavers would be on hand at the fair to show off their artisan abilities and colorful costumes. So began the first official *indigenista* project: to stereotype and stylize Indians in the service of national image making.[29] Otavalans were folklorized as the antithesis of the "common Indian," yet they remained as isolated as ever from the exclusive white nation.

As we step back from the historical canvas of highland Ecuador, it appears clear that the white nation-builders stood at an ideological and institutional crossroad in the late nineteenth century. Like their northern counterparts in Colombia, they bore witness to the gradual erosion of caste and the advance of cultural *mestizaje* in many highland areas. Southern Indian migration to the coast, as well as the bustling mestizo towns of the northern highlands – those nodal points of state control and plebian commerce – were symptomatic. And yet the conservative ruling elite remained deeply ambivalent about the historic role of the Indian and mestizo in the republic's past and future. For most of the century they eschewed unifying myths of the mestizo as historic agents of race mixture and cultural assimilation. The liberal Colombian project of whitening had little political resonance in nineteenth-century Ecuador.

On the contrary, the Church-sponsored republican project of Ecuador reinforced caste. Ecuador abolished tribute, but reinstitutionalized coerced Indian labor. Extractive modes of labor control, in turn, rested on discursive foundations that posited the immutability of race. By the 1870s, the white race had become

---

[29] Blanca Muratorio, "Nación, identidad y etnicidad: Imágenes de los indios ecuatorianos y sus imagineros a fines del siglo XIX," in her edited volume *Imágenes e Imagineros. Representaciones de los indígenas ecuatorianos, siglos XIX y XX* (Quito, 1994), 168–9.

synonymous with civilization and citizenship; the Indian race, with poverty and cultural depravity. As the backward race, Indians were biologically predestined to serve the nation as its laborers, servants, soldiers, and beasts of burden. They would build the nation's new roads but be denied membership in the imagined national community. They would pay taxes and serve in the military but be subject to a modern inquisition designed to root out idolatry, superstition, and shamanism. They would be effaced from Ecuador's censuses and silenced in public discourse but subject to discriminatory practices for purposes of public works, taxes, military conscription, and criminal and moral discipline. Still, elites thought there needed to be Indians. The evaporation of Indians into white peasants or laborers through progressive *mestizaje* and European immigration apparently did not grip the political imagination of most Ecuadorian leaders before the Liberal Party came to power in 1895. Too much was vested in colonial modes of exploitation. Even after the Liberals' victory, amidst heated Liberal–Conservative polemics, debt servitude and debtors' prison, as well as the degraded Indian peon, would remain fixtures of rural Ecuador until well into the twentieth century.

4

━━━━━━━━━━━━━━━━━━━━━━━━━━━━━━━━━━━━━━━

Peru

War, National Sovereignty, and the Indian Question

From the outset, the formation of the Peruvian republic was profoundly troubled. In 1810, the Creole aristocracy throughout the
Viceroyalty of Peru entered the age of independence with divided
loyalties and deep distrust of liberal ideals and popular politics. Still
haunted by fears of the Andean insurrection of the 1780s, many
landowners and merchants preferred to live under the iron fist of
Spanish absolutism than unleash the forces of revolution and rebellion. Indeed, Creole Peru witnessed the beginning of postcolonial dislocations and widespread peasant mobilizations in 1811 and
1812, when the Spanish liberals tried to dismantle tribute for *indios*
and *castas* (non-Indian castes) in Peru and the rest of America. The
restoration of the Bourbon dynasty in 1814 probably brought a
collective sigh of relief to most Creoles, but by then Peru's future
political fate was already being decided by the grand designs of
great liberators in distant lands. It was only a matter of time before
two invading armies, one led by José de San Martín and the other
by Simón Bolívar, would foist independence upon Peru's reluctant
Creole aristocrats.

Throughout most of the decade of the 1820s, Peru's transition
from colony to republic followed a circuitous process of liberal

reform and illiberal counterreform. As we discussed in Chapter 1, the critical issue of tribute was at the core of emerging political debates over the meaning and boundaries of postcolonial republicanism in Peru. Ever since the Spanish liberal constitutionalists had struck down Indian tribute in 1812, the Indian head-tax had continued to vex both indigenous authorities, fearful of incurring even more onerous tax burdens and of losing their customary and legal rights to community, and Creole elites, wedded to Spain's dual-nation system of colonial rule.

The restoration of tribute in 1814 did not survive the decade, however. When the liberating armies swept into coastal Peru from the south, José de San Martín proclaimed the end of "onerous tribute" by declaring that all Indians were to become citizens of the new republic, equal before the law, and henceforth known as *peruanos*. By abolishing tribute, San Martín took a decisive step in redefining the colonial basis of the Indian-state compact, based on the asymmetrical exchange of Indian tribute for access to communal land, self-rule, and legal protection. By liquidating tribute, the state also abrogated its obligation to protect and guarantee the internal social and agrarian order of indigenous communities. Without its formal obligations to render tributary services to the state, the juri-political existence of the *ayllu* would be thrown into jeopardy. It was Bolívar, however, who carried the implications of abolition even further, into the realm of agrarian reform. In 1824, the liberator decreed all state lands to be sold by lots in order to encourage new settlements. He granted land possession (in fee simple) to those "Indian tenants" occupying "state land." In particular, Bolívar targeted communal Indian lands (*tierras de comunidad*) to be divided up and distributed among indigenous families. Thus, both San Martín and Bolívar had a brief moment to impose their utopian visions and shape the legislative agenda of the new Peruvian republic. Perhaps inspired by the contemporary Jeffersonian ideal of agrarian democracy, Bolívar's early decrees pressed for the broad distribution and unrestricted circulation of land, the promotion of agrarian settlements, and the end of communal forms of authority and self-rule. But as Bolívar traveled into the highlands in 1825 and 1826, he bore witness to the complexities, disputes, and abuses that the new land reform laws had unleashed. Therein began a long, contentious process of diluting, even retracting, Bolivarian land reform laws. It would not be long before Indian tribute made its reappearance.

This imposed liberal experiment floundered under the early Peruvian republic. From the outset, most Creole politicians had choked on San Martín's liberal-Indianist rhetoric that condemned tribute, *mitas*, and servitude; recognized the Quechua language; and offered citizenship rights to Indians. And they resented Bolívar's imperious edicts. As soon as Bolívar left Peru to its own political fate, the new congress moved briskly to restore the Indian head-tax (under the euphemistic label of "*contribución de indígenas*) and to scale back the land reforms. Out of the lawmakers' furious debates and compromises came the Law of 1828 – a strange hybrid project that inscribed liberal notions of property (and implied citizenship) onto colonial notions of tribute and caste. Specifically, the Law of 1828 promoted individual peasant proprietorship, subject to certain restrictions designed to prevent the wholesale alienation of Indian lands to non-Indian landowners. In return, the Peruvian republic – now facing an enormous fiscal deficit in the aftermath of war – restored the postcolonial *contribución indígena* (1826–54). Indians would continue to pay a special head tax, after all, until the 1850s.[1]

In fashioning a compromise between Bolívar's liberal utopia of yeoman smallholders and the fiscal expedience of the state, Peruvian lawmakers abolished, not Indian tribute, but the colonial-Andean

---

[1] Nils Jacobsen, "Liberalism and Indian Communities in Peru, 1821–1920," in Robert Jackson, ed., *Liberals, the Church, and the Indian Peasants* (Albuquerque, 1997), 131–2.

heritage of communal lands, self-rule, and legal protection. Theoretically, Indians had possession of their subsistence plots of land
and, in return, paid a "tax contribution" to the new republic. This
episode was only the beginning of Peru's nineteenth-century saga
of Creole statesmen trying to position its Indian majority in the
slippery interstices of colonial caste and civil society. The Law of
1828 was a halfway measure, in which the notions of caste and civil
society were hopelessly entangled. For while it weakened the terms
of the old "tributary pact," by removing corporate rights and jurisdictions under the old *república de indios*, it theoretically opened
up the *possibilities* of indigenous claims to new rights and responsibilities as "propertied citizens" under liberal republican ideology.

But how, exactly, would indigenous authorities interpret this contradictory welter of reforms? What, after all, did it mean to be a
republicano in the peasant villages of, say, Huaylas, Ayacucho, or
Puno in the late 1820s, 1830s, and 1840s? How might *cabildos* negotiate the judicial politics of *republicanismo*, which both promised
and denied liberal citizenship rights to Indians? How might indigenous authorities, perhaps with the help of literate lawyers and
scribes, word their petitions so as to invoke their inherited folk-legal
rights to lands, self-rule, and protection under the colonial *república
de indios*? Indeed, indigenous people across the highlands found
themselves trying to interpret and deploy the ambiguous language
of early Peruvian republicanism to deal with urgent issues of taxation, land, and labor. Anthropologist Mark Thurner sums up this
moment of political and discursive flux in Andean Peru: "the useful
slippage between tributary subject and propertied citizen generated
a subaltern form of Indian citizenship wrapped up in the hybrid
notion of *republicano*."[2] Given the semantic and legal ambiguity

---

[2] Mark Thurner, *From Two Republics to One Divided: Contradictions of
Postcolonial Nationmaking in Andean Peru* (Durham, 1997), 35; Jacobsen
"Liberalism and Indian Communities," 135–8.

of the word "*republicano*" under the early republic, indigenous authorities might manipulate its multivalent meanings for all sorts of political purposes.

One thing is certain, however. Neither elite nor popular forms of liberalism suppressed the politics or demographics of Indianness during the early to mid-nineteenth century. Official census records reinforced caste divisions by continuing to use colonial-racial categories in sorting and counting the population. And those census records reveal a surprising degree of resurgent Indianness in the Peruvian highlands. At the time of independence, Peru was the most populated of the four Andean republics, with an estimated 1.5 million people. Historian Paul Gootenberg's astute analysis of little known 1827 provincial census records indicates that almost two-thirds of the population (62 percent) was registered as "Indian." More striking is the *persistence* of Indian population numbers over the nineteenth century. In spite of buoyant population growth of Peru's white, mestizo, and black populations, which were mostly confined to the cities and coastal areas, the indigenous sector remained remarkably in tact. Peru did not seem to share in the broad bio-cultural processes of *mestizaje* as did the northern republics of Colombia and Ecuador. To the extent that it did, cultural *mestizaje* was confined mainly to the coast.[3]

Historian George Kubler first published Peru's apparent anomaly of nineteenth-century "reindianization" in 1952.[4] Adopting the official classifications of *indio* and *casta* to compile aggregate population estimates and chart demographic trends between 1795 (following the last colonial census) and 1940 (the last national census

---

[3] Paul Gootenberg, "Population and Ethnicity in Early Republican Peru: Some Revisions," *Latin American Research Review* 26: 3 (1991), 109–57.

[4] George Kubler, *The Indian Caste of Peru, 1795–1940: A Population Study Based on Tax Records* (Washington, D.C. 1952). See the discussion in Nicolás Sánchez Albornoz, *The Population of Latin America: A History* (Berkeley, 1974), 109 ff.

before he undertook this study), Kubler highlighted the nineteenth century as the only era in Andean history that halted – even
reversed – the half-millennial trend of Indian depopulation and assimilation. (Indigenous populations had suffered drastic decline in
the sixteenth and seventeenth centuries, mainly due to devastating
European diseases.) More precisely, Kubler argued that Indian population rapidly recovered in the postindependence period (between
the 1830s and 1870s) before tapering off in the early twentieth century, with the onset of rapid migration, urbanization, market expansion, and transculturation. In the 1876 census (a census plagued
with errors, it might be noted), Peru's population had grown to
2.7 million, with "Indians" composing approximately 55 percent
of the total population. By contrast, the amorphous category of
"mestizo" was less than 20 percent of the total population in 1876.

Hidden behind these official population guesstimates, of course,
lies the republic's deliberate pursuit of tribute and its associated
ethnic-racial taxonomies. To most government officials, it was prudent fiscal policy to continue registering and taxing Indians while
there were few alternative sources of income. Only in the 1850s
would revenues from *guano* exports make abolition of Indian tribute a viable option. The spectacular boom in guano exports between
1847 and 1873 would lead to a fivefold increase of state revenues,
finally freeing the state from its fiscal dependence on the colonial
head-tax. Yet the reproduction of colonial categories of caste transcended their functional purpose. Republican officials would continue to register rural peasants as members of the "Indian caste"
long after tribute revenues had dwindled and tribute itself had
morphed into "labor," "property," or "poll" taxes. Racial-ethnic
classifications were never obliterated from Peruvian census taking, even in the heyday of nineteenth-century liberalism (1850 to
1870s).

Official perceptions of resurgent Indianness also had to do with
the *material persistence* of traditional forms of peasant livelihood,

community, and identity during the 1830s, 1840s, and 1850s. In his sweeping survey of liberalism and Indian communities, Nils Jacobsen concludes that the loss of Indian *tierras de comunidad* was quite limited in many parts of highland Peru before the 1850s.[5] Neither liberal policy making nor market forces made deep inroads into the Peruvian *sierra* in the postindependence period. Tulio Halperín Donghi's general observation that agrarian decompression and political fragmentation seemed to favor the survival of Indian communities (despite formal liberalism) bears up under the aggregate data thus far.[6] Although propertied communalism was formally banished by the Law of 1828, the highlands remained relatively isolated from the Creole national state and the locus of sputtering capitalist enterprise along the north coast. Furthermore, Peru remained huddled behind protracted protectionism until the 1850s. Did this postindependence relaxation of external market and political pressures provide a measure of reprieve? Did processes of rural dispersion and pervasive poverty encourage informal networks of *comunalidad*, to borrow Paul Gootenberg's term, wherein peasants continued to practice cooperative labor, exchange networks, fiesta systems, and other ritual expressions of communalism beyond the enforcement of liberal authorities? Did Andean peasants evolve effective political-judicial strategies to secure their communal niche in the interstices of the old and new *repúblicas*? Such queries invite new research, which might

---

[5] Jacobsen, "Liberalism and the Indian Community," 134, 136–7.

[6] Halperín Donghi, "Economy and Society in Post-Independence Latin America," in L. Bethell, ed., *Spanish America after Independence, c. 1820–1870* (Cambridge, 1987), 1–47. On Peru's sluggish economy and rural society, see Nils Jacobsen, *Mirages of Transition: The Peruvian Altiplano, 1780–1930* (Berkeley, 1993), chaps. 3 and 4; Charles Walker, *Smoldering Ashes: Cuzco and the Creation of Republican Peru, 1780–1840* (Durham, 1999), chap. 7; and Thurner, *From Two Republics to One Divided,* chap. 2.

help to explain the persistence of Indianness under the Peruvian republic.[7]

The political economy of reprieve did not signal, however, social stasis within rural Andean society in the early to mid-nineteenth century. Nils Jacobsen's work on the southern *altiplano* districts of Puno and Azángaro reveal intensive property and class realignments in the countryside. Beginning in the late 1820s, communal traditions adjusted to new smallholding patterns and shifting notions of land rights within the communities themselves.[8] Furthermore, as Thurner shows for the Huaylas region, indigenous authorities had to adapt their political strategies to fluctuating liberal and illiberal reforms. It is clear from the very intensity of indigenous political activity in these decades that Andean peasant authorities continued to broker all sorts of political negotiations between their own kin and republican institutions. Clearly, Bolívar's abolition of the hereditary office of *kuraka* (or *cacique*) in 1825 did not incapacitate peasant political leaders in this time of relative quiescence. Rather, it seems that Indian political authority and *comunalidad* were firmly rooted in the *ayllu* moiety or local head village (*cabecera del ayllu*). This was the consequence of a half-century or more of political readjustments within Andean society, in response to growing corruption among eighteenth-century hereditary (often mestizo) *caciques*. The fragmentation of Andean authority structures was hastened by draconian Bourbon policy, which had tried to destroy the Andean nobility in Cuzco and elsewhere after the general insurrection of the 1780s. In the postindependence era, the locus of communal self-rule was lodged in the Indian *cabildos* composed of various civil and religious leaders. In most regions, supreme authority

[7] Gootenberg, "Population and Ethnicity in Early Republican Peru," 149, 146–50; Heraclio Bonilla, "Peru and Bolivia," Leslie Bethell, ed., *Spanish America after Independence, c. 1820–c. 1870* (Cambridge, 1987), 246–7.

[8] Jacobsen, *Mirages of Transition*, chaps. 3 and 4.

was vested in the rotative office of *alcalde*, or *varayuq*. (The title *varayuq*, or staffholder, refers to annually rotating officers who held the silver-clad staffs of authority.) During times of agrarian compression or war, these local networks of ethnic authority could mobilize scattered communities in revolt or oil the machinery of Indian litigation and protest against land despoliation and other injustices. In short, Indian communities in much of Peru were neither so fragmented, nor beleaguered, nor atrophied as historians once thought.

This fact alone would make the Indian loom large in the Creole national imaginary. When President Ramón Castilla mandated the abolition of Indian tribute in 1854, Lima's politicians and intellectuals began to voice their doubts about the future of the nation's indigenous majority. As one progressive writer starkly posed the emerging Indian question in 1856: "and these Indians we call 'citizens' – what good will they do the Republic?"[9]

EMANCIPATION, EXTRACTION, CIVILIZATION, OR PROTECTION? CREOLE PERU CONFRONTS ITS INDIAN PROBLEM

Around midcentury, liberal politicians began to take that question rather seriously. Changing economic times – the economic promise of *guano* and railroads – called for institutional reforms that might open Peru to the world. In the 1840s, steamships began appearing in the waters of the Pacific, reducing the voyage from Peru to Europe to a mere forty-five days. Steamships also cut transport time to the ports of Chile, creating a lucrative market for Chile's wheat crop.

---

[9] Quoted in Alberto Flores Galindo, *Buscando un Inca: Identidad y utopía en los andes* (Lima, 1988), 3rd ed., 274. The writer was liberal intellectual, Santiago Tavara, posing the question in his celebrated essay, *Emancipación del indio decretada en 5 de julio de 1854* (Lima, 1856), 20.

Consequently, Peru's booming coastal economy in the 1850s and 1860s turned ever more seaward for its markets, and imported food, technology, investment capital, and European values. By contrast, the mountainous interior – a land of somnolent Indian villages, feudal landlords, and unruly *caudillos* – seemed to lag ever farther behind the coastal engine of outward growth. Such structural disparities so common to the *misdevelopment* of nineteenth-century Latin America took vivid shape in the political imaginary of Lima's liberal vanguard. Peru's familiar geo-racial fissuring into two incompatible republics – one coastal, white, and modern, the other mountainous, Indian, and backward – began to reemerge in the third quarter of the nineteenth century. Among other things, this spatial-racial idiom was a product of triumphal export liberalism turning its back on the Indian past.[10] This vanguard put its faith, however, in the power of free-trade liberalism to open the backlands to the benefits of order and progress. Booming exports encouraged the Lima-based oligarchy to imagine a nation of bustling markets and billowing smokestacks, industrious yeomen and European immigrants, commercial *haciendas* and teeming cities.

Peru's extraordinary windfall profits from *guano* did finance and shape the nation's first sustained experiment in free-trade liberalism (1850s to 1870s). The mountainous deposits of bird droppings on the arid islands off the coast of Peru proved to be a rich source of fertilizer. *Guano*'s utility was no secret, since native agriculturalists and later colonial planters had long used *guano* to fertilize arid, coastal

---

[10] Galindo, *Buscando un Inca*, 269–70; Benjamin Orlove, "Putting Race in its Place: Order in Colonial and Postcolonial Geography," *Social Research* 60 (1993), 306–8; Paul Gootenberg, *Imagining Development: Economic Ideas in Peru's "Fictitious Prosperity" of Guano, 1840–1880* (Berkeley, 1993); see also Pratt, *Imperial Eye: Travel Writing and Transculturation* (London, 1992), chap. 8, on the British and Creole "capitalist vanguards"' reinvention of geo-racial self and other in Spanish South America in the mid-nineteenth century.

croplands. But the advent of steamships and low transatlantic shipping costs, together with the opening of the English market, suddenly turned *guano* into Peru's legendary export commodity. England coveted the bird dung for its nutrient-hungry farmlands. Modern farming techniques depended on imported fertilizer to increase agricultural yields so landowners could provision Britain's cities and factory towns with cheap abundant foodcrops. For Peru, the explosion of overseas demand provided an unprecedented source of private wealth, as well as government tax revenue (some 60 percent of government income) between 1840 and 1880. No other export commodity in the greater Andean region generated the volume of revenue, or exercised such a powerful political mandate, as did *guano* for mid-nineteenth-century Peru. Although Peru's mishandling of these windfall profits has provided many scholars with a classic textbook case of an ephemeral boom-bust economy that never "took off" into agro-industrial development, historians now recognize the *guano* state's impact on a diversifying export sector (including silver, cotton, and sugar exports), foreign imports, credit, and state-financing. In short, *guano* revenues helped to finance a host of economic and political changes, from paying reparation costs to Creole slaveholders at the time of abolition (1855) to underwriting a national railway construction program beginning in the 1850s.[11] Suddenly, too, Lima finally consolidated power and put the rest of the nation under the influence of its centralizing military and bureaucracy. The federal state itself was, in large part, captive to Lima's emerging "*guano* bourgeoisie." Staking the nation's future on bird droppings, Lima's commercial plutocracy unfurled, once again, the tattered Bolivarian banner of economic liberalism.

---

[11] Paul Gootenberg, *Between Silver and Guano: Commercial Policy and the State in Postindendence Peru* (Princeton, 1989), chap. 5; and Heraclio Bonilla, *Guano y burguesía en el Perú* (Lima, 1974).

The Indian problem now began to demand the attention of Limenõ politicians. They were eager to promote market capitalism and free-trade liberalism in the Indianizing highlands, where the native population was clearly not going to disappear into *mestizaje* any time soon. Structural and "racial" roadblocks had to be removed so that market capitalism could travel from the Europeanizing seacoast into the mountainous interior. Specifically, the mandate demanded that Limeño statesmen take up the old issues of Indian tribute and land once again. More than those standard themes, however, the modernizing state would have to design the apparatus of cultural regulation and reform so as to hasten assimilative processes essential for building a unifying nation-state of Hispanized citizens. These liberal decades (1850s to 1870s) thus opened a new era in Indian-state relations. But like the earlier episode of "enlightened liberalism" of the 1820s, this period was one of liberal reformism and illiberal backsliding because the Limenõ oligarchy could not forge any kind of consensus, much less assemble a coherent government strategy, to diagnose and tackle the Indian problem. The midcentury liberal vanguard was torn between free-trade ideologies and authoritarian impulses, between assimilative programs and segregationist projects, and between economic optimism and racial anxiety.

These contradictions in official Indian policy assumed their starkest dimension in successive regimes during the heyday of liberalism (1850s to 1870s). Creole political leaders and intellectuals fashioned four basic "paradigms" of Indian policy reform: (1) the free-market reforms of the mid- to late 1850s; (2) a return to extractive and punitive actions in the mid-1860s; (3) the mobilization of a state-driven civilizing campaign in the early to mid-1870s; and (4) the discursive turn toward official paternalism on the eve of the War of the Pacific (1879–83). I briefly will explore each of these competing projects in contexts of political flux, with an eye on their lingering implications for Peru's evolving Indian-state relations.

The explosive export boom of the 1850s ushered in a new era of free-trade liberalism that rivaled the regimes of Ramón Castilla (1845–51, 1855–62) and José Rufino Echenique (1851–54). This climate of triumphal liberalism revived the emancipatory ideals of the early 1820s: the manumission of slaves, abolition of Indian tribute (the *contribución de indígenas*), and consolidation of private property. Both Castilla and Echenique pressed their abolitionist agendas, breaking the bondage of African slavery in 1855 and abolishing Indian tribute in 1854. Ideally, these acts would hurl Indian and African laborers into the nation's bourgeoning economy. In particular, Peruvian free-trade advocates looked to the nation's vast population of Andean peasants as potential agrarian producers and laborers, much as Bolívar had dreamed of creating a yeoman utopia in the Andes during the mid-1820s.

The 1854 law abolishing Indian tribute signaled to the nation that Indians would henceforth be subject only to "universal" property or poll taxes. It also removed the literacy clause that was meant to protect Indians from land alienation through fraudulent contracts. The midcentury liberal revolution also introduced Peru's first civil code of 1852 revoking three decades of republican tributary policy and its accommodation to Andean claims and practices of *comunalidad*. There is no doubt that these midcentury reforms represented an institutional and ideological benchmark, by removing all remaining colonial-Andean rights to communal lifeways. And their real-life implications would eventually play out, often violently, as peasant communities found themselves engulfed by land-hungry elites wielding dubious legal documents or judicial orders, in the late nineteenth century. Yet, curiously, Peru's political juncture passed peaceably, and it remains almost a non-event in nineteenth-century Andean historiography. Perhaps that is because there was no immediate wave of Indian divestiture in the mid-1850s, as a direct consequence of these liberal land reform acts. Whether by design or default, the Peruvian state did not directly outlaw the Indian community, or take immediate action to confiscate and auction off community lands, as did Mexico, perilously, with its draconian 1856 "Ley Lerdo." Rather than confront the territorial problem directly, Peru's liberal reformers simply effaced the Indian community from the public record. Nils Jacobsen notes this curious elision: "this was an era in which the Indian community nearly disappeared from public discourse.... When people did discuss the Indian at all, as during the mid-1850s and between 1866 and the early 1870s, the debate focused on a stereotyped individual, and whether [the Indian] was a proprietor or worker."[12] Peru's civil code of 1852, for example, did not recognize or even mention the Indian community. Its aims were to consolidate private property and contractual law under one unifying code, thereby reducing Indians to individuals subject to one body of law and to the forces of the market. But free-trade liberalism continued to imagine the Indian subject as both freeholder and laborer, preparing for his eventual entry into the nation as subaltern citizen.

The state's official stance toward the Indian question turned more hostile under the military general, Mariano Ignacio Prado (1866–8). Two key issues shaped his regime's Indian policy: Indian tribute (under a new guise) and peasant unrest and "pacification" in the remote border region of Puno. The issue of extraction had long been a subject of legislative debate, in spite of all the liberal fanfare accompanying tribute abolition in 1854. Some liberals, like Santiago Tavara, fought against the reinstatement of the head-tax (now under the guise of a "universal" male head-tax) on the grounds that it would target the poorest members of society, just after they had been emancipated from tribute.[13] But the prevailing viewpoint argued that the "*contribución personal*" was different from the

[12] Jacobsen, "Liberalism and the Indian Community," 139.
[13] Ibid., 143.

colonial-tributary head tax because it was imposed on the product of personal labor. Yet it was couched in resolutely colonial-racist terms: the republic needed to coerce the congenitally lazy and frugal Indians into the labor market by imposing a monetary head-tax. This recycled rationale was on the lips of every colonial administrator since Viceroy Toledo first rationalized Peru's extractive system of tribute and *mita* in the 1570s. Not content to leave the provisioning of cheap labor to the inner workings of a (non)self-regulated market, the pragmatists urged the adoption of this new "labor tax" on Indians.[14]

Why this discursive turn toward indigenous labor? *Guano*-age politicians were increasingly concerned about "structural bottlenecks" in the postabolition period, just at a moment when the north coast plantations required a massive injection of field laborers. Since the late 1840s, Peru had turned seaward for its immigrant plantation workers, to the Basque country of Spain and, more crucially, to the teeming cities of China. Once slavery was gone, planters

---

[14] Ironically, this notion that indigenous peasants, bound up in local subsistent economies, would not participate in regional market economies unless under coercive pressures of mercantile capitalism is a classic theme in Marxist studies on the peasantry, as well as in neo-Marxist studies on the uses of "extra-economic force" in Third World, predominantly peasant societies undergoing violent transitions to capitalism. On the latter point, see the influential model of "coerced cash crop labor" in colonized areas of the expanding "world capitalist system": Immanuel Wallerstein, various volumes in *The Modern World-System* (New York, 1974, 1980, 1989). For historical applications, critiques, and corrections in the Andean context, consult Steve Stern, "Feudalism, Capitalism, and the World-System in the Perspective of Latin America and the Caribbean," in Steve Stern et al., eds., *Confronting Historical Paradigms* (Madison, 1993), 23–83; Florencia Mallon, *The Defense of Community in Peru's Central Highlands: Peasant Struggle and Capitalist Transition, 1860–1940* (Princeton, 1983); and Brooke Larson and Olivia Harris with E. Tandeter, eds., *Ethnicity, Markets, and Migration in the Andes: At the Crossroads of History and Anthropology* (Durham, 1995).

preferred to procure laborers from China than rely on the seasonal trickle of migrant laborers from the Peruvian highlands. Over the long run, however, the "Chinese solution" to the labor problem turned out to be more problematic than expected. Chinese immigrants would submit to the miserable working conditions on the plantations only so long as they were kept under lock and key. Soon Chinese runaways began flooding into Lima and other cities along the coast, eventually mixing with and "perverting" (in the eyes of Creole policy makers) local native and black populations. Rather than "improving" Peru's racial stock, as white European immigrants were supposed to do, the invasion of Asian workers only "contaminated" the other nonwhite races, according to anxious Creole race theorists. For both economic and eugenic reasons, then, the capitalist planters began to look inward to the *sierra india* for its labor reserves. In the process, they devised an assortment of incentives and coercions to procure indentured workers. Their instrument of choice was the hook (*el enganche*), a binding seven-year contract of sweat work in the coastal cane and cotton fields. In the last decades of the nineteenth century, labor hookers (*los enganchadores*) swarmed across the northern highlands of Cajamarca and elsewhere in search of guileless, dislocated, or restless peasants willing to work for sweatshop agriculture on the northern Peruvian coast.[15]

---

[15] On the development of modern coastal plantations and their labor control problems, see Michael J. González, "Capitalist Agriculture and Labour Contracting in Northern Peru," *Journal of Latin American Studies* 12: 2 (1980), 291–315; and Peter Klaren, "The Social and Economic Consequences of Modernization in the Peruvian Sugar Industry," in K. Duncan and I. Rutledge, eds., *Land and Labour in Latin America* (Cambridge, 1977), 229–52. Apparently, "spontaneous" peasant migration to coastal plantations was more prevalent in the southern regions than previously thought, although labor demands were probably not so enormous there. See Henri Favre, "The Dynamics of Indian Peasant Society and Migration to Coastal Plantations in Central Peru," in K. Duncan and I. Rutledge, eds., *Land*

Urgent fiscal needs also dictated the Prado regime's imposition of an Indian "labor tax." Prado came to power at the end of a dangerous dispute with Spain. For a moment, Peru lost control of its rich *guano* islands of Chincha. The crisis discredited the free-trade liberals and catapulted Mariano Prado, a military man from Arequipa, into power in late 1865. He discovered to his dismay that Peru owed foreign concessionaires of *guano* over 20 million pesos in advances and loans. As the *guano* bubble burst, Prado's government heralded a new tax scheme, of which the centerpiece was the new head tax on natives. It represented a heavy burden on peasant families – the equivalent of twelve days of day wages. Moreover, the new lien was piled on top of myriad customary obligations that peasant villages were still forced to render to local political and priestly authorities. The government's *contribución personal* bore down most heavily on the Indian herding communities of the south, where a devastating drought was under way. Drought was not the only scourge of the southern *altiplano* district. As we shall see shortly, the region was being swept into the great funnel of the overseas wool market; as a result, a growing number of merchants were scouring the arid plateau for cheap wool. Mercantile and extractive pressures became inextricably linked and especially oppressive in that regional context. Peasant protests broke out in 1866, in and around the village of Huancané, near the city of Puno. Huancané people rose up against tax agents, but they also took the occasion to settle old scores with local landlords and merchants, who still deployed unpaid Indian labor services even as they prospered from trafficking in the cattle and wool trades on both sides of the Peru-Bolivian border.

and Labour in Latin America (Cambridge, 1977), 253–68, on the adaptive migratory strategies of the Astos Indians from highland Huancavelica. In contrast, Juan Martínez-Alier discusses social and cultural factors inhibiting many highland Indians from making seasonal treks down to the coast in his article, "Relations of Production in Andean Haciendas. Peru," in K. Duncan and I. Rutledge, eds., *Land and Labour in Latin America*, 141–64.

Despite its remoteness, the Huancané uprising jolted Limeño elites into immediate action, both conciliatory and repressive. The congress took measures to appease the indigenous masses, by revoking the labor tax in 1867. A deputy from Cuzco tried to push forward another law, abolishing the practice of personal service and the enforced sponsorship of religious fiestas in Indian communities. But another political faction sought punitive action and took steps to send a full army division to "pacify" the region. Before long, the government had engineered its first state-driven campaign of military repression. Fired up by the emergency "Law of Terror," the Peruvian army banded together with mercenaries and estate owners to massacre and imprison Indians. Insurgent villages of the *altiplano* were uprooted and sent into exile to the labor camps in the jungles of Carabaya. The army captured the peasants' mestizo spokesman and defender, Juan Bustamante. He was stoned to death in early 1868. The rebellion of Huancané was a terrible barometer of deteriorating conditions in the southern highlands. It also unmasked a harsher militarized republic in the mid-1860s, which veered between acts of extraction, repression, and criminalization in its dealings with this vilified region (known as *la mancha india*, "the Indian stain") of highland Peru.[16]

Yet out of this moment of brutality came the first stirrings of national conscience. Amidst the tumult surround the Huancané uprising, Juan Bustamante launched the first Indian-rights movement in the Andes. As a bilingual mestizo wool merchant, writer, and politician from Puno, Bustamante was perfectly situated to become the stereotypic provincial despot, swindler, land grabber, pen pusher, and producer of racist diatribe. But Bustamante put the lie to all such stereotypes by using his provincial position and

---

[16] Thomas M. Davies, Jr., *Indian Integration in Peru: A Half Century of Experience, 1900–1948* (Lincoln, 1974), 30–1. See Jorge Basadre, *La multitud, la ciudad, y el campo en la historia del Perú* (Lima, 1947), 243–4.

class privileges to bear witness to the daily forms of oppression and humiliation that local Aymara people suffered. He kept a notebook in which he catalogued the worst abuses that Indians suffered at the hands of local authorities and merchants, and after the Huancané revolt broke out, Bustamante took it upon himself to interpolate the rebels' grievances for the larger public. In 1867, he published an extraordinary little book, *Los indios del Perú*, which linked the future of the nation to the well-being of its Indian citizens, and he founded Peru's first pro-Indian civic organization, *La Sociedad Amiga de los Indios* (Society for the Friends of the Indian). Bustamante addressed himself both to Andean people, exhorting them to defend their rights to land and social justice, and to the Creole oligarchy, urging it to bring Indians into the nation. Specifically, Bustamante urged the state to promote rural schooling so that Indian children would learn to speak and read Spanish, dress in "modern" clothes, and bathe themselves. What distinguished Bustamante from other progressive pro-Indian thinkers, according to Nils Jacobsen, was that he believed such cultural reforms should not be imposed from above.[17] Philanthropic groups, like his own *Sociedad Amiga*, would serve as the agents of cultural reform. Set in the crucible of the "caste war" and legal terrorism on the *altiplano*, however, the view from Lima was anything but charitable. Bustamante's activism and agenda was deemed traitorous, and he was imprisoned and executed in short order.

Yet Bustamante's civilizing program soon became the centerpiece of reform under Manuel Pardo (1872–6). This new *"civilista"* coalition of coastal oligarchs, intellectuals, and politicians launched the first state-directed civilizing project in the Indian *sierra*. Inspired by liberal precepts, the new government hoped to spread the railway system across the mountainous backlands, bringing remote

---

[17] Jacobsen, "Liberalism and the Indian Community," 144–5.

regions into the ambit of the centralizing state.[18] Such technological miracles would demand that the government pursue the sorts of assimilative goals that Bustamante had outlined before his murder. If the highlands were to be colonized by entrepreneurs, Indians had to be released from their material and moral bondage (to feudal *haciendas*, subsistent communities, religious fiestas, and the like) and socialized to the work rhythms and demands of a modernizing Peru. Much as Colombia's free-wheeling liberals had, Peru's new prophets of progress manufactured a national vision of Indian redemption and assimilation – to be accompanied, of course, by aggressive efforts to import European immigrants. Although it borrowed the emancipatory and free-labor rhetoric of earlier liberals, Pardo's program nonetheless called for strong state intervention to coerce or cajole Indians into the modern political economy, without immediately striking racial categories from the public record. The *civilista* government strove for the selective assimilation of Indians, but whereas Colombia and Ecuador effaced race from their official records in the 1870s, Peru registered its Indian population in its 1876 census.

To reduce Andean peasants into disciplined laborers, Pardo's "civilizing mission" called for Indian education under a state-run system of primary schools. Although he never amassed the support he needed for his educational project, Pardo established one of Peru's first "Indian trade schools" in the city of Ayacucho. There, a select group of boys were trained to be carpenters, stone masons, and iron workers.[19] More than simply train Indians in the artisan trades, the civilizer wanted to massively deindianize Peru, which still registered Indians as the nation's demographic majority (55 percent) in the census of 1876. In much the same way that the late-eighteenth-century Bourbons had called for the

---

[18] See Gootenberg, *Imagining Development*, 71–89.
[19] Davies, *Indian Integration in Peru*, 31–2.

"extirpation of the Indian language," Pardo wanted to enforce the Hispanization of all indigenous peoples. But once again, Pardo's attempt to shake up racially segmented systems of labor and extraction in remote highland regions was bound to encounter stiff opposition from entrenched landed elites. In fact, well into the twentieth century, many provincial powerholders in both Peru and Bolivia saw Indian literacy and education as threats to the social order, and it was commonplace for landlords to forbid their peons from learning their letters. Such harsh realities of highland Peru reduced Pardo's grandiose schemes to token gestures. In 1876, Pardo ordered the state to print one thousand copies of a Spanish-Quechua dictionary for distribution among Indians! This was to be no "integrative revolution," to be sure. But it is arguably the case that Pardo laid the discursive groundwork for the prevailing "assimilationist paradigm" that later would drive Lima-based projects of *indigenismo* in the 1910s and 1920s.

When Nicolás de Piérola took office in 1879, that momentous year that brought the War of the Pacific, the republic reinvented Indian policy yet again. This time it was forged under the gun, as part of Peru's larger effort to defend the homeland against the Chilean invaders. Piérola reasoned well that if they were to prevail, he would have to mobilize the highlands behind the war effort. Of course that was not to be, and before long the central *sierra* roiled amidst the thunder of war. In 1879, while war loomed on coastal horizons, Piérola began to whip up the provincial bureaucracies to collect "war taxes" in cash and kind from its Indian constituencies. Local authorities reactivated the tributary apparatus and requisitioned money, supplies, and later soldiers from highland communities and *haciendas*. For the next several years, Indian communities throughout Peru virtually bankrolled the war effort.

Long before national and regional events spun out of control, Piérola made his pitch for Indian loyalty and obedience, not in the constitutional language of citizenship and patriotism, but in the older idiom of paternal absolutism. As the nation's father figure, he appealed to "his Indians" to make sacrifices for the national war effort, in return for which he promised his personal protection. Invoking the ideals of Spanish patrimonialism, Piérola proclaimed himself the "Protector of the Indian Race" against the tyranny of local government. He would serve as the ultimate arbiter of justice, with the right to intervene personally in situations brought to his attention by groups of aggrieved Indians who waited patiently outside his palace chambers. This self-styled Indian Protector wasted no time, however, in dispatching military men to comb the highlands for men, mules, and money. Was this a heinous example of political opportunism in a moment of national emergency? To be sure, but Piérola's belated experiment in coercive paternalism reveals how some members of the coastal oligarchy apparently understood the basis of their own legitimacy and authority in Indian society. Rather than appealing to Indians in patriotic or constitutionalist terms, Piérola reverted to the idiom of paternalism. It was empty rhetoric, of course, for it contained no legal reforms restoring communal rights or privileges. That far Piérola was unwilling to go. As we shall see, one of the great ironies of this period is that Indian soldiers themselves punctured the myth of Piérola's "Protectorate," revived the rhetoric of equality and citizenship, and thereby took political matters into their own rough hands. (So much for the power of paternalism!)

But we are getting ahead of the story. In the period between tribute abolition (1854) and the beginning of the Pacific War (1879), Indian communities confronted a fickle republic. The clashing paradigms of official Indian policy – from free-trade liberalism of the 1850s, the extractive-repressive regime of Pardo, Pardo's state-led civilizing mission, to the rhetorical protectionism of Piérola – bring to light the ineptitude that misguided Indian-state relations. Responding to both export market forces and political events in the hinterland, Limeño politicians and writers melded elements of liberalism, authoritarianism, corporatism, and racism into an amalgam of public policies and discourses on the future of the Indian race.

Yet it is possible to perceive important interpretive turning points during the liberal decades. First, the concept of the Indian community was rendered a nonentity in public and legal discourse during this period. The new language of liberal contractualism opened a huge gap between the juridical ideal of peasant freeholding under a formal regime of private property and on-the-ground customary practices that continued to govern real, everyday forms of livelihood, ritual, and community. The 1852 civil code also chose to ignore the pervasive coercive and servile relations that still burdened most Andean peasant families.

Second, early liberal discourses on the Indian as individual proprietor and laborer (1820s and 1850s) began to tilt toward the stereotypic Indian as reluctant laborer in the labor-hungry decades of the 1860s and 1870s. Earlier images of a propertied yeomanry, theoretically eligible for full citizenship rights, faded quickly before authoritarian prescriptions of new "labor taxes" to impel the sale of Indian labor, And indeed, private labor contractors were already deploying the infamous *enganche* to snare highland peasants for the coastal sugar plantations of the north. Equally significant, the reduction of the Indian peasant to landless "worker" forged crucial racial-class correlations in Creole public discourse, which simultaneously removed the Indian from the realms of propertied citizenship. Indians were cast, in other words, in the role of the nation's disenfranchised underclass.

Third, this growing interest in remaking Indians into the nation's laboring class called for aggressive programs of cultural and behavioral reform. Issues of immigration, education, production and consumption, religious ritual, family, and hygiene all became targets of Creole diagnosis and prescription. Ideally, the civilizing state would burrow into the inner recesses of Andean rural society in order to produce disciplined, hygienic, Hispanized laborers.

Finally, this era of political and discursive flux produced the nation's first pro-Indian movement, which assigned itself the role of interlocutor and defender of the Indian race. In the polarized climate of indigenous unrest and military reprisal of the 1860s, championing the civil rights of Indians was to invite disaster. But one long-term legacy of Bustamante's martyrdom was to create the basis of provincial *indigenismo*. In the early twentieth century, the highland cities of Puno and Cuzco emerged as crucial enclaves of *indigenismo* and regionalist projects, which defined themselves in opposition both to the coastal oligarchy and to entrenched regional elites, the reviled *gamonales* of the southern highlands. (The term *gamonal*, a Peruvianism coined by early twentieth-century *indigenistas*, conjures up the image of a "worm that corrodes the tree of the nation." It was used to define the parameters of local power, based on monopolistic forms of wealth [landholding, mercantile monopoly, access to servile labor, military bands, etc.] and the privatization of provincial power [control over local offices, judicial processes, etc.]. Indigenous peasants often referred to provincial authorities, *gamonales*, as *señores* or *mistis*.)[20]

As we shall see shortly, racial orthodoxies would harden in the years following the War of the Pacific, as Creole elites adapted positivist theories to explain away the disasters of war, poverty, and instability. Slowly and haltingly they gathered consensus that the state needed to take charge of domesticating the rural Andean world. Whether that project required methods of state repression, protection, or cultural regeneration continued to generate national debate. But I would argue that Peru's midcentury liberal hetero-doxies already contained the elements of a basic agenda: to forge the nation's racialized, laboring underclass, while denying their entry into the nation as political and "civil(ized)" subjects.

[20] Galindo, *Buscando un Inca*, 290. See also José Carlos Mariátegui, *Seven Interpretive Essays on Peruvian Reality* [1928] (Austin, 1971), 157–61.

EVERYDAY FORMS OF EXTRACTION, RESISTANCE, AND SOCIAL CLIMBING

Shifting liberal debates and policy making vis-à-vis the Indian were crucial for the exclusionary frameworks that emerged in the late nineteenth century. But historians have often noted liberalism's uneven material impact on indigenous communities in the prewar era. Nils Jacobsen writes: "the fate of the [Indian] community seems to have varied greatly during the third quarter of the nineteenth century." As he points out, "the strength and role of liberalism in the transformation of Andean peasant communities ultimately depended on local constellations of power, social structure, and the specific mechanisms by which communities were integrated into broader economic circuits."[21]

To carry this argument even further, it is clear from the historical evidence that commercial capitalism often proved to be a far more powerful force of rural change than did liberal policy making. Indeed, the pattern and pace of divestiture responded, not only to liberal land and tax reforms of the 1850s through 1870s, but also to the gathering "structural" forces of world market demand for Peruvian export commodities (wool, silver, copper, etc.) in the late nineteenth century.[22] Yet in considering the variegated impact of mercantile forces, we must still pay close attention to regionalism, which mediated and shaped the material and cultural effects of intense, albeit variant, forms of commodification. To take but two regional examples, which will be explored in some detail later: the advent of mercantile capitalism proved to be far more wrenching and violent for the villages of the southern *altiplano* of Puno, sucked into the vortex of the overseas wool trade, than for the buoyant, diversified peasant communities of Peru's central highlands. Regional

---

[21] Jacobsen, "Liberalism and the Indian Community," quotations on pages 147 and 125, respectively.

[22] Ibid., 156–7.

analysis also throws light on the intrinsic paradox of the spreading market economy. As the market unleashed threatening forces of communal divestiture and alienation, it also opened up pathways of economic and cultural mobility for some Andean people, driven or drawn into the modernizing urban sector.

Thus we can only begin to understand the different meanings and effects of liberalism and market forces if we plunk them down into local rural life and bear witness to the tangible forms of violence or opportunism they afforded. In the 1860s and 1870s, the southern highlands of Cuzco, Azángaro, and Puno seemed to be shot through with violence – driven not so much by the injustices of liberal-positivist doctrines as by the mundane brutalities of extraction. The booming overseas wool trade gave local commerce a violent edge it had not had in previous decades. As wool prices rocketed upward in the late 1860s and early 1870s, the lowly sheep and alpaca trade, the historic staple of southern Indian communities, turned into a hot prospect for wholesale exporters and their agents. The whole southern highlands, from the high plains of Titicaca to southern Cuzco and down into the valleys of Arequipa, was turning into a giant extractive economy feeding wool to the factories of northern Europe. This gradual transition climaxed much later, in the early twentieth century.

The export-driven wool trade picked up speed during the 1860s and 1870s, as British merchant and finance capital moved briskly into the Arequipa region and began to elbow aside indigenous wool traders. The capitalized wool business drove deeper into Aymara and Quechua zones – right to the thickest herds tucked away in the high *sierra* and clustered along the green and yellow lake shores of Titicaca. The interior *altiplano* was opened up to new forms of colonization after the iron rails reached Puno in 1874; from the north, the tracks moved southward to the lakeshore town of Juliaca in 1876. This triumph of European technology dealt a lethal blow to the centuries-old pack trade and wool industry that had sustained

Aymara and Quechua communities throughout the southern high-lands. Indigenous trading activities, muleteers, and markets were displaced, as the terms and conditions of overland trade shifted sharply against them. Throughout Peru, weekly retail markets continued to dictate the rhythms of local economic life, and their "picturesque characters" attracted the eye of European travelers (Figures 8 and 9). But in the southern wool zones, Vilque and other great market fairs and shrines faded in importance. Instead mestizo-dominated trade depots sprang up along the railroad tracks, and towns like Sicuani (Province of Canchis, in southern Cuzco) served as commercial outposts for British merchant houses located in the city of Arequipa. In the southern valley of Colca, for example, Indian llama drivers who had once traveled down the mountains to Arequipa to hawk their alpaca wool were dislocated by the arrival of the railroad and foreign export firms. They found themselves wheeling and dealing with commercial agents who rode the rails up into the highlands, looking to secure the best deals among Indian wool suppliers who now converged on the rail-side towns and markets. The Colca traders were not alone. All over the highlands a small group of commercial agents took over the management of the interior wool trade, often on behalf of Arequipa merchant houses.[23]

The new itinerant wool merchants walked a fine line between coaxing and coercing Indian suppliers into surrendering their wool on buyers' terms. Traders eager to bargain down prices often bypassed traditional peasant markets to purchase wool directly from Indian communities. As early as the late 1850s, Arequipa firms

---

[23] Benjamin Orlove, *Alpacas, Sheep and Men: The Wool Export Economy and Regional Society in Southern Peru* (New York, 1977); Nelson Manrique, "Gamonalismo, lanas, y violencia en los Andes," in Henrique Urbano, ed., *Poder y Violencia en los Andes* (Cuzco, 1989), 211–23; Jacobsen, *Mirages of Transition*, chaps. 5 and 6.

Figure 8. An Indian water carrier in the market of Cajamarca, in northern Peru, ca. 1880. This engraving was but one of hundreds that appeared in the published accounts of Charles Wiener, who wrote one of the century's most detailed, insightful, and richly illustrated travel-discovery accounts of the Andes. In his *Pérou et Bolivie: Recit du Voyage suivi archeologiques et ethnographiques et de notes sur l'ecriture et les langues des population indiennes* (Paris, Libraire Hachetter, 1880), Wiener, who undertook the journey for the French Ministry of Public Education between 1875 and 1877, conjoined ethnographic and archeological investigation to bring the rural Andean past and present into one field of inquiry. But like other contemporary European travelers to the Andes, Wiener used many of his engravings and the *cartes de visite* that he purchased in Peru and Bolivia to depict "popular types" by region,

began to send agents to tour the bandit-ridden Cuzco province of Chumbivilcas to buy wool directly from Indians. That practice spread rapidly across the southern Andes over the next two decades. Many wool traders managed to insinuate themselves into long-term relations with their Indian suppliers. Often they secured their wool supplies by advancing money to Indian herders. The sheep rancher would redeem the debt by delivering a certain quantity and quality of wool. The value of his herds and pastures would underwrite the whole transaction. Doing business in this way cost the merchant money and time – and perhaps much more, if he stalked sheep ranchers in dangerous provinces like Chumbivilcas. Even where rural trade was less treacherous, wandering wool buyers had to work through the rituals of community and kinship to establish client sheep-ranching communities. But after a certain point, as market

[*caption to Figure 8 (cont.)*] race, and occupation. Among the photographs he collected and categorized for the Musée d'Ethnographie, in Paris, were those that defined categories of Indian occupations, such as market vendors, healers, charcoal sellers, water carriers, porters, miners, agriculturalists, mule drives, domestic servants, and bandits. This particular engraving of a water carrier accompanied a lively description of market relations in the plaza of Cajamarca, in which water carriers (usually domestic Indians from the city) walked slowly and gravely through the city streets hauling their great *olla* of water to the marketplace, where suddenly their spirits lifted, as they smiled and laughed, greeted familiar merchants and hawkers, and made their way happily through the market's aisles and alley ways. When, suddenly, they were reminded of their servile station in life, they bid farewell to the pretty vendor, reassumed their "air of ennui and unhappiness" and headed reluctantly toward the mansion of their master (*Pérou et Bolivie* [Paris, 1880], 127). In the tradition of racial physiognomists like Hippolyte-Adolphe Taine who imputed moral, sentimental, and economic dispositions in the "racial-occupational types" they constructed, Wiener offers an entire scenario of affect and behavior to characterize the subject he was observing. In this case, Wiener explores the spaces of social freedom that marketplace culture (carnival and other popular-festive forms) offered, if only fleetingly, to indigenous traders, who were otherwise held in thrall by their masters. This would become a major literary, ethnographic, and historical theme in the twentieth century. See, for example, Mikhail Bakhtin, "The Language of the Marketplace in Rabelais," *Rabelais and His World* [1965] (Bloomington, 1984), chap. 2.

Figure 9. A married and rich market vendor of Puno, ca. 1880. Charles Wiener (in his *Pérou et Bolivia* [Paris, 1880], 385) was fascinated by the southern highland towns he toured. He especially loved market days, when indigenous men and women trekked into town from surrounding villages, *haciendas*, and *estancias*. Unlike Alcides D'Orbigny who perceived little difference in Peruvian "racial types," Charles Wiener differentiated Quechua and Aymara people by their physical characteristics (Aymaras were "shorter and darker") and by the dress of their womenfolk. He was particularly struck by the dress of Aymara women, such as that worn by the "rich merchant woman" shown here because of their adaptation of European dress, particularly the pointed headdress once worn, he noted, by the likes of Isabel de Baviere or Agnes Sorel of France. And adorning the head of such fashionable ladies, he hastened to point out, the coiffure is charming, but on the squat Aymara woman it only makes a mockery of her stature. Nonetheless, he recognized that their black hats served a function by making this "excellent cadre" stand out among the dark-skinned mass of haggling humanity that crowded the marketplaces of Vilque and other towns across the high plateau of southern Peru.

conditions shifted sharply against the raw wool suppliers, the brokers often grew impatient with these ritualized customs of trade. Professional wool merchants took advantage of things to entrap Indians into debt and eventually dispossess their flocks and lands.

Over the late nineteenth century, then, the southern Peruvian highlands experienced a dramatic shift in the correlation of social forces. Beginning in the 1860s, the wool export trade forged a new commercial axis connecting Arequipa (the merchant and banking city) to Puno (its commercial outpost in the sheep-breeding highlands). The arrival of the railroad in the 1870s clinched the wholesale trade by linking Puno and Arequipa to the Pacific ports. It was the beginning of the south's "commercial revolution" – one that consolidated itself around the turn of the twentieth century. Even though the wool trade tapered off during the War of the Pacific, the landed aristocracy of Peru's "new south" emerged from the war even stronger than before. Part of the reason for the rise of the south rests with the fortuitous events of the Pacific War, which spared the southern highlands from massive destruction and casualty. As we shall see, the central highlands bore the brunt of that war. But the tax burdens of war weighed heavily on Indian communities of southern Peru, and they suffered a wave of violent spoliations, enclosures, and evictions during and after the War of the Pacific.[24]

The wool boom that bore down on most Indian agricultural-pastoralist economies also opened molecular spaces for upwardly mobile rural entrepreneurs. Gradually commerce also created a thin layer of bureaucrats and professionals (schoolteachers, lawyers, police) staffing the towns across the Peruvian *altiplano*. In the countryside, a new breed of mestizo landowner cropped up. Poised on the interior "Indian frontier" of Peru's wool trade, the

---

[24] Nelson Manrique, *Yawar Mayu. Sociedades terratenientes serranas, 1879–1910* (Lima, 1988); Jacobsen, *Mirages of Transition,* chap. 6; and Alberto Flores Galindo, *Arequipa y el sur andino. siglos XIII–XX* (Lima, 1977).

social-climbing sheep ranchers were the country-bumpkin counterparts of the exquisitely civilized merchant/aristocrats conduct-
ing the export wool trade out of the city of Arequipa. Both kinds
of landowners – the white *latifundistas* and the mestizo sheep
farmers – owed their wealth and power to the booming wool export market and, ultimately, to their monopoly over Indian land
and labor. But it was the self-made mestizo landowners who directly subjugated Indian clients and who, in their growing power
and prosperity, seemed to violate all the standard ethnic and class
markers that white urban aristocrats so carefully maintained. Much
like the *tinterillo* who wandered both sides of the ethnic-class divide, the sheep ranchers of the Peruvian *altiplano* retained or assimilated elements of Indian culture. As Nils Jacobsen writes, "the
gamonales...constructed their own position in society both
through intimacy with the peasant world, from whence [sic] many
had come themselves, and through difference from that world."[25]

  This emerging regional subculture created dissonant ethnic
and class images. Travelers to the bleak backlands of Puno and
Azángaro brought back jarring images of Hispanizing Indian
bosses growing wealthy from their local monopsonies, or of white
landowners who seemed to be "sinking" into Indian lifeways. It
happened more than once that a European traveler, expecting to
be greeted by a wealthy Creole *hacendado* at the gates of his sheep
ranch, encountered instead a rustic man whose habits of life were almost indistinguishable from those of his Indian peons who watched
over his flocks and planted his potatoes. Anthropologist François
Bourricaud describes the experience of meeting one Señor López,
a man of European descent and the proud owner of some
1,500 hectares of land in Azángaro. But his rustic cultural ways
complicated his ascribed racial identity: his lips were stained green
by coca, and he uttered a vernacular Spanish, laced with Quechua.

[25] Jacobsen, *Mirages of Transition*, 333.

He had an "Indian wife" and two small sons, wearing ponchos and barefooted. According to Bourricaud, he was a kind of *declassé* mestizo who had assimilated into Indian culture.[26]

This profile points to local cultural transformations that broke down rigid 'race' and class categories into something more fluid and complex in Peru's *altiplano*. But out of an amorphous group of *misti* landowners and merchants arose a new stereotype: the predatory *gamonal* landowner living off the miseries of Indian underlings. In racial terms, this provincial elite crystallized into the archetypal highland mestizo. The social product of Peru's commercial wool revolution that wreaked havoc on indigenous herding communities, the mestizo *gamonal* came to represent in nationalist discourses all that was backward with rural Peru. Rather than being the bearer of civilization, the *gamonal* had refeudalized the countryside and, in the process, descended into barbaric (Indian) lifeways. By the early twentieth century, nationalist rhetoric had constructed a convenient straw man in order to promote official *indigenismo*. (*Indigenismo*, a blanket term for movements claiming to speak for Amerindian interests, in this case refers to a literary and political project promoted by Peruvian intellectuals.) In this version of rural reality, Indians became lost souls, victimized by mestizos, entrapped in feudal estates, and in need of rescuing by the Lima state.

There is a certain irony in the early-twentieth-century *indigenista* view of the hapless and helpless Indian, since late-nineteenth- and early-twentieth-century Peru was rocked by insurgent peasant threats of all kinds and intensities in both the southern highlands and the central highlands. Many southern wool zones erupted repeatedly in rebellion, reprisal, and counterreprisal along the cutting edge of the advancing *hacienda*. In 1895, Indian revolt spread across

---

[26] François Bourricaud, *Cambios en Puno* (Mexico City, 1967); cited in Galindo, *Arequipa y el sur andino*, 56.

the high pastures of Chucuito, near the Bolivian border, while local newspapers blasted "race-war" alarms across their banner headlines. Further south, in the province of Azángaro, where estates steamrolled over common pastures, early twentieth-century reports of Indian agitation, uprisings, and massacres punctured the precarious social peace in 1911, 1912, and 1913. Multiple uprisings on *haciendas* in those years, from Cuzco to Puno to Arequipa, climaxed in the massive peasant movement of 1915, led by the peripatetic visionary, Teodomiro Gutiérrez Cuevas, alias Rumi Maqui ("Stone Hand").

Equally important was the groundswell of subterranean, everyday forms of peasant resistance in both the center and periphery of Peru's wool districts after about 1870. Historical research lays bare the extreme vulnerability of local *haciendas* trying to colonize Indian peasant lands and labor in response to market incentives in the late nineteenth and early twentieth centuries. Much of this research has focused on those agrarian issues once shoved under the rubric of "the transition to capitalism" in rural Peru, but now with more interest on peasant agency, popular culture, and consciousness.[27] Juan Martínez-Alier's comment about the "basic conflict over the legitimacy of haciendas" also pertains to regions outside the southern wool districts in the late nineteenth century. The resilient traditions of communal land usage and peasant household economy in the central highlands, for example, served to block, and sometimes reverse, the rapid expansion of commercial *haciendas*. In the northern reaches of the Callejón de Huaylas, indigenous *estancias* (ranches) still controlled most pastoral lands on the eve of

---

[27] Alberto Flores Galindo and Juan Martínez-Alier, for example, have studied the power of Indian shepherds (*huacchilleros*) to resist modernizing sheep hacendados wanting to rationalize their use of land and labor. See Martínez-Alier *Los huacchilleros del Perú* (Lima, 1973), and Galindo, *Arequipa y el sur andino*, 114–27. Also, Jacobsen, *Mirages of Transition*, chap. 7.

the War of the Pacific. In the Mantaro Basin, peasant communities had managed to keep Creole hacendados at arm's length at least until midcentury. Even during the commercial boom of the 1870s, the regional elite did not manage to "break through the barrier of peasant resistance."[28]

Historians have begun to document this state of affairs for the buoyant, diversified peasant economies of Peru's central highlands. In the remote southwestern edge of the Mantaro Valley, for example, a raging war of drovers destroyed any illusions that legal entitlement (i.e., possession by deed) meant control over land. By night, pastoralists often drove their sheep, oxen, and cattle onto "stolen" pastures. Outright occupation, not title deeds, defined the status of "effective possession." In practice, the nominal landowner had to prove possession through the violent eviction of Indian herders and the impounding of their animals. This situation created private turf wars conducted on the edges of civil society. A title deed served not as a symbol of indisputable rights but as one of many weapons wielded in the struggle over land. Estate owners often armed their own service tenants with clubs and rifles, or hired mestizo townspeople, to drive out the encroachers and establish "effective possession" by driving their own herds onto the disputed lands and posting guards. Similar boundary wars raged across the central *sierra* after 1870.[29]

This ongoing contest over property claims, water rights, and grazing fees sabotaged and slowed the consolidation of commercial estates in the central *sierra*. Even by the late 1870s agrarian class balances remained more precarious and unstable in the central *sierra* than in either the Peruvian far north (where highland *haciendas* were more firmly entrenched) or the deep south (where

---

[28] Mallon, *The Defense of Community in Peru's Central Highlands*, 56.
[29] Gavin Smith, *Livelihood and Resistance: Peasants and the Politics of Land in Peru* (Berkeley, 1989), 57 passim.

the commercial wool revolution was delivering Indian lands and herds to brokers). A fledgling landed oligarchy, diversifying their holdings out of mining and *guano* and into cattle ranching, coveted the rich pastures. But most peasants were smallholding farmers and herders, living in rural communities and supplementing their home production with petty commerce, artisanry, and wage work. In the more commercially isolated and "Indian" region of Huaylas, provincial authorities continued to call upon highland *estancias* to send contingents of Indian workers to repair roads and buildings "for the republic." To the south, across the bustling Mantaro Basin, peasants also rendered gratuitous labor services to local authorities. But they participated in the buoyant regional marketing and mining networks that continued to thrive in the 1860s and 1870s.

Before the outbreak of war, then, there seemed to be no radical polarization between white aristocrats and dispossessed Indians in the central *sierra* district. Its fledgling landed-ranching elite remained vulnerable to the small arms fire of peasant resistance and sabotage. Further, the distant Limeño oligarchy proved too economically myopic, fickle, and weak to put muscle or mind behind its liberal land reform policies. Would-be estate magnates had to rely on their own retainers to carry out their nocturnal land invasions and evictions.

The most important shift in agrarian class relations in the central highlands took a more subtle, demographic, and cultural form. It flowed from the growing population of mestizo townspeople and landowners throughout the central *sierra*. A historic stronghold of cultural *mestizaje*, the region's peasantry became more economically stratified and culturally assimilated during the late nineteenth century. Regional commerce, mining, and bureaucracy opened new possibilities for bilingual social climbers who stitched together small-scale rural properties – usually on the outskirts of town and along river bottoms. They lived from localized trading, usurious, political, and productive opportunities that arose from Peru's expanding market economy and successive coastal booms in *guano* and agriculture. While this expansive regional economy attracted upwardly mobile peasants who could mediate capital, culture, and language, it ultimately reinforced ethnic and class differences – widening the difference between town and country, valley and highland, jacket and poncho. As elsewhere, *misti* fortunes in the central *sierra* often rode on the daily, grinding miseries of Indians. As a result, local society remained tense and precarious in the central highlands in the antebellum period.[30]

[30] Historians tend to agree about the deleterious impact of rising *mestizaje* on the climate of ethnic and class relations in the antebellum years. Nelson Manrique, Florencia Mallon, and, more recently, Mark Thurner point to the acute tensions that gripped peasant communities on the eve of the Pacific War, as petty and powerful regional elites tried to control and channel peasant labor and land to their own ends. They underscore the explosion of rural conflicts over land, labor, and credit as the best barometer of deteriorating ethnic and class relations.

Manrique and Thurner also examine rural-towns relations during traditional religious fiestas as political theatre that revealed deepening tensions and disengagement between rural Indians and town *mestizos*. Both historians note the gradual change in the climate of religious-municipal fiestas. Rather than serving as socially cathartic moments in which Indians and *mestizos* collapsed the social distance between them, letting off steam and channeling hostility, religious fiestas became an arena of mutual hostility between the highland Indians and the valley- or town-based *mestizos* and *cholos*. The latter viewed the fiestas as menacing moments of invasion by the ponchoed Indians of the interior highlands. The saints festivals allowed Indians to take over and remake the site and symbols of mestizo power in their own image (Mark Thurner, "From Two Republics to One Divided: The Contradictions of Nation-building in Andean Peru: The Case of Huaylas," Ph.D. dissertation, University of Wisconsin, 1993, 393–4; this discussion was omitted from the published version of the dissertation). Manrique, in turn, examines the efforts of the provincial council of Huancayo in 1880 to suppress the *baile de los Capitanes* and other dances, as well as bull runs and entire civil-religious festivals. These measures reveal the jittery nerves of Huancayo's political mestizo elite during the War of

PATRIOTS OR BARBARIANS? ARMED PEASANTS
IN THE WAR OF THE PACIFIC

When the War of the Pacific shattered this precarious peace in 1879, the nation's need to rely on an armed and mobilized peasantry – for the first time since the independence wars – radically altered power balances in the central *sierra*. The small arms fire of agrarian conflict of the 1870s rapidly gave way to a far more dangerous military situation: the rise of autonomous peasant guerrilla bands in the midst of foreign invasion, civil war, and the collapse of political authority across the entire central highlands – from the northern reaches of Ancash to the southeastern corners of the Mantaro Valley near the border of Huancavelica. It was there – in the mountainous tucks and folds of Ancash and Junín – where the fate of the nation hung in the balance during 1881 and 1882 and where the bloodiest dramas of war, repression, and revindication were played out.

If we are to understand this conflagration in the central highlands during the War of the Pacific (1879–83), we need to set it briefly in broader historical context. The War of the Pacific pitted Peru and Bolivia against an imperialist Chile, bent upon annexing the *guano* and nitrate-rich coastal territory of southern Peru and Bolivia. For the first time since the independence wars, Peru was invaded, occupied, and pillaged by a foreign army. Notwithstanding constant border disputes and territorial conquests during the nineteenth century, no other Andean republic experienced such a costly and humiliating defeat as did Peru at the hands of Chile. Peru shared its ignominious defeat with Bolivia, which also incurred territorial loss (and its only corridor to the sea). But Bolivia escaped the ravages of military invasion, as Chile focused its attack on the larger, more powerful nation of Peru (see Map 2).

the Pacific. Mestizo and Creole townspeople increasingly saw saints days as dangerous moments in the civil calendar, when the Indian "barbarians" came down into town (Manrique, *Yawar Mayu*, 43–50).

A foreign army tore the nation apart, decimating entire regional economies and dividing the country among factious regional elites who ultimately failed in forging a common front against this foreign enemy. They split over military and diplomatic strategies. The northern elites of Cajamarca pursued a policy of appeasement toward Chile, hoping to cut their losses and consolidate their own power base. The main body of troops in the central highlands, however, stood fast against the invaders and increasingly looked upon their northern allies as little more than traitors. By 1883, then, the international conflict was rapidly devolving into a civil war between the northern army (under General Iglesias) and the motley, "irregular troops" of General Cáceres who controlled the central highlands. Ultimately Iglesias's victory drew Cáceres into a political pact and thus began the third phase of the war: political pacification, repression, and demobilization.

In short, the period of warfare evolved through several phases: (1) Peru's defensive war against Chile's territorial invasion (1879–83); (2) the implosion of Peruvian civil and regional warfare (1883–4); and (3) the consolidation of allied military forces against the nation's "internal enemies" – armed peasants, now branded as "bandits" and "barbarians" (1884–90). Thus, Chilean aggression proved the unraveling of fragile paternal and coercive bonds that had barely contained ethnic and class hatreds during the 1860s and 1870s. The war initially catalyzed masses of rural peoples, creating a series of ephemeral yet pivotal moments for peasant-soldiers to grab the political limelight, forge multiethnic alliances, and force alternative visions and power constellations onto the political landscape – until the republic turned irreversibly against them. It is this hidden underside of the Pacific War that has recently come to light and that I recount here.

When the War of the Pacific left the sea lanes, it soon became a campaign of territorial conquest that engulfed the northern and central highlands of Peru. In June 1880, after Chile took the southern

port of Arica and effectively annexed Peru's southern nitrate-rich
Province of Tarapacá, her naval ships sailed up the coast to begin
battering Peruvian ports, cities, and plantations. By early 1881 as
Lima lay smoldering, 22,0000 Chilean soldiers pushed into the interior highlands and began its three-year-long military occupation.
Although Chile had no imperialist designs beyond its southern territorial conquest, it needed to bring Peru to the negotiating table.

Blocking Chile's way was the military commander, General
Andrés Cáceres. After Lima's fall in 1881, he had retreated to the
central highlands to begin organizing a national "campaign of resistance." His retreat into the province of Junín made sense for two
reasons. First, the central highlands continued to serve as the main
inland route from Lima. Just as the foreign liberators had found in
the 1820s, the Chilean invaders had to control this corridor if they
were to bring down Peru. Second, Cáceres himself had deep family
roots in the central *sierra*. He could call on an extensive clientele
network to build and supply his regular armies.

The beginning of Cáceres's resistance campaign inevitably thrust
the peasant communities of the greater Mantaro Valley into the middle of the war. Almost immediately, the general decreed that they
provide monthly quotas of potatoes, corn, cattle, and other food to
feed his ragtag armies. Meanwhile, estate owners in the northern areas of Junín began organizing and arming their own peasant cliente-
les to defend the region and nation against the foreign enemy. Under
Cáceres's leadership, they were to fight a defensive guerrilla campaign, relying on their ingrained knowledge of the land and village
support networks. Even so, the regular armies of Cáceres, which
numbered no more than 1,500, were unprepared for the brutal realities of Chilean invasion (Figure 10). Between 1881 and 1882,
thousands of Chilean soldiers moved into the central highlands in
two separate invasion forces. The second one, carried out in early
1882, was particularly devastating. Some three thousand enemy

Figure 10. A Peruvian foot soldier, his *rabona*, and a cavalryman on the eve of the War of the Pacific. In the text that accompanies this engraving, E. George Squier, in his magnificent travelogue (*Peru: Incidences of Travel and Exploration in the Land of the Incas*, [New York: Harper and Brothers, 1877], 46–7), expressed the profound moral ambivalence that most "enlightened" foreigners and Creole nationalists felt toward Peruvian Indians who apparently were "brave but stupid," "patriotic but apolitical" – suitable, in other words, for soldiery but not citizenship. In spite of this racist form of ambivalence, Squier offers here insightful observations about racial divisions within the military and the informal participation of Indian women in military campaigns. He wrote: "The Peruvian army is made up almost exclusively of Indians and negroes, or *sambos*. The Indians constitute the infantry, and, being accustomed since infancy to travel on foot in the mountainous interior, they are quick-footed and stoical on the march. . . . The Peruvian soldiers are tractable, and, if well led, as brave as any in the world. The native Indian tenacity and stubbornness are excellent elements in the composition of the soldier. Almost every Peruvian foot soldier is attended by his *rabona*, who may be, but is not generally, his wife. She marches with him, cooks and mends for him, often carries his knapsack, sometimes his musket, and always the little roll of matting which, when unfolded and supported on a couple of sticks, constitutes his tent. It is of little moment on which side the Indian fights. He knows nothing about the political squabbles of the country, and cares less."

181

soldiers combed the countryside looking for provisions and booty, all the while threatening to burn down the city of Huancayo if the hacendados did not meet their demands. Cáceres's armies retreated to Ayacucho, leaving the central highlands wide open to Chilean pillage and terrorism.

This proved to be a pivotal moment in the war, in that both regional elites and peasants began to take matters into their own hands. Throughout 1882, peasant villages began to organize guerrilla bands (*montoneras*) to fight the Chileans. Although poorly armed and vastly outnumbered, they managed to inflict casualties, capture weapons, and erode the confidence of the Chilean patrols. In fact, in their sporadic rearguard actions, the guerrillas waged the famous "resistance campaign" in the absence of Cáceres and his regular army, which had retreated temporarily from the region. In the eyes of the region's landowning elite, however, the specter of armed guerrilla fighters was terrifying. Their sudden rise to power as resistance fighters – free to roam the countryside, invade *haciendas* and towns, control the highways, and demand provisions, ammunition, and booty from merchants and hacendados – seemed far more treacherous than the presence of the Chilean army.

Many merchants and landowners soon began to conspire against the peasant-soldiers, hoping for an early peace agreement with Chile that would restore order to the countryside. In the meantime, the soldiers saw the writing on the wall. While there is some controversy among historians over the timing, patterns, and motivations of peasant invasions of rural properties, there is little doubt that by mid-1882 the guerrillas began to look upon regional elites as "Peruvian traitors." By then, Cáceres had returned to command the military campaign against Chile, but he continued to rely on the peasant-guerrillas to rout the Chileans and punish their Peruvian collaborators. It was during the winter months of 1882 that guerrilla activity became more violent and menacing toward collaborationist landlords, particularly in the southern Mantaro Valley.

As nationalist resistance fighters, the peasant guerrillas empowered themselves to take reprisals against the traitorous landlords, who had forsaken the nationalist front to save their own skins and properties. It is not surprising to find that many of those properties in the southern Mantaro were high *puna* regions only recently (and dubiously) acquired through enclosure and legal chicanery.

Here, then, was an extraordinary political opportunity for local peasants: to turn their patriotic struggle against their own immediate class enemies and, in the name of national defense, legitimately appropriate crops, cash, and livestock to feed their own armies and, in some cases, to reclaim their stolen lands. It is in this moment of national and regional crisis, Florencia Mallon argues, "with class and national concerns intermingled and reverberating against each other, . . . [that] the various land invasions and other actions in the area must be viewed."[31]

The central highlands thus became the main theatre of national resistance and class warfare between 1881 and 1883. But while peasant soldiers were fighting against the Chilean invaders and their Peruvian collaborators, a new threat to the patriotic forces of Cáceres loomed on the northern horizon. In 1882, General Miguel Iglesias, a wealthy landlord from Cajamarca, organized a "Free North Government" and began to negotiate the terms of surrender to Chile. Iglesias wanted to cut Peru's losses, and Peru's wealthy bankers, planters, and politicians supported him. They found natural allies among the landed elites of the central *sierra*, who feared the onslaught of "guerrilla-bandits." For Cáceres and many others, however, the 1883 Treaty of Ancón mocked his military campaign and disgraced the nation. No less important to the ambitious Cáceres, it catapulted the Iglesias faction into the presidency in

---

[31] Florencia Mallon, *The Defense of Community in Peru's Central Highlands*, 98. See also her book, *Peasant and Nation: The Making of Postcolonial Mexico and Peru* (Berkeley, 1995), chap. 6.

1883. The general now turned his war efforts against this partisan enemy, and the international conflict rapidly turned into civil war.

The formal end to the Pacific War in October 1883, then, did not restore the social peace. It unleashed the second phase of warfare – this time between partisan armies. As drought came and conditions sharply deteriorated in late 1883 and 1884, the civil war between Iglesias and Cáceres rampaged across the Mantaro Valley. The *montoneras* continued invading *haciendas* and combing the land for arms, livestock, and other meager provisions. To make matters worse, crops failed, food prices spiraled, and hunger spread. Even where *haciendas* and villages were not burned or abandoned, there was nothing left to sustain the escalating civil war between Iglesias and Cáceres. Military commanders resorted to draconian measures, wrecking local economies for years to come.

In the meantime, the shifting tides of partisan warfare during 1883–4 dealt a lethal blow to the Mantaro guerrilla movements. Already by early 1884, Peru's factious elites were beginning to put aside their differences and close ranks against the growing threat of rural anarchy in the central highlands. In June 1884, Cáceres turned his back on his own peasant-soldiers to forge tactical alliances with Iglesias and other power holders. The civil war was over. Cáceres could capitalize on his heroic resistance efforts, but only if he threw his weight behind coastal oligarchs and *serrano* landlords. He especially needed the landowners in his own province of Junín to support his bid for political power. And to win it he had to crush the guerrillas who had once defended the nation in his name. This he did in one brutal gesture. In July 1884, barely a month after Cáceres agreed to honor the infamous Treaty of Ancón, he captured, tried, and executed a guerrilla leader, Tomás Laimes, and his three aides in a plaza of Huancayo.

With that public massacre, Cáceres launched a military and rhetorical campaign of repression. Later, as president, he turned the full force of his office against the *montoneras*. In May 1886, he joined the conspiracy of officials to discredit and defile the guerrillas, and to expunge them from the official memory of war heroes. Stripped of their status as patriots and veterans, the guerrillas were transfigured into savage hordes and common criminals who preyed upon the peace-loving landlords and peons of the region. As we will see shortly, this effort to "barbarianize" the *montoneras* was not simply a feeble attempt to legitimate state violence against the guerrillas. It was part of a deeper debate within Creole political and literary circles over the culprits and causes of Peru's humiliating defeat.

But however Cáceres himself tried to justify military aggression against the guerrillas, he in fact underestimated their capacity to survive. Postwar pacification became the most protracted phase of Peru's crisis. As late as 1888, guerrillas still occupied dozens of *haciendas*, stretching along the length of the central highlands – from Cerro de Pasco in the north to the southern edge of the Mantaro. One of the last strongholds of guerrilla resistance was the peasant confederation of Comas, located in the isolated eastern mountains beyond Jauja. But like any semiautonomous *"republiqueta"* (self-governing area unofficially detached from the state much like a large maroon community), its existence fundamentally threatened the basis of national sovereignty, particularly in a fragmented and war-torn land like Peru. Inevitably, the Comas federation became the target of state violence and cooptation. In 1902, long after Cáceres was gone, Lima's strategy of combined negotiation and repression finally smashed it.

It is worth pausing for a moment to consider the political experiences and discourses of the Comas and Acobamba guerrillas during the 1880s. Having borne the brunt of the war, they emerged as the most autonomous guerrilla movement throughout the central *sierra*. More than other armed peasants, they came to understand the changing significance of the international and civil wars for

themselves and their own communities. They bore witness in 1881
to the atrocities the Chileans committed against their lands and people, and they organized the first successful military strikes against
them. Therein lay the wellspring of an incipient "peasant patriotism," which expressed itself in their words and deeds. But just as
they assumed the gravest burdens of national defense as the ragged
vanguard of Cáceres's floundering resistance movement, they saw
the regional elite begin to cave in to Chilean demands. In their eyes,
treasonous landlords not only compromised the nation's honor before the Chilean "bandits" but also denied what was most precious
to the guerrilla fighters: their hard-won dignity and legitimacy as patriotic "citizen-soldiers." In an extraordinary communication sent
to a prominent hacendado in April 1882, the Acobamba guerrillas exploded the hypocrisy of traitors like him, who "are in this
province communicating and giving explanations on how they can
ruin the Peruvians, to those treacherous Chilean bandit invaders."
Meanwhile, they wrote, hacendados had the audacity to stigmatize
the guerrilla patriots as "barbarians" just because "we with reason
and justice unanimously rose up to defend our homelands." Their
written words hardly contained their anger and disdain. Yet the
peasant correspondents were careful to couch their outrage in reasoned, even defensive, language. The letter concluded by denying
that they had committed barbarous acts: in wartime, they argued,
"any hacendado should be able to tolerate us [peasant guerrillas]
as patriotic soldiers."[32]

An eloquent cry for justice, this letter reveals the racial and
class antagonisms that cut deeply into the national front against
Chilean occupation in early 1882. But, as Florencia Mallon sug-
gests, this letter also hints at the political hopes and moral expectations that newly empowered veterans harbored: to command

---

[32] Quotations in Mallon, *The Defense of Community in Peru's Central
Highlands*, 89–90.

the tolerance and respect the nation owed them as veterans of the La Breña campaign. They demanded entry into the nation as citizens, not denizens, in return for having spilled their own blood in defense of Peru. And in so doing, they constituted themselves as political subjects engaging nationalist ideals of honor and self-sacrifice to press their own alternative, inclusive notions of citizenship. This collective sense of moral empowerment and self-confidence, and their ability to subvert the codes of political virtue to justify their rites of violence, were precisely what became intolerable to the regional and national elites.[33]

THE REBELS OF HUAYLAS

Only two hundred miles to the north of the Mantaro Basin, another political drama of war, rebellion, and repression unfolded along the Callejón de Huaylas. The agrarian crisis of 1883–4 had been devastating for the region. And just as the drought cracked open the fields, the civil war arrived with a vengeance. Towns and villages along the Callejón de Huaylas were subjected to successive military requisitions and cash-raising campaigns. Amidst these hardships, local Creole authorities suddenly decided to enforce the collection

---

[33] As the cockpit of insurgent peasant politics, the Mantaro guerrilla movements of the 1880s and 1890s have been the source of lively debate among historians. At base, the debate engages theoretical notions of peasant mentalities and the historical conditions that gave rise to translocal political coalitions and popular nationalist imaginings. The Mantaro guerrillas hold particular interest precisely because, for a brief period, they used the crisis of the Peruvian state to forge multiethnic solidarities, subvert the authority of regional landlords, and capture the public forum to redefine notions of civic virtue and citizenship in opposition to the oligarchic state.

On this point, historians tend to agree. Where consensus breaks down is around three questions: (1) the genuine "nationalist" content of the Mantaro guerrilla movement; (2) whether the Montaro rebels represented a regional anomaly; and (3) the ambiguous legacies of peasant insurgency and guerrilla

of the 1879 war-tax. This double "poll-tax" (a quasi-tributary tax that carried none of the customary rights or privileges associated with Indian tributary status) was to prove the proverbial precipitant of rebellion. In 1885 the town of Huaylas exploded in a mass of rural and urban uprisings that briefly turned the whole Callejón de Huaylas into a ribbon of insurgency and repression.

On the surface, the political events of state violence and Indian rebellion in Huaylas appear to have all the hallmarks of a classic anticolonial rebellion: the perpetration of state violence against the region's peasant villages (a double poll-tax, heaped on top of customary *corvée* labor obligations and military impressment); Indian petitions for tax relief, only to be met by the imprisonment and torture of their chief *vara*, known as Atusparia; the explosion of ethnic revindication against local "bad government," culminating in their defeat at the hands of army troops dispatched from Lima. Furthermore, the main target of Indian violence – the prefecture archive – was a powerful symbol of Indian grievances against heavy taxes. In short, Andean insurgency in Huaylas would appear to be a defensive, conservative, insular "Indian rebellion" – a study in contrast to the precocious peasant nationalists of the Mantaro region, who were plunged into the middle of the War of the Pacific.

---

warfare for the regions and villages involved and, more generally, for the nation in the postwar years. For a lively exchange, see Heraclio Bonilla, "The Indian Peasantry and 'Peru' During the War with Chile," in Steve J. Stern, *Resistance, Rebellion, and Consciousness in the Andean Peasant World, 18th to 20th Centuries* (Madison, 1987), 219–31; and Florencia Mallon, "Nationalist and Anti-State Coalition in the War of the Pacific: Junín and Cajamarca, 1879–1902," ibid., 232–79. See also Mallon, *Peasant and Nation*, 230–42. For a retrospective on the unfolding debate, as it shaped subsequent research on "peasant politics" in Peru and elsewhere, see Steve Stern, "Between Tragedy and Promise: The Politics of Writing Latin American History in the Late Twentieth Century," in G. Joseph, ed., *Reclaiming the Political: Essays from the North* (Durham, 2001), 43–8.

To understand these regional contrasts, whether superficial or not, it is important to root this insurgent movement – the so-called Atusparia rebellion of 1885 – in the specific regional and cultural context of nineteenth-century Huaylas. How did preexisting local power relations and political-cultural traditions of struggle shape indigenous responses to war-related pressures and events? How did the particular contingency of national events, particularly during the civil war phase, bear upon the internal evolution of the Huaylas's political strategies, agendas, and horizons – as they were thrust into the national arena of struggle after 1885? The Huaylas case is particularly interesting because it brings to light precisely how the rise of ethnic militancy necessarily implicated the morality of nation building as it affected indigenous citizens.

That this insurgent movement originally coalesced around indigenous leaders and concerns in part reflects the fact that preexisting power relations in Huaylas were still negotiated largely through ethnic intermediaries. Mark Thurner notes that most Indians in Huaylas were semiindependent smallholders, grouped in land-hungry *estancias*, administered by rotating Indian authorities directly subordinate to provincial officials.[34] These village leaders served a vital function in provisioning *corvée* laborers for local public works projects. On the other hand, many of those communities had recently lost their use rights to alpine pastures, woodlands, and glacial ice, under a new wave of land privatization and enclosure. These local power dynamics set the initial parameters of Indian negotiation and protest when the war came to Huaylas in early 1885.

Apparently all that was needed was a precipitant: one more assault on Indian integrity and self-respect. That came in early 1885. Under the leadership of Pedro Pablo Atusparia, recently elected to the highest office of his rural district Independencia, the

---

[34] Thurner, *From Two Republics to One Divided*, 333–4.

varayoc of Huaylas submitted a petition asking for a 50 percent reduction of the double poll-tax and more time to deliver the updated tribute lists. Prefect Noriega denied the request and instead had Atusparia imprisoned, tortured, and made to "confess" his guilt. And in a brutal gesture hailing from the colonial Inquisition, Atusparia's jailers cut off his braid (a symbol of chiefly rank and authority) to make a mule's cinch. After a second delegation of Indians confronted intransigent authorities, they resorted to direct actions. Thousands of Huaylas peasants converged on the mountain slopes surrounding the provincial capital of Huaráz in March 1885. Noriega's belated concessions could not contain peasant political violence.

This narrative throws into bold relief the historical contingencies of peasant political action and discourse in this region. As in the Mantaro Valley, here too the complex alchemy of war, betrayal, and partisan politics shoved Huaylas peasants into the center of national turmoil. But they experienced neither the empowerment, nor the ultimate betrayal of Cáceres's resistance movement, which first emboldened and then embittered the Mantaro guerrillas. Instead, the Huaylas people came face to face with the war only through the coerced extortions of local authorities, long after the Chilean invaders had gone home. Huaylas peasants were targeted for tax hikes because they were "Indians." They were not called up to join a national resistance campaign as "citizens" or "patriots" fighting against Chilean bandits. And when faced with a double war-tax slapped on them during a terrible drought, they resorted to the time-worn rituals of Indian protest, carried over from colonial times, to mount a collective defense against this new tyranny. Thus, the Huaylas villages initially shaped their politics of protest in response to the real and symbolic violence they experienced at the hands of the provincial state, by wielding the well-worn political and discursive weapons at their disposal.

Such vivid images of localized Indian protest soon fade into the background, however. What began as revindicatory violent actions by aggrieved Indians soon evolved into a transregional, multiethnic, multiclass movement that harnessed ethnic defensiveness, memories, and moral legitimacy to broader political goals and historical consciousness. Three aspects reveal the 1885 Atusparia rebellion to be far more complex and significant than once thought: its fluid and heterogeneous social makeup; the submergence of political violence in broader indigenous strategies of legal petition and negotiation before the provincial and national state; and the volatile mixture of ethnic and constitutional idioms with which Indians articulated their political grievances, claims, and visions in an effort to reach rapprochment with the state following their military defeat. Let us consider each of these factors turn.

First, the notion of a defensive "Indian rebellion" ignores the fact that the Huaylas rebels were plunged into the larger theatre of war raging between Iglesias and Cáceres in the early 1880s, and that this civil war pulled dissident elements from all niches of the region's ethnic-class hierarchy. William Stein notes that the movement attracted peasants and plebians, Indians from *estancias* and *misti* townspeople – hardly an undifferentiated *indiada* (native mob) that Lima newspapers depicted in 1885.[35] The escalation of violence also

---

[35] William Stein, "Town and Country in Revolt: Fragments from the Province of Carhuaz on the Atusparia Uprising of 1885 (Callejón de Huaylas)," *Actes du XLIIe Congrés International des Américanistes*, 10 vols. (Paris, 1976), 3: 171–87. In sheer geographic scope, the uprising eventually came to encompass the entire interior of the Department of Ancash. In the early months of 1885, it spread like wildfire through the river valley, from the Department's capital of Huaráz to the towns of Yungay, Carhuaz, and Caraz, and fanned out across the Cordillera Negra and the Pacific slopes. How many people participated in the movement is unknown. Alarmist reports from Lima inflated the rebels into some 20,000 or more, branding them all as "Indian hordes." However suspect those numbers,

spawned guerrilla fighters only tenuously connected to Atusparia.[36] The movement's heterogeneous ethnic and class composition could be seen in the faces and actions of its leaders. Upon seizing Huaráz, Atusparia rebuilt the provincial government. Among others, he appointed two prominent Creoles: Manuel Mosquera, a lawyer, and Luís Felipe Montestruque, a journalist, writer, and orator. Both men joined the movement partly out of partisan interest. The Indian rebels had assaulted the prefect, a diehard Iglesista, and thus stood on the side of Cáceres, who by 1885 was en route to the presidency. These alliances at the top were politically convenient to all parties for a brief period. Atusparia's delegation of authority to Indians and mestizos was a fascinating, albeit brief, moment of provincial

historians have documented the rebellion's expansive regional scope and heterogenous makeup. (See Thurner, *From Two Republics to One Divided*, chap. 6.)

[36] Curiously, while most historical accounts have affixed the name of Atusparia on this movement, local oral histories often remember Uchcu Pedro (or Tunnel Pedro) as the more colorful and heroic leader. Not an Indian peasant, but a "tough-minded mine operator and trader" of some wealth, Ucuchu Pedro emerged as the most fearsome guerrilla leader. He fought alongside Atusparia, taking one river valley town after another in March 1885. And after Atusparia was wounded and captured, Uchcu Pedro and his forces escaped into the highlands. Ensconced in the high *sierras* of the Cordillera Negra, he continued to raid and attack valley towns and estates even after government troops came to pacify the region. The guerrilla-miner called their bluff, and soon became a legend in the local lore of Huaráz. Eventually, he was coaxed down from the mountains, ambushed, and executed in September 1885.

In his monumental work on crowds in Peruvian history, Jorge Basadre described an epic figure standing tall before his executioners at the bitter end of the rebellion (Basadre, *La multitud, la ciudad, y el campo en la historia del Perú*, 248). The fate of Atusparia is shrouded in ambiguity, on the other hand. As he died neither in battle nor before the firing squad, but perhaps in disgrace and by his own hand, Atusparia did not cut such a defiant, honorable or colorful figure as did Uchcu Pedro in the local lore. See Stein, "Town and Country in Revolt," 177 and 180.

reconstruction under the *vara's* leadership. In any event, this insurgent movement soon escalated into a broad regional movement caught up in the chaos of Peru's civil war.

Second, if we expand the temporal scope beyond the early months of 1885 when popular political violence reached its apotheosis, we can see how those violent incidents were embedded in an ongoing, contentious history of political engagement by Huaylas peasants; how the rituals of violence and justice were part of the same repertory of political struggle that Indians had improvised and deployed for generations. On this point, Thurner's study of Huaylas is enlightening. He shows that between 1886 and 1889, the *varayoc* of Huaylas waged a paper campaign – petitioning and litigating for various reformist and restorative measures. Conventional historical accounts that focus on the violent episodes of the Atusparia rebellion tend to overlook the crucial political war-of-words that Atusparia and other *varayoc* waged in the mid- and late 1880s. Unlike the Mantaro rebels who broke rank with Cáceres once he betrayed them, the Huaylas insurgents continued to manipulate partisan and paternalist strategies to wrest small concessions from him. Just as their ancestors had trekked over the mountains to the viceregal courts and palaces of Lima, the *varayocs* of Huaylas traveled down to the coast, seeking audiences with the supreme commander, "Tayta Cáceres." Among other things, their petitions defined the terms under which the Indians would deliver, or not, the poll tax and *corvée* labor to the republic. In particular, they demanded a reduction of the poll tax that Cáceres had tried to reimpose in 1886. But as we shall see later, this petition campaign raised issues that transcended local concerns. In effect, it bid the republican state to restore its authority over Indian peoples, as their protector and ultimate arbiter. Rather than turn inward to create an alternative, oppositional *republiqueta* as did the Comas peasants in the same period, however, the peasants of Huaylas struggled to cast themselves as Indian *republicanos* of the Peruvian state. Ultimately, they sought a return to "good government." Toward that end, they defined a covenant under which Cáceres would bestow republican rights that granted the material and cultural conditions necessary for their villages to survive. In the end, their threats and petitions scared off the republican tax collectors and other authorities until early in the twentieth century. Thurner writes that "for two decades after 1885 Indian peasants in Huaylas successfully resisted what they considered to be the illegitimate exactions of an unprotective state."[37]

Third, indigenous politics before and after the uprising widens our perspectives on the political aspirations and values that Huaylas people harbored. In particular, peasant political thought can be gleaned from the (highly mediated) petitions they pressed upon provincial and central authorities during the mid-1880s. Although the petitions were drawn up and submitted by *misti* lawyers and signed with the thumb-stamps of dozens of *varayoc*, they show how the Huaylas leaders improvised political strategies and rhetoric to curry favor with the President-Protector Cáceres and, at the same time, map out the moral principles by which the republic could rightly ask Indians to pay taxes, give labor, and otherwise partic-ipate in the nation as Indian subjects and citizens. At base, their petitions went far beyond their request for tax relief, land rights, and good local government.

By 1886 and 1887, long after Atusparia had retired from the political scene, the *varas* mounted a scathing moral critique of the Peruvian republic. They argued that the republic had violated all the protective laws and policies toward Indians since the time of in-dependence, and that with the abolition of tribute, the government had become their worst enemy. For they had "watched with pain as [mestizos and Spaniards] began to place obstacles in the . . . exercise of [their] rights, pretending that the community of pastures, wooded

---

[37] Thurner, *From Two Republics to One Divided*, quote, 416; see also, 344–6.

ravines, and waters had disappeared." Why, they asked rhetorically
in the 1887 petition, should they give tribute and labor when they
received in return only misery, hunger, and hardship?[38] Their deployment of an "insurgent nostalgia," of course, was but part of an
arsenal that indigenous mediators had used since the beginning of
the republican era. But in the postwar period of Chilean invasion
and national humiliation, racial hysteria, and ongoing guerrilla warfare in parts of the central *sierra*, the Huaylas peasants' petition
campaign crystallized a powerful historical critique of Peru's experiment in nineteenth-century nation making. Not only did they
indict the hypocritical elites for not recognizing their own patriotic
contributions to the republic before and during the Pacific War, but
they also mounted a dissident history of the republic to challenge
the moral basis of the posttributary state. Already in the 1880s,
the politics of ethnicity were beginning to implicate the ethics of
nationalism.

BANISHING INDIANS FROM HISTORY
AND THE NATION

The Mantaro and Huaylas peasant movements had repercussions
far beyond the central highlands during the last two decades of the
century. They forced the Lima elite to confront the full measure of
their failure as nation-builders. Not only had the country disintegrated under the impact of Chilean firepower, but the government
had witnessed its own rural masses rise up against Peruvian landlords and political authorities in a moment of national crisis.

To make matters worse, the postwar state could not pacify
the countryside. In 1885, newspapers reported gruesome details
of "race wars" raging in the highlands of Huaylas and Mantaro.
By the late 1890s, rural unrest, smuggling, and border wars were

---

[38] Ibid., 356.

escalating across the southern *altiplano* provinces of Azángaro and Chucuito. Various "salt rebellions" in the Departments of Ayacucho and Puno in the late 1890s demonstrated the dangerous limits of Lima's control over the *sierra*, even under President Piérola's putative "Protectorate of the Indians."[39] In this deteriorating climate, the Indian race assumed the role of scapegoat in Creole accounts of Peru's defeat in the war. By the late 1880s and 1890s, ongoing news of indigenous uprisings in distant provinces only hardened Creole narratives of savage Indians, rural bandits, and race wars. It became self-evident among Peruvian elites that the war was lost because Indians, by their nature, were unmoved by sentiments of patriotism or civic virtue. In a letter written immediately after the war, Ricardo Palma, a popular folklorist-belletrist, crystallized this sentiment:

The principal cause of the great defeat is that the majority of Peru is composed of a wretched and degraded race that we once attempted to dignify and ennoble. The Indian lacks a patriotic sense; he is a born enemy of the white and of the man of the coast. It makes no difference to him whether he is a Chilean or a Turk. To educate the Indian and to inspire in him a feeling for patriotism will not be the task of our institutions, but of the ages.[40]

[39] Jacobsen, *Mirages of Transition*, 337–56; Michael Gonzáles, "Neo-colonialism and Indian Unrest in Southern Peru, 1867–1898," *Bulletin of Latin American Research* 6 (1987), 1–26; Wilfredo Kapsoli, *Los movimientos campesinos en el Perú* (Lima, 1987); Rosalyn Gow, "*Yawar Mayu*: Revolution in the Southern Andes, 1860–1980," unpublished Ph.D. dissertation, University of Wisconsin, 1981; and Dan Hazen, "The Awakening of Puno: Government Policy and the Indian Problem in Southern Peru, 1900–1955," unpublished Ph.D. dissertation, Yale University, 1974.

[40] Quoted in Efrain Kristal, *The Andes Viewed from the City: Literary and Political Discourse on the Indian in Peru, 1848–1930* (New York, 1987), 97–8. But see especially the foundational study of divergent *indigenista* images and debates in the Andes: Angel Rama, "El area cultura andina (hispanismo, mesticismo, indigenismo)," *Cuadernos Americanos* 33 (1974), 136–73. See also Deborah Poole's recent book, *Vision, Race, and Modernity:*

These sentiments were more pessimistic perhaps than most. Certainly there were various diagnoses and debates about the quintessential Indian character and the problems it posed to the nation. But amidst postwar angst, those debates grew sharper and more intense. On the one hand, imported theories of biological determinism allowed Creole scientists, writers, and politicians to exercise more authority over issues concerning the Indian race. European blood to whiten the nation assumed more importance, even urgency. On the other hand, hard-line racial theorists found worthy rivals among a younger generation of positivist and radical dissidents, who pointed to deep-rooted historical, social, and environmental causes of Indian backwardness.[41] Among them were criminologists, physicians, and other positivists who proposed regulatory reforms to "improve" Indian hygiene, morality, productivity, and discipline in the long hard process of assimilating them into a homogenizing nation. Like the *civilistas* of the early 1870s, they advocated massive state investment in rural education, prison reform, road building, communication, and industry in order to open up the *sierra* and integrate Indians into their allotted niches in the nation. A leading politician made the case succinctly: "Through wise tutelage, we must make the Indian a laborer or a soldier to liberate him from his local traditions and from his depressing and drab setting."[42] Order and progress depended on remaking Indians into

A *Visual Economy of the Andean Image World* (Princeton, 1997), chap. 5; and Marisol de la Cadena, *Indigenous Mestizos: The Politics of Race and Culture in Cuzco, Peru, 1919–1991* (Durham, 2000), chap. 1 and 2.

[41] Deborah Poole, "Ciencia, peliogrosidad y represión en la criminología indigenista peruana," in Carlos Aguirre and Charles Walker, eds., *Bandoleros, abigeos y montoneros: Criminalidad y Violencia en el Perú, siglos XVIII–XX* (Lima, 1990), 335–67.

[42] Francisco García Calderón quoted in Kristal, *The Andes Viewed from the City*, 182. See also Frederick Pike, *The Modern History of Peru* (New York, 1967), 159–68.

laborers and soldiers. And so now, it seemed, did Peru's territorial sovereignty.

Manuel González Prada and Clorinda Matto de Turner stood out among the more militant social critics and reformers of this period. In their writings and speeches, they tried to prick the conscience of the oligarchy. Although they shared the prevailing belief that Peru had lost the war because Indians were devoid of patriotism, they put the blame on Peru's antiquated feudal oligarchy. It was the highland *gamonal* in particular who was responsible for the degradation of Indians. In her best-selling novel, *Aves sin nidos* (*Birds Without Nests*), Matto de Turner threw open a window on that remote feudal-colonial world, shaded by her childhood memories, to expose the brutality and exploitation that Indians endured at the hands of landlords and their agents (corrupt judges, governors, and priests). On pragmatic grounds, Matto de Turner and González Prada (and other neopositivists) looked to a renovated and aggressive national state to bring in foreign capital, industry, and technology to break the back of Peru's landed oligarchy. They believed that emancipated Indians were capable of being educated and assimilated. In the short run, however, the enlightened White Man's Burden was to protect Indians from abusive treatment.

This strain of muckraking and reformism was to inspire later incarnations of *indigenismo* (particularly the writings of José Carlos Mariátegui), as well as the Indian policy reforms undertaken by the second administration of Augusto Leguía in the 1920s. By then too Cuzco intellectuals, such as Luís Valcarcel, were engaged in a vibrant regionalist project that lay claim to the Inca utopia and contemporary folklore as the nation's "authentic cultural patrimony" (in sharp opposition to Lima's mimetic version of Eurocentric modernity).[43] Invoking the region's Inca heritage, Cuzco's cultural

---

[43] On the relationship between peasant activists and urban dissident *indigenistas* in the early twentieth century, see Galindo, *Buscando un Inca*, 323–43; José Deustua and José Luís Rénique, *Intelectuales, indigenismo, y*

vanguard projected a noble "Quechua race" of Indians onto the national imaginary (Figure 11). This redemptive racial discourse flourished in the first decades of the twentieth century, a time when much of Latin America was beginning to forge national cultures rooted in their own interior (non-European) soul and soil, as well as in the pre-Hispanic past. In the immediate aftermath of the War of the Pacific, however, Peru's pro-Indian dissidents confronted the virulent racism and intransigence of the fractured oligarchy eager to rebuild its power base. Eventually (although under different circumstances), both González Prada and Matto de Turner grew more pessimistic. Manuel González Prada left Peru for Paris in 1891 and returned only in 1898, newly armed with revolutionary socialist ideas. Clorinda Matto de Turner fell from grace in 1895 after Piérola returned to the presidency, and she went into a lonely exile until her death. Their sacrifices were not totally in vain, however, because they left a legacy of social criticism, which began to chart the way toward early twentieth-century nativist, anarchist, and socialist ideologies.

But the formation of legacies takes time, and the immediate postwar era of Indian-state relations remained bleak. One of the bitter ironies of the War of the Pacific was that Lima's elite – from the conservative to the iconoclastic – basically wrote Indians out of the national script as potential or proven political subjects.[44] As the official story of Peru's defeat crystallized around the image of the ignorant, apathetic Indian, the Indian race became unfit for citizenship. Silenced, suppressed, or forgotten were the voices of Andean peasants – from the rebels of Huaylas to the guerrillas of Junín – who

---

descentralismo en el Peru, 1897–93. (Cusco, 1984), chap. 3; Marfil Francke Ballve, "El movimiento indigenista en el Cuzco, 1910–1930," in Carlos Iván Degregori et al., eds., *Indigenismo, clases socials y problema nacional. La discussion sobre el 'problema indígena' en el Perú* (Lima, 1979), 107–86.

[44] Mallon, *Peasant and Nation*, chap. 6; Thurner, *From Two Republics to One Divided*, 131–6.

Figure 11. Portrait of a Quechua man in Cuzco, ca. 1909. This photograph (photographer unknown) represents a subtle aesthetic variation from the standard form of late nineteenth-century *cartes de visite*. It places its emphasis not on the purported occupation or emotional disposition of the indigenous subject, but on the material artifacts that depict (in a disembodied, decontextualized way) the semblance of a *cultural* identity. Posing before the ornate colonial doors of a Church or monastery, gazing with head held high at distant horizons, dressed in rustic *bayeta* clothing, and surrounded by the accoutrements of country life, this man exudes a certain sense of nobility and dignity in his exoticism, indicative of the emerging bohemian and regionalist *indigenista* movement of Cuzco that began to flourish in the early twentieth century. (On this regionalist-indigenist aesthetic, see Poole, *Vision, Race, and Modernity* [Princeton, 1977], chap. 7.) (Reprinted with permission from the Peabody Museum of Archaeology and Ethnology, Harvard University.)

had thrown themselves into the maelstrom of war by serving as patriotic soldiers, taxpayers, and laborers of the floundering republic. The new orthodoxy widened the political, cultural, and biological distance between the highland Indians and the coastal (or urban) whites. Race differences became immutable, coast and *sierra* unmoored, and the Indian problem almost intractable.

In a country where most people were still considered by the elites to be Indian and therefore beyond the bounds of nation and civilization, in a republic that had just been brought to its knees by foreign invaders, how could Peru enter the company of modern nations? There, in brief, was the social dilemma that Peruvian intellectuals had created for themselves toward the end of the nineteenth century. Cultural *mestizaje* offered no obvious solution, since most reformers considered the social-climbing mestizo to be a social pariah, barely a leap beyond the Indian on the evolutionary scale. Postwar racist discourses had no way yet of positioning the mestizo as the unifying, or healing, race to help in the project of national reconstruction and political reopening. Thus postwar recovery and reconstruction turned into a lost opportunity for reinventing Peru around more inclusive principles of nationhood. Like its neighbor to the south, Peru carried into the early twentieth century the dead weight of its violent, repressive, and exclusionary republican past. Yet it is also true that strong indigenous political and cultural movements eventually sprang out of the rural villages of Cuzco and the southern *altiplano* and projected their political visions onto the broader canvas of Peruvian history during the early twentieth century.

5

<hr />

Bolivia

Dangerous Pacts, Insurgent Indians

Almost as soon as Simón Bolívar had bequeathed his illustrious name to the new republic, emancipating it from both Spain and the neighboring Viceroyalties of Peru and Buenos Aires, the British began to eye Bolivia's economic prospects. The British vice-consul in Lima dispatched his secretary, one J. B. Pentland, into Bolivia with instructions to collect economic and demographic data, chart the topography, and collect specimens for the British Museum. In 1826, Pentland took on the assignment with dispatch, wandering the countryside and compiling information on Bolivia's mines, settlements, government, laws, and institutions. But as he came to contemplate the enormity of the problems facing the newly independent Upper Peru, including the economic devastation left by the war of independence, Pentland injected a note of caution into his appraisal of Bolivia's future.[1]

To this British traveler, coming up over the mountains from the desert seacoast, Bolivia's towering *cordillera* must have given him

<hr />

[1] John B. Pentland, *Report on the Bolivian Republic, 1827* (United Kingdom, Foreign Office), 61/12 (microfilm). See also J. Valerie Fifer, *Bolivia: Land, Location and Politics since 1825* (Cambridge, 1972), 18–19.

pause. Pentland quickly realized that the new republic had inherited an unenviable geographic location, especially since it had recently lost the Pacific port of Arica to independent Peru. Except for the tiny panhandle port of Cobija (which would be stolen by Chile in the War of the Pacific), Bolivia suddenly had turned into a land-locked nation, and its only access to the sea was across three hundred moonscape miles of the Atacama desert. Moreover, the republic's internal topography offered little relief from this bleak view. Through his arduous travels, the Englishman saw a spectac-ular landscape of desolate peaks, desert, savannah, swamp, and rain forest. The core mountainous area contained more than three-quarters of the total population (est. 1.1 million in 1826), whereas Bolivia's dissected eastern *sierras* (host to Quechua-speaking com-munities and a smattering of Creole cities, towns, and *haciendas*) comprised the most isolated and inaccessible portion of the *cordilleras*. Westward, the great high-altitude plateau served as a magnificent north-south corridor of long-distance traffic and trade between Peru and Bolivia, as well as a densely populated settlement focus of Aymara-speaking communities around the Titicaca basin. But Pentland's greatest impression was that of a pseudo-republic composed of fractious regions cut off from one another by desolate and rugged mountains, etched only by rutted llama and mule trails. This jagged land and segmented regions made it all the more difficult to bring some sort of unity to the fledgling republic. Creole rivalries and secessionist conspiracies simmered in the old colonial capital of Chuquisaca, the rival and more populous *altiplano* city of La Paz, and the traditional *hacienda* valleys of Cochabamba. Already in 1826, Pentland perceived these strong disintegrative forces at work within the republic's pronounced patterns of physical, cultural, and regional diversity. Under such adverse circumstances, the strength and tranquility of the new republic would surely be thwarted – a clear warning to naïve British merchants and speculators, if not to Bolivia's fractious elites.

Pentland's demographic imbalances must also have tempered British commercial ambitions in the 1820s. Pentland discovered just how "Indian" Bolivia really was: it was inhabited by an estimated 800,000 native peasants, composing nearly three-quarters of the population. But unlike in Creole Peru, Bolivian nation-builders could not take comfort in the geographic remoteness of its indigenous majority. Whereas *guano*-driven Lima might turn its back on the Indian highlands, Bolivia's major cities were located in the very midst of Aymara and Quechua communities. Indeed, the topography of the city of La Paz served as a terrifying metaphor of the city's vulnerability to the Aymara masses, which might gather at any moment on the towering rim of the *altiplano*, before sweeping down into the city's basin to take their revenge. Just as Creole Peru entered the republican era burdened by memories of the 1780 Andean insurrection, so too did stories of Tupac Catari's six-month 1781 siege of La Paz still haunt the nightmares of its upper-class inhabitants.

No less important, there was the territorial issue. In the early nineteenth century, Bolivia's indigenous peasantry was almost evenly divided between the servile tenantry (*yanaconas* or *colonos*) living on landed estates and the *comunario* members inhabiting independent communities, or *ayllus*. Bolivia's first national census (1846) registered 138,104 families as members of an *ayllu*.[2]

---

[2] The first Bolivian census, taken under the supervision of José María Dalence, registered some 1.4 million "Bolivians," with another 700,000 "unpacified" tribal peoples inhabiting the eastern tropical lowlands and plains. Using such cultural markers as language, "customs," dress, place of habitation, and rural poverty, Dalence estimated that 80 percent of the population was indigenous or monolingual (or bilingually conversant in more than one indigenous language). Fewer than 20 percent of Bolivians spoke Spanish in the 1840s. Quechua remained the predominant language (and, in fact, became the rural *lingua franca* throughout the highlands over the course of the eighteenth and nineteenth centuries). Aymara remained the second most important language, spoken predominantly by peasants and herders who

If we accept the census' estimate of family average, we come up with an estimated total population figure of some 620,000 Andean people (or 51 percent) who belonged to the world of communal landholding.[3] What these vague estimates suggest is that enormous tracts of land throughout the western highlands continued to be under the control of semiautonomous communities. Historical research confirms this impression. In scrutinizing a thick set of Indian tribute registries (*padrones*), historian Erwin Grieshaber discovered a remarkable revival of highland Indian communities in the rural regions of La Paz, Oruro, and Potosí (the homes of 80 percent of Bolivia's Indians), in spite of Bolivia's overall population decline. Specifically, the *comunero* population (that is, village or *ayllu*-based) grew by 24 percent between the years of 1838 and 1877 – in spite of severe economic recession and successive waves of epidemic. In contrast, the *haciendas* saw their tribute-paying, servile tenants dwindle (by somewhere around 4 percent) over the same period.[4] The vast majority of Bolivia's *indios tributarios* continued to claim membership in communal villages, so that by 1877 (the last year for which official tribute records were kept), they

inhabited the high plateau. The Dalence census also revealed the preponderance of *ayllu*-communal Indians (some 620,000), compared to the smaller group of Indians attached to estates (between 375,000 and 400,000). The national census of 1900 reveals little change in these regional, ethnic, and institutional balances. See José María Dalence, *Bosquejo estadístico de Bolivia, 1846* (La Paz, 1975). See Map 2 for the spatial distribution of ethnic groups.

[3] Herbert Klein, *Bolivia: The Evolution of a Multi-Ethnic Society* (New York, 1982), 124.

[4] Erwin Grieshaber "Survival of Indian Communities in Nineteenth-Century Bolivia: A Regional Comparison," *Journal of Latin American Studies* 12: 2 (1980), 223 and 236. In his study of tribute registries and other records, Herbert Klein found similar demographic patterns in the *ayllus* and *haciendas* of the Department of La Paz during the same period, in his *Haciendas and 'Ayllus': Rural Society in the Bolivian Andes in the Eighteenth and Nineteenth Centuries* (Stanford, 1993), chaps. 4 and 5.

contributed about 75 percent of all head-tax revenues. In short, the peasant communities still held half the land and half the population in 1880. Rather than dissolving the official tributary and territorial basis of Indianness, the Bolivian republic seemed to be *advancing* it!

In the city and countryside, colonial-caste hierarchies not only insinuated themselves into the everyday practices but also shaped the juri-political relationship between Indians and the state under colonial notions of *republicanismo*. As everywhere in the Andes, Bolivia's peasants occupied very different institutional locations in the social order, depending upon whether they were *ayllu*-based *comunarios*, *hacienda*-bound *colonos*, or peasant freeholders. Despite these different, often overlapping, positions in relationship to land and the state, and the proliferation of cultural *mestizos* and *cholos* in Bolivia's eastern valleys and cities, the republic cemented the system of socio-racial stratification. The *ayllus* had a relatively institutionalized relationship to the law and bureaucracy, but so too did the landless Indians (*forasteros*) who lived in Indian communities, *haciendas*, or small parcels of land. But whereas the communities had a stake in the tributary regime, most landless peasants did not. It should be no surprise, then, that nineteenth-century tribute registries show a steady decline in the tributary population on *haciendas*. Historians have shown us that landless peasants, particularly those who lived in regions like ethnically mixed cities and provinces, managed to evade the tribute collector and eventually disappear from the official tax rolls.[5] In sum, then, Indians had different relationships to the official structures of bureaucracy and the social order. Obviously, this difference did not translate directly into differences in elite perceptions of Indians, or in conditions of material welfare. To be perceived as Indian, or as one of the amorphous

[5] Grieshaber, "Survival of Indian Communities"; Brooke Larson, *Cochabamba, 1550–1900: Colonialism and Agrarian Transformation in Bolivia* (Durham, 1998), 2nd ed., chap. 9.

mixed strata (*mestizos, cholos, castas*), was not simply a legal-administrative fiction but an everyday reality, reconstituted through daily practice. Landed and regional elites often saw Indians as belonging to one seamless race, destined by birth, history, and biology to a life of field labor, servility, and humility. By contrast, they tended to distrust the racially ambiguous plebe as a threat to caste and the larger social order. Such colonial perceptions could turn on a dime, however, when the gravest threats emanated from mobilizing *ayllus*, rather than from the "transgressive" hybrid races.

In the aftermath of independence, the reconstitution of servile Indian subjects, whatever their tributary status, was essential to the maintenance of local power relations. Civic-religious festivities, public works, and even the postal service all functioned thanks to indigenous authorities continuing to supply Indian laborers for public and private works. Indeed, whole provincial bureaucracies in the Department of Northern Potosí, for example, continued to function on the basis of Indian tribute and *corvée* labor long after tribute was formally abolished in 1874.[6] Thus, official forms of colonial extraction and caste hierarchy were rooted in the subsoil of colonial habits and practices not easily described in words because they had become so implicit, natural, inevitable.

Travel writers and artists, on the other hand, were drawn to Bolivia's enduring *sociedad de castas* and to render it scientifically or picturesquely to an urban literate audience. Among the mid-nineteenth-century European travel writers to Bolivia, Alcides D'Orbigny was by far the most serious student of the Andes, and the first travel writer/scientist to borrow elements from the late-colonial genre of *casta* paintings to render a hierarchical composite of ethnic-racial, regional, and gendered "types" (Figure 12). The

[6] Tristan Platt, *Estado boliviano y ayllu andino. Tierra y tributo en el Norte de Potosí* (Lima, 1982), 140–7.

Figure 12. Quechua-speaking Indians and *mestizos* of the southern province of Chuquisaca and environs, ca. 1833. Among the first Europeans to explore the interior of South America after the independence wars, Alcides D'Orbigny commenced his journey in 1825 under the auspices of the Museum of Natural History in Paris "to investigate thoroughly the language and physiological characteristics of the South American peoples" (quoted in Poole, *Vision, Race, and Modernity* [Princeton, 1997], 79). D'Orbigny's racial-tribal map of South America appeared in his two-volume report entitled *L'Homme américain (de l'Amerique mēridionale) considéré sous ses rapports physiologiques et mor aux* (Paris, 1839). A few years later, D'Orbigny published his nine-volume journal of his travels and explorations in South America. It remains one of the finest post-Enlightenment products of ethnographic, geographic, and historical description of the early nineteenth century.

D'Orbigny's journey from the eastern lowlands of the tropical jungle to the highlands of Potosí and Oruro took him through the city of Chuquisaca in 1833. He described the great number of "cultured people" who inhabited the city of Chuquisaca, making it a "pleasant and civil" place to reside. He also remarked upon the gulf separating the "people of breeding" from the "inferior ranks," including the mestizo (or *cholo*) artisans and, below them, the Indians. He was taken with what he considered to be the outlandish, yet sensual, appearance of the city's *cholas*. Full-breasted, coquetish, and adorned, the *mestiza* (pictured on the far left) displayed a medley (*mescolanza*) of European and Indian styles, combining Spanish balloon sleeves and full pleated skirt trimmed in ribbons with a regional variation of the indigenous *lliqlla* (Quechua term for a rectangular piece of woven cloth used as a shawl). "When they promenade clutching their hankies, with their hair adorned in showy beads, and their feat clad in silk slippers, they might as well have just emerged from a ball" (Alcides D'Orbigny, *Viaje a la America Meridional... realizado de 1826 a 1833* [1844], 9 vols. [Buenos Aires: Ed. Futuro, 1945], 4: 1486], Illustr., p. 1352).

Frenchman was intrigued by the elaborate clothing and bodily codes of racial-ethnic identity, which distinguished Indians and *cholos* from one another, as well as separated them from their "social superiors." D'Orbigny's delight in Bolivian racialisms and regionalisms perhaps also sprang from his surprise at Bolivia's distinctiveness. Compared to Peru, where "all [Indians and mestizos] dressed in the same manner," Bolivia's racial groups were strikingly set apart by dress and demeanor, if not by physiognomy.[7]

No matter how entrenched, everyday forms of colonialism and racial hierarchy can survive only so long as favorable conditions prevailed, and Bolivia had a good political-economic climate. First, economic collapse enforced an early restoration of tribute, as in Ecuador and Peru. Far more than its northern neighbors, however, Bolivia was a war-weary and economically depressed region at the end of the independence era. Herbert Klein notes that between 1803 and the late 1840s, the economy suffered from progressive decapitalization of its mining industry, a crisis in overseas trade, and a severe loss of urban Creole population.[8] Pentland first recorded this alarming demographic index of Bolivia's economic collapse. He discovered that almost all Bolivian cities had suffered great population losses. Demographic decline was most dramatic in the cities of Potosí and Oruro, whose mines and smelters were wrecked by the war. As late as 1846, some 10,000 mines were still abandoned, not for lack of silver ore, but as a result of the flight of capital,

---

[7] D'Orbigny quoted in Deborah Poole, *Vision, Race, and Modernity: A Visual Economy of the Andean Image World* (Princeton, 1997), 80. Along with European travelers' reports, mid-nineteenth-century *costumbrista* paintings often rendered intricate ethnic hierarchies carefully encoded by physiognomy, costume, body language, and context. Gendered, racial, class, and regional classifications were masterfully rendered in the watercolors of Bolivia's greatest *costumbrista* painter, Melchor María Mercado. See the splendid edition of his work in, *Albúm de paisajes, tipos humanos y costumbres de Bolivia, 1841–1869* (Sucre, 1991).

[8] Klein, *Bolivia: The Evolution of a Multi-Ethnic Society*, 101.

equipment, and enterprises.[9] Once abandoned, the mineshafts tended to flood, requiring the use of expensive, imported steam engines to pump them out. But with Bolivia's export sector mired in long-term depression, there was little incentive to restore mining. And so the vicious cycle of war, destruction, depopulation, and decline continued.

Nor was that all: Bolivia's domestic market in food crops and overland trade was also badly hurt by the war. After Upper Peru was severed from the old Viceroyalty of La Plata, the new Bolivian republic lost its direct access to the Argentine port, provincial cities, livestock ranches, and commercial outlets of the late colonial era. Across the northern edge of its new border, Bolivia continued to be severed from its older, overland circuits of trade with Cuzco, Arequipa, and other highland Peruvian cities. Overland trade circuits did not totally disappear, but now political borders, internal customs houses, and highway bandits plagued indigenous and mestizo traders and pack drivers. On the other hand, Bolivia's postwar economic woes hit the landed elites especially hard. Most *haciendas*, already debt-ridden in the late colonial period, suffered from acute market decline, if not from outright physical destruction, during and after the independence war. Ecclesiastical estates might well have flourished, either by propping up or filling the void opened up by decaying *hacendado* class, much as happened in highland Ecuador, but for radical anti-Church policies under the new republic. The liberator, Antonio José de Sucre, launched one of the most radical attacks on the Church in nineteenth-century Latin America. Anxious to impose state control over Church lands and tithes, the new government annexed vast tracts of Church land, drastic reforms from which it never recovered.[10] But the larger point here

---

[9] Pentland, *Report on the Bolivian Republic*; Klein, *The Evolution of a Multi-Ethnic Society*, 104.

[10] Erick Langer and Robert Jackson, "Liberalism and the Land Question in Bolivia, 1825–1920," in Robert Jackson, ed., *Liberals, the Church, and*

is that the wholesale collapse of mining and the *hacienda* regime after independence drastically dislocated Upper Peru's traditional political economy, leaving in tact only the indigenous communities, which now were tapped for the government's only major source of income – tribute. The bottom line was tax revenue, as the 1846 census made perfectly clear. José María Dalence's census revealed the startling fact that all economic sources of revenue had declined steadily over the 1820s, 1830s, and 1840s. Only Indian tribute had kept the government afloat. As Herbert Klein notes, the relative importance of Indian tribute in the sum total of state revenue had increased to 54 percent in 1846, up from 45 percent in 1832.[11] The impoverished Bolivian republic rode on the back of its rural indigenous population more than ever before.

Little wonder that Creole policy makers were quick to fashion a policy of appeasement toward its indigenous communities as the basis for restoring the tribute-for-territory equation. At the end of the independence wars, many *ayllu* authorities in the southern highlands of Northern Potosí and across the northern *altiplano* struggled to adapt political languages and strategies to restore or protect traditional territorial and political jurisdictions. Although we still have few historical studies of Indian-state relations in the postindependence era, Tristan Platt's early discovery of Chayanta *ayllus* petitioning for the right to pay tribute, and even to serve on the *mita*, offers a stunning example of "Indian ambiguity over the question of [liberalism and] citizenship." Platt agues that

most Indian communities in early nineteenth-century Potosí defended what they called their "single native contribution" (*única contribución de naturales*). They sought a hybrid status...[or] "tributary citizenship." As "citizens," they could demand enlightenment,

---

Indian Peasants: Corporate Lands and the Challenge of Reform in Nineteenth Century Spanish America (Albuquerque, 1997), 172–6.

[11] Klein, *Bolivia. The Evolution of a Multi-Ethnic Society*, 114.

education, and individual legal protection from the state and its judiciary, while as "tributaries" they could demand state recognition of
their colonial titles to the ethnic territories (*repartimientos*).[12]

Other historians, working in the late nineteenth century, have documented a frenzy of indigenous litigation in defense of their colonial
entitlements in the face of aggressive liberalism in the 1870s and
1880s, a theme to which I will return. Suffice it to say here that
indigenous support for "a hybrid tributary-citizenship status" and
for protectionist economic policies was evident from early on. And
Bolivia's early republican leaders quickly bowed to indigenous
claims (as well as to the general antiliberal sentiment) because they,
too, were eager to restore the tribute system in the late 1820s –
albeit for different purposes. In contrast to the Peruvian republic,
which honored Bolívar's law to privatize Indian land titles, the new
Bolivian republic revoked outright the liberator's smallholding
utopia imposed in 1824–5. Fortified by an astounding degree of consensus, the administration of Andrés de Santa Cruz (1829–30) not
only restored the tributary system (much as Peru and Ecuador did
in the same period) but also confirmed the legal existence of Indian
communities. Through political intrigue and instability, this policy
of informal appeasement persisted amidst all sorts of other changes.
In the Ballivián era (1841–7), the state tried to bring some semblance of stability to political life by taming the military, balancing
the national budget, and promoting European colonization of the
eastern lowlands. The regime was particularly active in promoting
internal tariffs and taxes, including a tax on coca production, an

---

[12] Tristan Platt, "Simón Bolívar, the Sun of Justice and the Amerindian Virgin:
Andean Conceptions of the *Patria* in Nineteenth-Century Potosí," *Journal
of Latin American Studies* 25 (1993), 161. This article goes on to explore the
religious dimensions of these surface political objectives. For Platt's primary
work on Andean communal politics, see his *Estado boliviano y ayllu andino.
Tierra y tributo en el Norte de Potosí* (Lima, 1982).

item consumed exclusively by Indians. Yet amid all those reforms, Ballivián still offered state protection over communal lands, which were now converted to "state-owned lands" carrying long-term usufruct rights. This 1842 land reform was notable, not so much for its theoretical nod at contractual notions, as for its tolerance toward communal forms of landholding and self-governance. The penurious Bolivian state still had a stake in maintaining the tributary regime.

Not for long, however. By the time liberalism finally rode into the interior of Bolivia on the back of its sputtering export economies in the early 1870s, the era of official tributary pacts and tenuous appeasement was fast fading. Yet grave questions remained. How would liberalism be imposed on a society in which indigenous people still had such an enormous stake in autonomous communities? How might the liberalizing state press its agenda on Quechua- and Aymara-speaking communities without setting the republic on a collision course? And would liberalism ultimately lead to Indian integration, along the lines of *mestizaje*, or polarize the nation as never before, by turning Aymara and Quechua peasants into racialized outcasts in their own land?

BETWEEN CONQUEST AND RECONQUEST: THE COMMUNAL LAND QUESTION

The slow recovery of silver mining in the highlands during the 1860s and 1870s brought with it feverish investment activity along Bolivia's short stretch of Pacific coast. *Guano*, nitrates, and mines drew Europeans into the highlands and coast, including the disputed southern Atacama region, where the borders of Chile, Bolivia, and Peru converged. Although Bolivia had no capital to invest, its narrow stretch of coast acted as a magnet for her neighbors and foreign capitalists. Soon Bolivia's revenue-starved governments began signing away the commercial, and even territorial, rights of its coastal resources to Chile and Peru. Even the eastern tropical low-lands began to attract vanguard capitalists after quinine and rubber were discovered there. The Brazilian giant also took notice and gained valuable territory. But while Bolivia's political leaders gave away pieces of its territorial patrimony, the government created new sources of revenue from the sudden coastal wealth in *guano* and nitrates. Meanwhile, the silver mining revival began to attract migrants and settlers to highland towns and cities, which exerted more market demand for traditional agricultural products. Thus the 1860s also fortified the Creole landholding class, which began to covet neighboring lands under the control of the *ayllus*.

A new breed of modernizing silver miners appeared on the political scene, advancing their free-trade ideas. Fired up by the feverish activity in *guano*, nitrates, and silver, this tiny oligarchy touted the benefits of government deregulation of mining and minting, the end of protectionism, and the promotion of railroad building to give the mine owners cheaper access to the world market. The rising spirit of economic liberalism sparked a revival of Bolivarian ideals as well. And that put the "Indian problem" at dead center of elite political debates for the first time since the 1820s.

Already by the early 1860s, liberal reformers were gathering consensus among themselves that the juridical basis of Indian communities had to be destroyed once and for all. Their arguments were both philosophic (the ideological incompatibility between caste and citizenship, communalism and private property, etc.) and pragmatic (the need to shift the tax base from Indian tribute to universal property taxes, to raise immediate revenues from the sale of land titles, to promote commercial agriculture on newly privatized lands, etc.). But, as we shall see shortly, the naïve and reckless proposals for Indian land reform of the 1860s did not anticipate a violent backlash. By the early 1870s, liberal reformers came face to face with the frightening reality of peasant insurgency – of living under a

weak, coercive, and unstable government largely incapable of disciplining an increasingly refractory *indiada*. Bolivia as yet had no
rural police or professional military, nor could it rely upon Indian
rural schools, a modern juridical system, or government agents to
assimilate the Indian masses into civilized life. The advent of tribute
and land reforms therefore was pressed upon a resentful peasantry
under extremely precarious political conditions. And by the early
1870s, liberal reformers were painfully aware of this fact. From
that point on, they argued interminably among themselves about
the least dangerous way to proceed. Not surprisingly, factious reformers introduced a series of half-hearted, contradictory "reforms
and counter-reforms" aimed at waging economic and cultural warfare on Indian lifeways, while trying to contain the threat of violent
insurrection. Such efforts were to prove impossible.

The decade of 1860 saw two major efforts at Indian land reform
fail: the aborted decree of 1863 under President José María de Achá
and the fundamental land reforms of 1866 and 1868 implemented
by President Mariano Melgarejo. Although they failed in different ways (the 1863 decree was stillborn, and Melgarejo's decrees
were eventually repealed), they are interesting for their competing
utopian visions of rural Bolivia and the fate of its peasantry under
a modernizing nation. The proposal of 1863 revisited Bolivarian
ideals of Indian smallholding. As with the earlier land reforms in
Ecuador and Peru, Achá advocated the subdivision of communal
lands and their redistribution to Indian households. According to
his plan, Indians would buy or sell lands at will and, motivated
by market incentives, improve agricultural production, eventually
becoming prosperous yeoman. In the meantime, the state would
compel them to adopt civilized ways of life: fining Indians ten pesos, for example, if they did not build "comfortable, spacious and
ventilated houses" on their lands within the year, or erect school-
houses for their offspring. As with other land reforms in neighboring

countries, however, the state had a vested financial interest in selling off vast acreage of "vacant lands" to the highest bidders. To politicians, the sale of vacant lands seemed an easy solution: it would put wastelands into production while raising immediate state revenues. Such proposals showed abysmal ignorance of Andean patterns of land rotation (high altitude crop land lay fallow for years at a time), as well as little awareness of the lingering effects of the 1856 epidemic. In any event, while the 1863 decree was abrogated that same year, it crystallized the "peasantization" view of liberal reformers.[13] Those promoting the smallholder-yeoman solution, however, were hardly Jeffersonian democrats; they were hard-nosed pragmatists imbued with positivist notions of racial backwardness. Thus their proposals to redistribute lands to Indian families were embedded in a more ambitious project of cultural reform aimed at the compulsory civilization of Indians.

Foreshadowing the famous land reform act of 1874, these early liberal ambitions were immediately swept aside by the larger-than-life *caudillo*-president, Gen. Mariano Melgarejo. He rode into power on the crest of the silver mining boom, determined to throw open Bolivia to international capital and markets and to bolster state power. After seizing power in late 1864, he initiated a package of reforms that dismantled the whole edifice of protective tariffs, modernized the currency system, sold off large chunks of Bolivian territory, and launched the first sustained attack on Indian communal property rights since the Independence era. By the terms of the 1866 confiscation decrees, Melgarejo declared the state to be the owner of all communal properties. All Indians residing on state-owned lands were now required to purchase individual titles at the sum of between 2 and 100 pesos within a sixty-day period. Titles would allow Indians to hold the land for five years, after which

[13] Erick Langer, "El liberalismo y la abolición de la comunidad indígena en el siglo XIX," *Historia y Cultura* 14 (1988), 59–95.

time they would again have to repurchase titles. In effect, Indians would be advancing ground rent for five years, while absolute ownership rights would still rest with the state. Those Indians unable to purchase titles under the stipulated terms would have their lands confiscated and auctioned to the highest bidder. The 1868 decree added salt to the wounds inflicted by the earlier law: it allowed whole communities to be auctioned off as a land unit and imposed a "universal" head-tax, with Indians liable for double the standard tax rate.

Many features of Melgarejo's land reform paid lip service to the liberal goal of converting Indians into property owners, once they purchased land titles. But the notoriously harsh terms he imposed set the stage for large-scale despoliation, and Melgarejo's 1868 edict legitimated the sale of entire communities to one landowner. Thus Melgarejo aligned himself with the pro-*hacienda* faction of the oligarchy. By the early 1860s, the seigneurial viewpoint was articulated as the preferable, and most likely, long-term outcome of liberal land reforms. Traditional landowners, as well as merchants and mining entrepreneurs, began to argue that advancing *latifundismo* held the secret to Bolivia's deliverance from rural backwardness. Some advocated *hacienda* expansion on paternalist grounds: private landlords would step into the role of Indian protector recently shed by the modernizing state. At the same time, it was argued, landlords would improve agriculture and supply the growing urban markets with food. Others tinged their arguments with assimilationist ideals: Indian absorption into the private estate sector would bring them into more contact with industrious mestizos and whites, eventually leading to their racial miscegenation. Here, then, was a Bolivian analogue to Colombia's popular "whitening solution" to justify the pro-*latifundista* polemic, or what their critics called the "refeudalization" position of greedy landowners. While Mariano Melgarejo never defined his position in those terms, his policies in effect endorsed the seigneurial stance.

While historians disagree about the global and regional effects of Melgarejo's reforms on Indian land divestiture, most agree that the government fell far short of its fiscal goals. By the end of the Melgarejo era in 1870, over 1.25 million pesos of land had been sold to whites and mestizos. But because most land purchases were made with devalued government bonds, the government actually made very little money. Furthermore market conditions were only beginning to ripen, and Creole demand for Indian lands was still sluggish in many regions. Nonetheless, Melgarejo's decrees shattered the agrarian peace in the thickly populated Aymara provinces of Sicasica, Omasuyos, and Pacajes, where despoliation was concentrated. Overnight indigenous peoples unable to prove land possession through colonial titles or too impoverished to purchase entitlement watched their common fields and pastures pass into private hands at the bidding of rich speculators. The beneficiaries were political clients of Melgarejo, traditional landowners who expanded their frontiers into indigenous territory, medium-scale miners and merchants, and prosperous Indians (often of *cacique* lineage), who frequently privatized the former *cacique* lands, which had once covered communal ritual and tributary costs. Certainly, in the *altiplano* provinces surrounding the city of La Paz, we see the outlines of a diversified regional oligarchy beginning to consolidate power in this transitional period. Their windfall properties were soon jeopardized, however, by the rising tide of Indian resistance and rebellion. Indigenous violence escalated over a three year period (1869–71) – to a degree unprecedented since Túpac Catari's siege of La Paz almost one hundred years earlier. Most of the violent opposition gathered fury in Aymara communities of Pacajes and Omasuyos, but by January 1871 thousands of Indians allied themselves with Melgarejo's political enemies to lay siege to La Paz and drive the *caudillo* into permanent exile.

On a more prosaic but no less threatening level, Aymara communities mounted their everyday counterattacks against the land reforms. By day, they challenged the legitimacy of tributary and land reform, as well as denounced the extortion of individuals involved, in local notary offices, government chambers, and courts. By night they waged guerrilla warfare over contested boundaries and pastures: posting sentinels at ancient landmarks, driving llama herds and sheep onto disputed pastures, and squatting on potato fields stolen by the state or its private agents during Melgarejo's violent enclosure movement.

The lesson was not lost on Creole reformers, who realized that such a frontal attack on communal land was sheer treachery. Trying to placate the masses, the 1871 Constitutional Convention voided all laws passed during the Melgarejo era. But the land reform issue continued to vex and divide lawmakers. On the one hand, they condemned Melgarejo's annexation of communal lands, arguing that the early Bolivarian decrees had given individual property rights to Indians. On the other hand, many legislators believed in the *hacienda* solution, publicly stating that the interests of indigenous peoples would be better served by paternal landlords who protected them from predatory mestizo lawyers, officials, and priests.

Out of these debates (and a deep-seated fear of rural insurgency) came the 1874 *Ley de Ex-vinculación*. Although not implemented until the 1880s, it set the basic terms of Indian landholding rights from that moment until the mid-twentieth century. At base, the 1874 law conceded the right of individual landownership to Indians, abolishing the community as a juridical, taxpaying, and landholding unit. In its rejection of Melgarejo's efforts at annexation, the law leaned toward the Indian smallholding solution. But it was every bit as radical a break with the recent past: in law, propertied communalism was gone, and so were customary ethnic jurisdictions and traditions that had survived, even flourished, under Bolivia's tributary republic. The law dismantled the tributary apparatus, establishing a universal property tax (*catastro*) to be paid in the new devalued currency of *bolivianos* (which effectively raised Indian taxes by some 20 percent). After the Conservatives' electoral victory in 1880, and under growing fiscal pressures (as the War of the Pacific escalated), the central government rationalized the land-tax structure and dispatched tax commissioners to draw up the first blueprints of propertyholding patterns and begin collecting taxes. In their own traditional roles as ethnic mediators, Indian authorities were swept aside. From then on Indians would be juridical subjects of civil law, directly subject to the authority of white and mestizo agents and to the siege of the land market.

Yet again the rising tide of Indian unrest in the 1880s rapidly forced new concessions from the Conservative regime. Whether by design or confusion, the government created legal loopholes through which indigenous communities could evade or contest the new tax and land policies. In innumerable cases, local reports of Indian unrest or noncompliance forced government authorities to suspend tax collection or land sales during the early 1880s. In October 1885, for instance, appointed Indian authorities (*indios apoderados*) from the Departments of La Paz, Oruro, and Potosí petitioned the Bolivian senate to rescind the tax increases, annul Indian land sales, and call off government land surveys. The senate hedged, telling the leaders to address their grievances to the executive branch. Frustrated by government indifference, Aymara peoples began organizing night meetings throughout Omasuyos to plan for further action. Reports of Indian disturbances also came in from Sicasica. In both cases, white authorities petitioned for troops to crush the insurgents, setting off a vicious pattern of indigenous legal protest followed by military massacre. That same year, the southern highland villages of Macha, Pocoata, Aymaya, and Condo (all located in northern Potosí) forced the tax commissioners to suspend their operations under the threat of Indians invading the silver mining town of Colquechaca. Three years later, a more militant movement erupted in the northern Potosí village of Sacaca, where Indians demanded the head of the land-tax commissioner, while envisioning a neo-Inca social order in alliance with the local branch of the dissident Liberal Party based in the nearby mining town of Colquechaca.[14]

What these reported incidents of violence hide, however, is the massive paper campaign that Indians began to wage in the 1880s for the restitution of their communal rights. The whole confusing welter of legislation over land and tax reforms, together with officialdom's corruption and inefficiency, were perverse ways of encouraging (and tying up) legal challenges by aggrieved Indians. Under pressures of indigenous protest, the government watered down the 1874 law in two basic ways. First, in November 1883, the state agreed to exempt from government title inspections all communal lands entitled by the colonial documents. This legal concession (*la ley pro-indiviso*) flew in the face of the 1874 land reform by allowing Indian communities to legitimate their collective claims if they presented proper colonial titles. Second, the government created labyrinthine procedures whereby new landowners had to consolidate, or "ratify," their property titles. In effect, the ratification process created some "cooling off" time for aggrieved Indians seeking a legal means of redress. In fact, most Indians used these procedures in the late nineteenth and early twentieth centuries to argue for the annulment of land sales on the basis of legal fraud.

With what success did Indians use these laws to slow or reverse the earlier land reform acts? Certainly, most Creole landowners had little respect for these protectionist measures. Indeed, social commentators wrote prolifically about the disastrous effects

[14] Tristan Platt, "The Andean Experience of Bolivian Liberalism, 1825–1900," in Steve Stern, ed., *Resistance, Rebellion, and Consciousness in the Andean Peasant World, 18th to 20th Centuries* (Madison, 1987), 307–9; Erwin Grieshaber, "Indian Reactions to the Acquisition of Communal Land: La Paz, 1881–1920," unpublished paper presented at the FLACSO Conference on "Las comunidades indígenas de los Andes en el siglo XIX," Quito, March 27–30, 1989.

the land reforms were having on indigenous peoples. One of the most prominent writers around the turn of the century was Rigoberto Paredes. An intellectual, lawyer, and *latifundista*, he commented on the sorry state of *altiplano* communities in his book, *Tiahuanaco:*

The legal abolition of the communities has done serious damage to the Indian. Being accustomed to the collective form of cultivation, he lived perfectly peacefully and kept out of reach of covetous land-grabbers. But as soon as he was transformed into a proprietor he became their victim. Illiterate, unaware of the value of his landed property, and without guarantees of any kind, he was stripped of his lands, usually by means of violent spoliation. And thus the great estate was formed and the Indian was reduced to serfdom; [he] lives in hope of reclaiming his rightful ancestral heritage one day.[15]

Recent historical research has tried to measure the scope of Indian land divestiture in the late nineteenth and early twentieth centuries. Erwin Grieshaber, for example, estimates that among 7,616 land-sale contracts registered in the vast Department of La Paz between 1881 and 1920, only about two dozen were annulled and the Indian lands returned.[16] Looking back over a forty- or fifty-year period of vigorous real estate sales, there can be no doubt about the massive alienation of indigenous lands throughout the country. Herbert Klein sums it up: "still holding half the lands and about half the rural population in 1880, the communities were reduced to less than a third of both by 1930. The power of the free Indian communities was definitively broken."[17]

---

[15] Rigoberto Paredes, *Tiahuanaco y la Provincia de Ingavi* [1914] (La Paz, 1965), 31.

[16] Grieshaber, "Indian Reactions to the Acquisition of Communal Land," 18–26.

[17] Klein, *Bolivia: The Evolution of a Multi-Ethnic Society*, 152.

However, it was not broken everywhere, nor shattered completely. La Paz was still a turf of raging territorial wars. *Latifundista* frontiers advanced rapidly in those districts of Omasuyos and Pacajes, which had easy access to the growing urban market of La Paz and the railroad network. Land values soared, as booming mines, rails, and markets opened up commercial opportunities for highland agriculture and livestock raising across the north. Estate owners tended to be absentee landlords and prominent members of the oligarchy, playing politics in Sucre or La Paz. In their shadow, a new layer of commercial intermediaries articulated rural and urban exchanges. Petty provincial bureaucrats, lawyers, merchants, and moneylenders: these rural "mestizo" brokers arose in the institutional crevices opened by the collapse of Indian communities and their local authorities.[18]

So the experience of Indian enserfment was less than universal throughout rural Bolivia at the end of the nineteenth century. The tug and pull of state and market pressures, as well as the forms, forces, and consequences of indigenous response, worked out differently from place to place and region to region. Here we need only point to divergent peasant responses to liberal land reforms in the contiguous departments of Cochabamba and northern Potosí in the late nineteenth century. In the eastern maize valleys of Cochabamba, a region quilted by *haciendas* and smallholding peasants deeply integrated into regional product markets, the liberal land policies gave many peasants a chance to own small parcels of *hacienda* land they had once cultivated through sharecropping or leasehold arrangements. Many *haciendas* also pushed against the

---

[18] Silvia Rivera, "La expansión del latifundio en el Altiplano boliviano. Elementos para la caracterización de una oligarquía regional," *Avances* 2 (1978), 95–118; Carlos Mamani, *Taraqu, 1866–1935. Masacre, Guerra y 'Renovación' en la biografía de Eduardo Nina Qhispi* (La Paz, 1991); and Herbert Klein, *Haciendas and 'Ayllus.'*

borders of nearby Indian communities. The historically weak, engulfed nature of communal landholding in the rich lower valley of Cochabamba, together with a strong peasant tradition of petty commodity production on the edges of valley towns and landed estates, created the regional context for accelerated "peasantization" – especially in the early twentieth century, as peasant household economies revolved more and more around the maize-*chicha* complex. This region also began to expel some of its "surplus" peasants – those unable to live off their shrunken parcels of land – to distant silver, nitrate, and tin mines.[19]

The northern part of the department of Potosí lies across the mountains and valleys to the southwest of Cochabamba. There the historically resilient *ayllus* of Chayanta (a province in the Department of Northern Potosí) had posed strong opposition to earlier cycles of liberal reform and continuously struggled over the republican period to restore ethnic authorities and jurisdictions at the moiety level—the axis of their extended, interecological kin networks and ritual cycles. Under the early tributary-protectionist republic of Bolivia, these *ayllus* seemed to negotiate kin and cash economies in ways that maintained a semblance of political and social equilibrium.

The collapse of protectionism dealt the *ayllus* their first blow. Free-trade policies in the 1870s and 1880s opening Bolivia to cheap

---

[19] Brooke Larson, *Cochabamba, 1550–1900*, chaps. 9 and 10; Gustavo Rodríguez Ostría, "Entre reformas y contrareformas: las comunidades indígenas en el Valle Bajo cochabambino (1825–1900)," in Heraclio Bonilla, ed., *Los Andes en la Encrucijada* (Quito, 1991), 277–335; and Robert H. Jackson, *Regional Markets and Agrarian Transformation in Bolivia, Cochabamba, 1539–1960* (Albuquerque, 1994). Compare the southern valleys and highlands of Chuquisaca in Erick Langer, *Economic Change and Rural Resistance in Southern Bolivia, 1880–1930* (Stanford, 1989).

Chilean and Peruvian wheat flour dislodged the Chayanta *ayllus* from their privileged position as wheat suppliers in regional and urban markets. The second blow came with the land reform acts in the 1880s, when the region became an enclave of *ayllu* protest and rebellion. However, the *ayllus* operated in a very different regional field of force than did the besieged Aymara communities of the northern *altiplano* or the peasant-artisan smallholders of Cochabamba. Their growing economic isolation, the small proportion of lands held in *hacienda*, the vested interest of provincial bureaucrats in maintaining Indian tribute (as it continued to finance local government), and the historical legacy of indigenous struggle and insurrection in the area (a site of massive Indian rebellion during 1780 and 1781) all conspired against the onslaught of applied liberalism and *latifundismo* in northern Potosí. If anything, smallholding mestizos grabbed more lands and turned their political back on *ayllu* Indians. But Chayanta was one region where liberal land-tax policies met with repeated resistance, and Creole authorities eventually retreated. In fact, Tristan Platt notes that "in spite of economic crisis and growing pressure from private property, the *ayllus* entered the twentieth century with a substantial increase in fiscal autonomy." They had managed to scare off the land-tax commissioners and restore Indian tax collectors, chosen from among the *comuneros*. These *kurakas recaudadores* symbolized not only the reassertion of *ayllu* control over critical aspects of communal life but also the renegotiation of an informal "tributary pact" with provincial authorities (in opposition to the central government's liberal policies and discourses of the day).[20]

---

[20] Tristan Platt, "The Andean Experience of Bolivian Liberalism," 318. See also Platt's "Liberalism and Ethnocide in the Southern Andes," *History Workshop* 17 (1984), 3–18, and "Simón Bolívar, the Sun of Justice, and the Amerindian Virgin: Andean Conceptions of the *patria* in Nineteenth-Century Potosí," 159–183.

Such strong regional variations unseat earlier assumptions about the inexorable enserfment of communal Indians. Clearly we cannot reduce local and regional variations of indigenous-state relations to one seamless "Andean experience of liberalism" – whether it be construed as massive *ayllu* divestiture and "ethnocide" under liberalism, resurgent ethnic movements of communal defense, or peasant family strategies of land acquisition. Under particular regional and class conditions, Andean peasants did take advantage of commercial expansion, which fundamentally transformed local landscapes of power in the late nineteenth century. Even across the northern *altiplano*, new opportunities opened for bilingual, literate lawyers, merchants, labor contractors, and others who used their indigenous roots for accumulative ends. Yet there is no doubt that the booming export, land, and product markets came at the price of social justice and peace for most other indigenous peasants across highland Bolivia. Economically, most highland Indians were reintegrated into the market under sharply more disadvantageous terms under the liberalizing regime. Many were displaced from traditional market circuits, subjected to new commercial monopolies on top of their traditional *corvée* obligations, hit with heavier head or land taxes, and threatened by laws and practices of divestiture. Accompanying this economic transition were deep cultural incursions into the most intimate corners of communal life – violating intra-*ayllu* norms of political succession; the administration of local justice; the allocation of lands, taxes, and ritual responsibilities; and the coordination of the "ethnic calendar." In theory, indigenous jurisdictions evaporated as Indians became subject to law and bureaucracy controlled by and for whites and mestizos, landlords and merchants.

Yet liberal incursions had a contradictory effect on highland indigenous communities. Although the reforms half-heartedly, at times timidly, tried to abolish indigenous communities as legal entities, the imperatives of communal defense and survival revitalized a sense of communal identity and ethnic memory among a spreading transregional network of Aymara people. This was a slow, uneven grassroots process that assumed national scope in the final years of the nineteenth century, as local indigenous struggles merged briefly with the oligarchic north-south conflict of 1899. Ethnic militancy reached its apotheosis during the "cycle of Aymara rebellions" between 1910 and 1930. It was only then – during the frenzied growth of *haciendas*, rails, and tin mining; the modernization of La Paz's bureaucratic and military apparatus; and the beginning of an aggressive "civilizing" crusade – that local rebel actions began to fuse and articulate into a broader, national ethnic movement.[21]

Yet there is no doubt that the roots of modern Aymara ethnic militancy reached deep into the colonial past and grew stronger and more entangled under the liberal assault of communal land rights in the 1880s and 1890s. It was then that many Aymara communities first began to confront the consequences of the 1874 agrarian reform, the onslaught of fraudulent land sales, and the wholesale conversion of *ayllu*-based *comunarios* into an atomized mass of landless *colonos* newly attached to private estates. The rise of a grassroots movement of communal defense and land restitution was spurred by the state's confusing welter of liberal laws (in particular, the so-called *pro-indiviso* clause of 1883), which opened the way for some indigenous communities to press their claims to "indivisible lands" on the basis of court-ratified, Spanish colonial land titles. In the meantime, ongoing land disputes turned putative property boundaries into perpetual war zones, as indigenous people waged legal battles in the courts by day and tried to take back their stolen lands and pastures by night. Historian Juan Martínez-Alier's old axiom about the "dubious legitimacy" of private property in highland Peru is an understatement for the Bolivian *altiplano*.

---

[21] See Silvia Rivera Cusicanqui, *'Oprimidos pero no vencidos.' Luchas del campesinado aymara y qechwa, 1900–1980* (La Paz, 1986), chap. 2; and Mamani, *Taraqu, 1866–1935*.

In 1900, the new *latifundia* regime was under full attack by indigenous leaders, small town lawyers, and peasant intellectuals, who gathered colonial land titles, tribute and *mita* registers, and other colonial documents to defend their claims to communal territories and the right to self-rule. Just as *caciques* in the eighteenth century had once produced legal depositions and litigated property rights in the colonial tribunals, so now did peasant leaders make pilgrimages to colonial archives in the cities of Sucre, Lima, and even Buenos Aires in search of "ancient documents" that might provide the legal proof of *ayllu* entitlement. By means of the colonial document, reinterpreted through the prism of liberal and constitutional legality, indigenous intellectuals would advance their claims to *comunario* status (with its right to territorial justice, communal sovereignty, and legal protection) as an alternative to the atomizing forces of divestiture, impoverishment, and servitude. Taken together, these local-level legal battles reveal the contours of an extraordinary movement of *ayllu* self-empowerment beginning to spring up across the Bolivian highlands around the turn of the twentieth century. Like the Páez Indian movement and other subaltern projects that rested on ambivalent combinations of modernity and tradition, Aymara projects of communal defense, or *ayllu* restitution, tried to articulate indigenous understandings of the colonial past, ethno-genealogies and geographies, and individual rights under the "Constitutional Law" of the Bolivian republic. Popular uses of the colonial past did not represent a unilateral embrace of all things colonial, however. Indigenous leaders strategically deployed the "colonial pact" by simultaneously contesting the injustices of coerced labor and tributary extractions, still widely practiced throughout the rural provinces, and invoking colonial-corporatist rights to landholding and self-rule. Thus they began to interweave disparate strands of colonial memory, ethnic descent, and contemporary land claims into a broader project of ethnic resurgence and territorial justice under the modernizing Bolivian state.

ZÁRATE WILLKA AND THE AYMARA
PEASANT MOVEMENT

Living on the edge of violent despoliation and repression, many Aymara communities began to reorganize themselves as communities of opposition in the 1880s and 1890s. Rhetorically ready for reconciliation with a redemptive, protectionist republic, yet poised for violent counterattack against aggressive land grabbers, Aymara peoples began to fashion multiple modes of struggle, inside and outside the bounds of Creole law. As the jittery La Paz elite often warned, that incipient Aymara movement could escalate at any moment, sending the "savage warriors" across the northern *altiplano* to the edge of the dusty bowl that shelters the city of La Paz. And so it happened in 1899 – ironically at the invitation of the Liberal Party.

Already by the late 1880s, political and social conditions began to encourage some Liberals to enlist Indians in their crusade for power. In 1888, a presidential election year, there was a groundswell of indigenous protest against the tax and land reforms that the Conservative Party had been pushing for some eight years. In the southern highlands of Sacaca, Macha, and elsewhere, armed peasants set fire to municipal buildings and drove off government authorities trying to inspect properties and collect land-title fees. These areas proved to be fertile ground for cultivating strategic alliances between defensive, antigovernment *ayllus* and dissident, anti-Conservative Liberals. For the rebellious *ayllus* of Chayanta and Charcas, the silver mining town of Colquechaca became a hotbed of Liberalism in the late 1880s. Liberals campaigned openly for Indian support, and party propaganda and slogans circulated through intricate rural webs of communication among large numbers of transient Indians trekking between their *ayllus* and the mines, markets, and shrines of Colquechaca. These transitory alliances with Liberal mestizo townspeople probably emboldened Indians to oppose government land reform policies openly. In any event, Indian and mestizo protests against the new land commissioners in the region escalated in the late 1880s and early 1890s, and Indians continued to petition sympathetic legislators with the help of dissident Liberal lawyers and agitators.[22]

By the mid-1890s the Conservative oligarchy began to see its political and economic fortunes dissolve. Collapsing silver prices on the world market eroded the economic base of the Conservatives. The tin mines of the center and north of Bolivia would soon catapult La Paz into Bolivia's preeminent economic and political center, the country's rival capital city. But for the moment, the Conservative Party tried to cling to its political monopoly against the opposition party operating out of La Paz. Partisan elite politics increasingly manifested regional and economic schisms (the economic and political rise of the north and fall of the south), but the parties differed little in their promodernization stances. And yet the Liberal Party would only begin to champion order and progress, capitalism and civilization, after they seized power in 1900. In the 1880s and 1890s, they defined their goals in narrow political terms: to share power at the top and restructure the bureaucracy along federalist lines. Most of all, they wanted clean elections, and they were willing to forge unholy alliances and espouse pro-Indian causes (e.g., the restitution of communal lands and the repeal of land reforms) to mobilize Indians against their Conservative enemies. As we saw,

---

[22] Platt, "The Andean Experience of Bolivian Liberalism," 311–12. Note that both the Conservative and Liberal Parties advocated liberal reforms and economic progress, while each party scrambled for popular support at the polls.

Liberals had already established local enclaves of Indian clientelism in northern Potosí during the late 1880s. But in the election year of 1896, a new political opportunity arose for La Paz Liberals to broaden their indigenous base of support in the north, by hooking into a vast preexisting web of insurgent Indian communities scattered throughout the rural districts of Oruro and La Paz.

The powerful, new Liberal-Indian coalition was built by two men: Colonel José Manuel Pando and Pablo Zárate Willka. They became historic partners (and later enemies) in the Federalist Revolution of 1899, which finally broke the Conservatives' political monopoly. Both were supreme political and military leaders that forged their own constituencies and agendas into a fragile popular-partisan front. For Pando, the enemy was simply the opposition party that had kept the Liberals out of power since the beginning of civilian oligarchic rule in 1880. For indigenous communities under siege for more than two decades, the enemy transcended narrow party politics and implicated the whole social and moral order. Their common ideological ground was shallow, at best.

Still, the first signs of political coalition between Pando and Zárate Willka were hopeful. On the eve of the 1896 election, they approached each other in mutual need and respect. Zárate Willka had already established himself as a widely respected, well-traveled, literate Aymara leader, mediating land conflicts in different communities, petitioning politicians on behalf of aggrieved *comunarios*, and spinning kinship and political webs across the *altiplano* (Figure 13). This figure was no accidental hero spawned by the circumstances of war. He was a powerful Indian *caudillo* who participated in national-level war and rebellion, and who brought to the political partnership a rural constituency of aggrieved Indians. Mobilized and harnessed to the Liberal cause, they could terrorize the Conservatives into submission. Or, so Pando believed.

Figure 13. General Willka Condori and his troops in Arque, 1899. According to historian Ramiro Condarco Morales, the standing figure in the center of the photograph is Feliciano Condori Willka, the "Third Willka," in charge of indigenous troops through the western highlands of Cochabamba. This photograph was taken during the early phases of Bolivia's Federalist War (1899), while the indigenous forces were still allied to General Pando's Liberal Party grab for power. (Photo courtesy of the Archivo de la Paz, Bolivia.)

By the 1890s, Pablo Zárate Willka enjoyed widespread political influence.[23] In correspondence with Pando on the eve of the

[23] Little is known about Pablo Zárate Willka's formative years, and his persona remains shrouded in rival black-and-white legends. At his trial, he stated his birthplace to be Sicasica, although he was probably born in the small village of Imilla-Imilla, located in the western mountains of the Province of Sicasica, in the Department of La Paz. Stretching across mountains and *altiplano*, the province was located midway between the cities of Oruro and La Paz. In 1899, it became a battleground between the northern and southern armies locked in civil war. But long before then, Sicasica was legendary for its bellicose Indian communities: it was the cradle of Indian rebels and successive uprisings – in 1781, 1811, and most recently under Melgarejo in

elections in 1896, Zárate Willka alluded to the broad peasant constituency he already commanded. The letter, dated June 27, 1896, was written from the village of Taraco, poised on the edge of Lake Titicaca. Zárate Willka had been engaged in settling land disputes between local hacendados and *comunarios* to their mutual benefit (or so he reported). The letter also told of his perambulations among other lake shore villages and offered to take Pando's greetings to other *caciques*. One of his next destinations was the shrine of Copacabana, across the lake from Taraco, where he would beg the Virgin's blessings for Pando. Finally, he asked Pando for a favor: to bring back news from Sucre about congressional deliberations over the petitions that he and other Indians had sent. The letter reveals the kind of reciprocal relations already obtaining between Zárate Willka and Pando, even before military action began.

Here, then, are glimpses of a literate, bilingual Aymara man who had cultivated political and kinship links in villages across the northern *altiplano*, far from his own homeland. He had established himself as a political *caudillo* and interlocutor among Taraco villages, on the defensive against rampant *latifundismo*. His travels, political connections, and diplomacy had laid the groundwork for the rise of a broad Indian political movement, which Zárate provisionally offered to deliver to the Liberal Party. And as the Liberal Party turned to military action (following another electoral defeat in 1896), it turned to Zárate Willka to mobilize an Indian army to fight the Conservatives (now called the Constitutionalists). It was a pact of political convenience – inevitably, precarious and dangerous.

1871. Zárate Willka's political sensibilities were undoubtedly influenced by local oral traditions about Sicasica's insurgent past.

For the following discussion of the Zárate Willka and the 1899 rebellion 1899, I am indebted to Ramiro Condarco Morales, for his pioneering study, *Zárate, el 'Temible' Willka. Historia de una rebelión indígena de 1899* (La Paz, 1982), 2nd ed. This interpretative synthesis is my own, however.

From the beginning Pando never effectively subordinated the Indian leader to his own direct command. Although Zárate Willka's stature was enhanced by his long political connection to Creole Liberals, he was no mere client of Pando. His primary allegiances and power base were rooted in Aymara communities throughout the north, where he had spent long years of networking, mediation, and struggle on their behalf (Figure 14). As politics became militarized in 1899, Zárate Willka was determined to enter the war as both ally and equal of Pando. He conferred upon himself the combined military title of "General of a Division in the Federal Army" and "Commander-in-Chief of the Indigenous Army." It reflected his double identity: as Pando's military ally of equal rank and as supreme leader of indigenous soldiers (and, by extension, all Indian communities) brought into the war effort. Incipient ideals of social equality and cultural pluralism were embedded in these formal titles, which later Zárate Willka expressed more openly through his words and deeds.

But if Pando was unable to subordinate Zárate Willka to his own military command, the Indian leader himself had difficulty containing grassroots peasant violence amidst the chaos and brutality of civil war. As the Conservative-Constitutionalist and Liberal-Federalist armies swarmed over the villages of Sicasica and other provinces, committing all kinds of atrocity, partisan politics faded rapidly before the brutal logic of ethnic and class warfare and survival. The very presence of troops victimized peasants no matter what their political allegiance: "each march of an army brings [peasants] the same damage and terror as the most furious earthquake would bring," commented one sympathetic journalist in 1895.[24]

---

[24] *El Comercio* (La Paz, 1 April 1895), quoted in Andrew Pearse, *The Latin American Peasant* (London, 1975), 134.

Figure 14. The high ministers of Zárate Willka's army and government, 1899. This formal portrait of the various "Willkas" who served as *ministros* to Pablo Zárate Willka vividly demonstrates the collective, indeed consciously federative, nature of the high command. To the degree that historians have focused on elite images of Pablo Zárate as a "terrifying," "irrational," or "savage" Aymara Indian, or on his *caudillo*-style of governing, or even his opportunistic impulses, they overlook the crucial political and territorial base of support and hierarchy of leadership that undergirded this extraordinary indigenous peasant movement. The Willka mobilizations built upon enduring Aymara traditions of local self-rule and indigenous authority networks, as well as on *ayllu* resentments over the growing danger of land divestiture, in order to spread the movement among Aymara and Quechua peasants across several highland regions. Zárate Willka himself consciously decentralized political and military power among a handful of other newly designated "Willkas" in the northern zones, including the crucial "Third Willka" of Tapacarí, Feliciano Condori (pictured here in the top hat). His other highly ranked authorities included at least two "presidents" of southern districts: Juan Lero of Peñas and Mariano Gómez of Challoma. (Photo courtesy of the Archivo de La Paz.)

Furthermore, as we saw happen among Peru's Mantaro guerrillas during the War of the Pacific, nationalist or partisan politics may serve to inspire and legitimate peasant violence against ancient class and ethnic enemies. In the towns and villages of Sicasica, Pablo Zárate Willka's peasant-soldiers hunted down *alonsistas* (supporters of the Constitutionalist government), but this hunt was an opportunity for peasants to settle old scores among hacendados and townsfolk. Throughout the war-torn provinces, the Federalist Revolution of 1899 set indigenous peasants against mestizo towns – the administrative site where servile labor had to be rendered, taxes paid, commercial monopolies set, and Indian justice mocked. In a similar vein, peasant irregulars who saw their own communities sacked and their women raped began to turn against the regular (white) armies of both camps, even as they shouted *"viva Pando!"* After a certain point, the civil war became submerged in an indigenous rebellion, the likes of which had not been seen in Bolivia for more than a century.

The turning point came in February 1899 in the town of Mohoza. A squadron of well-armed Federalist cavalry encountered a roadblock of hostile peasants, who took them hostage. Through that terrible night, the white soldiers were taken to the parish courtyard and cemetery where they were executed, one by one. Several townspeople, on both sides of the partisan divide, also met their death that night. The exact circumstances of this mass extermination were never cleared up and remain obscure to this day. But that this autonomous peasant action had shattered the pact was all too clear. On the eve of his murder, a terrified commanding officer whispered to the local priest, "we are lost, father. The peasants have risen. The war is not between factions, but between races. We cheered Pando and the Federation, and they answered '*viva* Willka!'"[25]

---

[25] Quoted in Ramiro Condarco Morales, *Zárate, el "Temible" Willka: Historia de la rebelión indígena de 1899*, 273.

There is some controversy as to Zárate Willka's role in these events, although the tribunal later accused him of commanding the mass execution. Certainly, in the weeks to follow, Zárate Willka continued to profess his loyalty to the Liberal cause and to carry out military operations in many places. But as the doomed cavalry officer realized, the events of Mohoza reflected the radical drift of peasant violence. It also seems clear that Zárate Willka, while never disavowing partisan loyalty, increasingly indicted the injustices of Bolivian society and summoned peasants to take direct action against their local oppressors.

Yet Pablo Zárate Willka never unleashed an all-out "race war." In fact, he was caught on the barbs of his own past and identity as an Indian leader in postcolonial society. On the one hand, Zárate Willka had achieved the stature of a military and political *caudillo* through his astute partisan politics and long season as a widely respected mediator of local ethnic and class disputes. On the other, he was a militant Aymara advocate and activist, deeply committed to the ideals of territorial autonomy and cultural pluralism under republican rule. No wonder his later military actions were full of ambiguities and contradictions that few contemporary observers cared to figure out. Thus he sent circulars to his Indian troops to exercise self-restraint toward "whites and *vecinos*" and to remember their common goal (the overthrow of Alonso and the "regeneration of Bolivia"). But he also took radical actions to subvert the moral and symbolic order of ethnic oppression. While he never openly declared war on the white citizens' world, he envisioned a new order of social equality and mutual respect that would give real social content to the empty rhetoric of the Liberals. "We Indians are of the same blood," he said, "and [we are] all children of Bolivia."

In his uniquely daring practice, more than ideology, Zárate Willka actually inverted the hierarchy of caste. For what better way to impose one's vision of social and cultural equality on this deeply divided society than to coerce the "Indianization" of whites? To reverse the onward march of "Creole civilization" and compel the cultural assimilation of non-Indians into native Andean society? Breaking all the cultural codes, he ordered all "whites and *vecinos*" in the western Cochabamba province of Tapacarí to dress in rustic homespuns and sandals (*traje indígena*) as they prepared to meet the Constitutionalists in battle. Later during his public trial, testimony described Zárate Willka holding "court" in the village of Tambo de Iro, where "serfs and gentry paid their respects; where men with...golden beards and pale skin put their pride in their pockets...and came to pay homage...picturesquely dressed in sandals and *bayeta* homespuns in the native style."[26] No whimsical act, this was subversive political theatre aimed at putting into practice the deep ideals that he had stood for all his life. Nurtured by the oral traditions of Aymara insurgency in his homeland of Sicasica, Zárate Willka performed acts of cultural defiance that his Aymara ancestors had carried out during the 1781 uprisings in Sicasica, Oruro, and La Paz. A century later, the ghost of Túpac Catari lived on in the villages of Sicasica. But even if we cannot trace the genealogy of Zárate Willka's insurgent actions directly back to the rebels of 1781, those actions assume deep symbolic significance when read against the political and cultural ideals he projected by his other actions and writings. In his proclamations and circular, Zárate Willka hints of an imagined nation-state that not only redeemed Liberal Party promises of land restitution but invited indigenous communities into a new political covenant. His agenda embraced a kind of "federalism" attuned to indigenous aspirations of autonomy, equality, and cultural respect.

But that, of course, was not to be. The victorious Federalist army and the Liberal Party unleashed their fury against their indigenous

[26] Testimony recorded during the Mohoza trial, quoted in ibid., 299.

allies, capturing, trying, and eventually executing Zárate Willka and
288 other "guilty" Indians. The famous trial (*el proceso Mohoza*)
dragged on for several years, in Mohoza, Inquisivi, Oruro, and La
Paz. It became a roving public spectacle, through which Creole elites
scrutinized and judged the native defendants and, through them, the
Indian race. The trial incubated multiple racist theories explaining
the biological and social origins of Indian inferiority. Journalists
passionately engaged these legal, scientific, and philosophical debates and, in turn, propagated images of the savage or forsaken
Aymara race. After the turn of the century, scientific teams were
imported from France, and later Belgium, to conduct studies measuring the cranium capacity of Indians. Physical anthropologists
and other early-twentieth-century "experts" proclaimed the Indian
race fit to become the nation's productive peasants, mineworkers,
and soldiers, but essentially unfit for participation in public culture
and politics. The French anthropologist, Arthur Chervin, went so
far as to predict Bolivia's "racial improvement" to the extent that its
Indian races were absorped into a homogenizing mass of mestizos
(Figure 15).[27]

In the meantime, progressive *indigenista* intellectuals in La Paz
plunged into literary, geographic, and ethnographic studies of indigenous attributes and anachronisms, turning a critical eye on the
feudal structures that kept Indians in a state of backwardness. La
Paz *indigenistas* became the font of racial and environmental theories, positivist studies, and exotic images of Bolivia's Indian other.
From whatever conceptual angle these new racial diagnosticians
worked, they came to a common conclusion: there was no getting
around the centrality of race to the nation's future. Just as Peru had
to come to grips with the Indian problem and the question of national sovereignty following the War of the Pacific, so Bolivia had

[27] Arthur Chervin, *Antropologie bolivienne* (Paris, 1908), I.

Figure 15. Sample *cartes-de-visite* featuring Aymara "Indian types," 1910. The *carte-de-visite* was a popular aesthetic and social convention that circulated "exotic" or "artistic" images through society. Applying the same standards as those used in bourgeois portraiture, photographers in La Paz (and elsewhere) froze anonymous Indians in standardized poses, gaping out at the viewer, perhaps holding a signifying water or *chicha* jug (as in the two photographs here) or wearing the ubiquitous leather straps used for hauling heavy sacks of flour, firewood, or other loads that burdened rural men (as we see in the photograph of the man), but removed from any humanizing cultural or social context and set against a blank backdrop of the indoor studio. These stark racialized subjects give only the barest hint of the subjects' occupations (which interested Wiener, as in Figures 7 or 8, for example) or their cultural heritage (alluded to

Figure 15 *(cont.)* by the careful placement of certain "ethnic artifacts" in Figure 11). Postcard portraits like these were collected by the hundreds and analyzed by scientists to construct "composite types" and racial taxonomies that might be useful for genetic theories of race, criminology, or Creole debates over Indian legislation, education, and civilizing potential. For example, French scientist Arthur Chervin used *cartes de visite* (in conjunction with his anthropometric studies) to assess Bolivia's racial makeup so as to be able to prognosticate its future development! (See his *Antropologie Bolivienne*, 3 vols. [Paris, 1908]. Discussed in Poole, *Vision, Race, and Modernity* [Princeton, 1997], 134–5.) (Photographs reproduced with permission from the Peabody Museum of Archaeology and Ethnology, Harvard University.)

to deal with its internal enemy: the Indian Other. Out of the 1899 crisis came a new national obsession with the Indian race and the determination to conquer it once and for all.[28]

This, then, became the historic burden of the triumphant Liberal oligarchy. While they inherited the mantle of modernization from their Conservative rivals, and while they paved the way for unbridled capitalism in tin mining, railroad building, and land grabbing after 1900, their main mission necessarily had to be the domestication of the Indian race. The 1899 rebellion proved it to be a fundamental condition of sustained economic progress and stable oligarchic rule. Political alliance, or even coexistence, was no longer a viable political option. And starting with Pando himself, the Liberal Party expunged from official memory all earlier collaborations with Indian allies. Zárate Willka was barbarianized into the "fearsome Willka," as intellectuals and policy makers argued about the linked destinies of the Indian and the nation.

For now they were inevitably conjoined. Much like the postwar intellectuals of Lima, Bolivian writers found no easy exit from their national dilemma. They could not harbor much hope of racial assimilation in the near future, given the preponderance of native peoples. Extermination campaigns could be (and were) carried out against specific tribal groups in Bolivia's vast tropical frontier, but they were unfeasible in the highlands. Thus thwarted, writers and politicians looked into the national soul and saw "mestizo" but could not agree on the worthiness of the mestizo to carry forth the national mandate. Indeed, until deep into the twentieth century, cultural *mestizaje* did not become an ideological rallying point of

---

[28] Marie-Daniele Demelas, "Darwinismo a la criolla. El darwinismo social en Bolivia, 1880–1919," *Historia boliviana* 1 (1981), 55–82; and Marta Irurozqui, *La armonía de las desigualdades. Elites y conflictos de poder en Bolivia, 1880–1920* (Cusco, 1994).

national identity. On the contrary, Alcides Arguedas and other prominent writers found the mestizo to be a contemptible race – indeed, the main cause of Bolivia's barbarous republican history of *caudillaje* (leadership by charismatic armed men). The orthodoxies of Social Darwinism may have held out some hope that over time the superior white race would prevail. But in a nation where whites comprised less than 20 percent of the population, how long would that process take?

This dilemma called for an intermediate solution to the Indian problem. If cultural *mestizaje* offered no easy way out, then the government had to design policies to exclude Indians from the political sphere, remove them from their lands now coveted by a new breed of La Paz-dwelling landowner, contain Indian unrest, and convert them into disciplined manual laborers who were anchored in the countryside. Intellectuals, lawyers, and policy makers tried to fashion an informal system of apartheid: Indians would be civilized and molded into a laboring class yet simultaneously separated, protected, and their political aspirations contained.[29] An emerging visual language of race undergirded this inchoate project of turning highland Indians into subaltern laborers. In particular, photography provided a crucial medium for penetrating the physiognomic interior of the Indian psyche and soul (Figure 15). Biologized race differences naturalized Indians as exotic, potentially useful, but possibly dangerous "others." This new race-based knowledge authorized La Paz reformers to develop institutions capable of imposing tutelage, social control, and moral improvement on the rural Indian

---

[29] See Brooke Larson, "Redeemed Indians, Barbarianized Cholos: Crafting Neocolonial Modernity in Liberal Bolivia," in N. Jacobsen and C. Aljovín, eds., *Andean Political Cultures, 1750–1850* (Durham, forthcoming); Marta Irurozqui, *La armonía de las desigualdades: Elites y conflictos de poder en Bolivia, 1880–1920* (Cuzco, 1994), chap. 4; and Laura Gotkowitz, *Within the Boundaries of Equality: Race, Gender, and Citizenship in Cochabamba, Bolivia, 1880–1952* (Durham, forthcoming), chaps. 2 and 3.

masses. Notwithstanding their racist, positivist, and civilizing impulses, however, La Paz Liberals had no unifying program of reform, and, in any event, market forces proved far more virulent than any such policy agenda during the Liberal Party's twenty-year reign (1900–20).

As a result, the rapid expansion of *latifundismo* across the northern *altiplano* after 1900 created the de facto basis for the "seigneurial solution" to land reform. Many indigenous communities were swallowed whole by expanding *haciendas*, although not without long struggles.[30] But the alleged immutability of racial difference, and the deepening of racial tension after 1899, shut Indians out of the Creole notion of nation-state. Ideals of political and cultural assimilation through education were deemed unrealistic, even dangerous. Instead, policymakers began to tailor a "civilizing" mission to keep Indians back – to socialize them to perform manual labor, to stay in the countryside, and to keep their own customs. Indians were to be instructed in agricultural skills, temperance, hygiene and crafts, but not in literacy. They were to cultivate their crops, but not on their own communal lands. And they were to render their usual labor services and pay property taxes, but they were to remain disenfranchised.[31]

---

[30] Victor Hugo Cárdenas, "La lucha de un pueblo," in Xavier Albó, ed., *Raíces de América. El mundo Aymara* (Madrid, 1988), 495–534; Xavier Albó, "From MNRistas to Kataristas to Katari," in Steve Stern, ed., *Resistance, Rebellion, and Consciousness in the Andean Peasant World, 18th to 20th Centuries* (Madison, 1987), 379–419; Taller de Historia Oral Aymara (THOA), *El indio Santos Marka T'ula. Cacique principal de los ayllus de Callapa y apoderado general de las comunidades originarias de la República* (La Paz, 1986).

[31] Roberto Choque et al., *Educación Indígena:¿ ciudadanía o colonización?* (La Paz, 1992); Roberto Choque, "La problemática de la educación indigenal," *Data: Revista del Instituto de Estudíos Andinos y Amazónicos* 5 (1994), 9–33.

Much like the other Andean republics, then, Bolivia entered the twentieth century more fragmented and divided than ever before. But those fragments of the modernizing Bolivian nation contained the seeds of ethno-identity politics that would flourish, under changing conditions, throughout much of the twentieth century.

Conclusion

Postcolonial Republics and the Burden of Race

This book has traced the dynamic interactions among highland indigenous peasants, factious Creole elites, and emerging "mestizo" sectors swelling the interstices of Andean rural society. It maps diverse national and regional landscapes, which became more textured, fluid, and differentiated over the course of the nineteenth century. Against that rich tapestry of Andean socio-cultural flux and transformation, this book has also explored the hardening *conceptual landscape of race* in the Creole national imaginary. For it seems that in varied contexts, the imagined Indian was almost invariably cast in contradictory terms – as both essential and anathema to the forces of order, progress, and civilization. In their varied expressions, racial discourses proved to be crucial props in the second half of the nineteenth century, after Creole reformers began dismantling the legal-discursive framework that had continued to bind Indians to the state through their partially restored tributary status.

At base, the emerging postcolonial relationship mandated the redefinition of Indianness from a corporate group, endowed with codified tributary obligations and rights, to an inferior "race" sentenced to the margins of nation and civilization. In social and juridical terms, this reformulation dealt a double blow to indigenous

246

communities. First, Indians lost their legal rights to collective existence and protection and became individuals subject to universal contract law. Gone, too, was the common ground on which Indians, regional elites, and states had tried to work out their fundamental differences over indigenous entitlements under colonial rule and the new republics. Second, Indianness was modernized into a degraded biocultural race, whose essential character rendered it unfit for civil society and citizenship. By 1910, Creoles had reorganized their nation-states around rigid concepts of race, culture, and geography, which aimed at controlling the ambiguous spaces of racial-ethnic crossing and mediation, while securing the boundaries of whiteness, urbanity, and civilization. Concretely, progressive state policies aimed at preparing Indians for their eventual entry into the segmented labor market as a rural underclass of farmers, laborers, and (in times of war) foot soldiers at the margins of political life and public culture. Converging racial-class correlations (the Indian race as rural underclass) thus cemented modern forms of social inequality and marginality under liberalizing "republics without citizens" (to borrow the late Alberto Flores Galindo's unforgettable phrase).

As chronicled in this book, these postcolonial Andean passages from colonial rule to independence, and from early republicanism to late-nineteenth-century liberalism, racism, and modernity, were wrought with conflict, violence, and reversal. And how could it be otherwise in regions where racial-ethnic divisions were stark, states were weak, and peasant politics resided at the very core of national identity making? But while the dialectics of liberalism and racism might sound familiar to cultural theorists of Western modernity, especially as played out on the margins of nineteenth-century European empires, the specific historical struggles that surrounded and shaped postcolonial relationships in the interior of the Andes need to be studied in greater depth. The historical literature is still vastly uneven, and national narratives still tend toward the teleological tracings of modernization. Yet we know, of course, that the Andean republics did not set off on a brisk march toward order and progress over the nineteenth century. Rather, the century unleashed a cacophony of clashing visions, voices, and interests that reverberated across these broken landscapes and sundered early Bolivarian utopias. It was not until the late nineteenth century that Creole political cliques managed to hitch their tenuous class interests to the resurgent export sector and launch aggressive liberal-positivist reforms in the indigenous interior of their nations.

Over the course of the century, highland Andean peasantries had no choice but to cast themselves as political subjects and meet the challenges of nation-building. In so doing, indigenous leaders found themselves negotiating their own meanings of the colonial past and the national future, and struggling to locate their rightful place in that tumultuous temporal passage. In the process, Andean peasants often evolved their own ambivalent modernities, which might still accommodate sacred traditions of propertied communalism, local self-rule and ritual, and state protection under a modernizing nation. To be sure, there was no unifying popular vision, either Incan, colonial, or liberal, that sprang from some sort of primordial Andean experience or seamless culture. Nor did Andean farmers, herders, artisans, traders, migrant laborers, servile tenants, or domestic servants possess a unity of economic interest from which they might mount a collective challenge to the liberalizing state, or even lay claim to a collective heritage. But what was singular about the Andes, at least in many parts of the South Andes, was the powerful legacy of communalism, reinforced by colonial and early republican policies of tribute, segregation, and protection. Thus armed (or perhaps, burdened) with local folk-legal traditions, honed in the colonial courts under the *república de indios*, local Andean authorities evolved a variety of political, cultural, and discursive strategies to recover local autonomies under the new republics. Although Andean peoples did not blindly adhere to the colonial past, they did draw bitter experiential lessons from warfare, intrusive reforms, and political repression that had accompanied independence. Gradually, many rural people came to understand that the advent of liberalism and modernity might pose terrible threats to their most significant colonial-cultural patrimonies.

For many Andean communities, then, the abolition of tribute in the 1850s (later in Bolivia) marked a watershed in the long history of Indian-state relations. Andean people found themselves more vulnerable to the riptides of labor extraction, liberal reformism, and mercantile and landlord violence. Stereotypes aside, Andean peasants certainly were not isolated from either world-historical or national forces. Thus it was that Andean *corvée* laborers (latter-day *mitayos*) built Ecuador's modern trans-Andean highways and laid Peru's first iron rails. Bolivian *ayllus* sustained federal and provincial officialdom with tribute monies until well after 1850, when the sputtering silver mines finally began to disgorge profits for the mineowners and revenues for the state. Local peasant villages across the Andes were still required to fulfill their ancient labor quotas to municipal authorities, by clearing mountain roads, constructing irrigation works, carrying mail, staffing highway inns, digging graves in municipal cemeteries, and serving local monasteries. During war, too, Peruvian peasant were suddenly converted into Indian patriots, conscripted into militia bands, and sent to the front to defend the *patria* against the barbarian Chilean invaders. Little wonder that many Andean people came to expect territorial justice, protection, and even citizenship in return for their labors and sacrifices.

But as we have seen, liberalism-cum-divestiture was not the whole story. Subtle paradoxes of the market were also at work in the countryside. For on the other side of dispossession and mercantile violence lay *the potential* for individual prosperity, cultural adaptation, and mobility. Late-nineteenth-century political and economic flux opened narrow exit routes out of the poverty and stigma of Indianness. Bustling world and local markets in wool, coca, chicha, and other local commodities; the recovering silver, copper, and nitrate mines throughout the highlands; the expanding wage work opportunities on coastal plantations, and, not least, new opportunities for political clientelism and favoritism under emerging party systems all seemed to provide a certain measure of geographic and social mobility, which in turn created new streams of labor migration, urban-rural circuits of exchange, and sites of popular culture and identity. Such social transformations wreaked havoc on colonial ideals of Indian segregation, protection, and purity. And many a Creole writer and statesman looked with alarm at this amorphous mass of semiliterate, politicized *cholos* and *mestizos* threatening to invade their cities, public culture, and electoral politics. But for countless other rural people, the exit from rural life represented a violent rupture. For how often did wholesale divestiture, expulsion, or displacement in the countryside serve as motor forces behind those migratory streams into the mines, plantations, and cities?

The midcentury was also a moment of acute tension among splintered elite factions – as liberal ideals, partisan interests, and colonial practices clashed head on. Although liberal reforms slowly gained ground, political regimes across the ideological spectrum had trouble defining (much less implementing) their Indian policies. This is starkly revealed in the Peruvian republic's welter of contradictory reforms and counterreforms between the 1850s and 1870s. Four successive regimes reversed and reinvented Indian policies alternately to emancipate, crush, assimilate, and segregate its highland Indians. In Ecuador, tribute abolition coincided with the state's efforts to conscript Indians to build the nation's trans-Andean highways. And in both Colombia and Bolivia (albeit under very different circumstances), late-nineteenth-century liberal reformers were quick to reverse their policies to quell rural unrest.

These intramural battles subsided somewhat in the early twentieth century, partially due to the desire of small but prospering export oligarchies to rally around new positivist-authoritarian variants of liberalism. More than ever before, Creole nation-builders (of whatever partisan stripe) began to link the national question to the Indian problem. Modernity fostered orientalism, as aspiring urban political leaders, writers, and naturalists turned their cosmopolitan gaze inward in order to rediscover authentic Indian cultures, the pre-Hispanic and colonial-Hispanist pasts, and the Humboldtian majesty of their mountainous and jungle landscapes. In each republic, the production of a new scientific and literary canon (travelogues, ethnography, regionalist novels, romantic poetry, race science, muckraking essays, *costumbrista* portraiture, and later photography) created a "new age of discovery." Armed with these textual tools, a new generation of social reformers set out to diagnose the essential, perhaps ultimately redeemable, Indian race. Liberal-positivists may have disagreed over the root causes of Indian backwardness, or argued over their nation's racial destiny, and, indeed, the Indian race often served as a rhetorical pawn in elite power struggles. What drew them together was their collective self-authorization to arbitrate and police the boundaries of nationhood, race, and territorial space. In so doing, Creole ruling elites largely rejected homogenizing ideals of *mestizaje* as an imperative to capitalist modernity. Instead, most Creole writers and reformers embedded Indian subordination in modern racial-cultural lexicons of difference. In the process, they did not hesitate to describe contemporary Andean peasants in essentializing ways that made Indians the scourge, or the shame, or even the soul, of their nation. But few Creole writers or politicians bothered to listen to Andean voices, or thought they possessed the capacity for political participation, or that their history was anything but ancillary to the development of the Andean republics. Abandoning the ideal of universal citizenship, and fearful of "degenerate" race-mixing projects, Creole oligarchies concentrated instead on civilizing projects designed to remake Indians into vigorous underclasses of laborers, yeomen, and artisans. Elements of liberalism, racism, and colonialism once more intermingled in binary discourses of race, class, civilization, and geography.

For Andean peasants and laborers, the transfiguration into mute biocultural subjects narrowed the compass of what was politically possible and morally acceptable. It shut them out of the nation at the very moment they were catapulted into the middle of national and international wars and increasingly subject to violent despoliation under liberalizing laws in the 1870s, 1880s, and 1890s. At the local level, however, Indians possessed a variety of legal, rhetorical, and communal resources they might call upon to forge local solidarities and confront encroaching landlords, census takers, or other state agents. In case after case, from the Páez warriors and Otavalo weavers of the North Andes to the Aymara and Quechua *ayllus* of the South Andes, we have seen how indigenous leaders and their councils continued to deploy folk-legal discourses to defend customary or colonial legitimacies, manipulate liberalism's ambiguities, and forge transitory political pacts. In the process, rural Andean people rediscovered and revitalized their own ethnic pasts and traditions of struggle, thus laying the foundations for the rise of modern class and ethnic militancy in certain times and places over the course of the twentieth century.

Even before the rise of radical class and ethnic movements in the early twentieth century, however, Andean peasantries briefly burst onto the national scene in Peru and Bolivia amidst the din of military invasion and warfare during the War of the Pacific in the early 1880s. These moments of crisis significantly altered the site and scope of struggle, as well as tipped the balance of power in certain regional contexts. Equally important, they now afford us glimpses into the politics of Andean peasant-soldiers, who redefined themselves as patriotic subjects entitled to justice, respect, and protection within their own nation-states. Indigenous leaders, such as Atusparia, Laimes, or later, Zárate Willka, did not necessarily map ideological blueprints of an alternative nationhood or subscribe to any nativist orthodoxy. But in diverse and fragmentary ways, these indigenous leaders affirmed the right of their communities to a collective place in a reimagined polyethnic nation.

It is not necessary to identify the origins of "modern social movements" in these local mobilizations in order to appreciate their transformative potential. All we need do is project ahead into the mid- to late twentieth century to see the explosive potential of indigenous movements for Indian rights, territorial justice, and participatory democracy. In recent times, Colombia, Ecuador, and Bolivia have produced indigenous movements with broad constitutional and political ramifications for those nations, as well as for the vigorous Indian rights movement across the Americas. The roots of these modern ethnic movements grow deep, and late-nineteenth-century peasant mobilizations around land, community, and citizenship proved to be a crucial episode in this long, still largely unexplored, history. In the 1880s and 1890s, a full century before the explosion of contemporary indigenous movements in the Andes, Andean peasant petitions and actions were already rehearsing crucial issues of democratization, cultural pluralism, and collective rights (their colonial-Andean heritages). In so doing, they were attempting to become a counterforce – albeit, still more hopeful than real – to the polarizing forces of liberalism and race at the end of the nineteenth century.

Bibliographic Essay

Traditionally nineteenth-century Andean historiography has been the province of political historians who chronicle the instability of republican governments and of economic historians critical of export-driven economic growth and oligarchic regimes toward the end of the nineteenth century. Ethnohistorians and anthropologists, in contrast, have tended to focus most attention on contemporary Andean cultures or on the transition from Inca to Spanish rule. Much of this colonial scholarship forms the basis of Kenneth Andrien's fine synthesis, *Andean Worlds: Indigenous History, Culture, and Consciousness under Spanish Rule, 1532–1825* (Albuquerque, 2001). In addition, Andean ethnohistorians have been drawn to the topic of indigenous culture and politics during the late eighteenth-century in Ecuador, southern Peru, and Bolivia. Among the indispensable classics are the studies by Alberto Flores Galindo (including his anthology, *Túpac Amaru II – 1780: Antología*[Lima, 1976] and his interpretive cultural history, *Buscando un Inca. Identidad y utopía en los Andes* [Lima 1988]); Jan Szeminski, *La utopía tupamarista* (Lima, 1984); Scarlett O'Phelan Godoy, *Un siglo de rebeliones anticoloniales. Perú y*

Bolivia, 1700–1783 (Cusco, 1988); Manuel Burga, *Nacimiento de una utopía. Muerte y resurrección de los incas* (Lima, 1988); and Steve Stern's compilation, *Resistance, Rebellion and Consciousness in the Andean Peasant World, 18th to 20th centuries* (Madison, 1987). On the northern Andes, see the classic study on indigenous unrest in Ecuador's central highlands by Segundo Moreno Yáñez, *Sublevaciones indígenas en la Audiencia de Quito, desde comienzos del siglo XVIII hasta fines de la colonia* (Quito, 1985), and Mario Aguilera Peña's research on Colombia's 1781 "Comunero rebellion," *Los comuneros; Guerra social y lucha anticolonial* (Bogotá, 1985). A more traditional political study of the late colonial Colombian uprising is John Leddy Phelan's *The People and the King: The Comunero Revolution in Colombia, 1781* (Madison, 1978). However, most recent historical research on the "Age of Andean Insurrection" focuses on Cuzco and surroundings. See, for example, Charles Walker, *Smoldering Ashes: Cuzco and the Creation of Republican Peru, 1780–1840* (Durham, 1999), and Ward Stavig, *The World of Túpac Amarú: Conflict, Community and Identity in Colonial Peru* (Lincoln, 1999). On the evolution of Indian-state relations and internal communal organization among the *ayllus* of Bolivia, see Sinclair Thomson, *We Alone Will Rule: Native Andean Politics in the Age of Insurgency* (Madison, 2002), as well as the doctoral theses, soon to be published by: Sarah Elizabeth Penry, "Transformations in Indigenous Authority and Identity in Resettlement Towns of Colonial Charcas (Alto Perú)," unpublished Ph.D. dissertation, University of Miami, 1996, and Sergio Serulnikov, "Peasant Politics and Colonial Domination. Social Conflicts and Insurgency in Northern Potosí, 1730–1781," unpublished Ph.D. dissertation, Stony Brook University, 1997. For insightful synthesis of some of this literature, see Luís Miguel Glave, "The 'Republic of Indians' in Revolt (c. 1680–1790)," in F. Salomon and S. Schwartz, eds., *Cambridge History of the Native Peoples of the Americas: South America*

(Cambridge 1999), III, 2: 502–57, and Kenneth J. Andrien, *Andean Worlds: Indigenous History, Culture, and Consciousness under Spanish Rule, 1532–1825* (Albuquerque, 2001), chap. 7.

Traditional historiographical neglect, as well as the severe limitations imposed by thin, discontinuous, and opaque republican sources, have long discouraged social and anthropological histories of Andean peoples under republican rule. (A stunning exception is the magisterial 30-volume *Colección documental de la Independencia del Peru*, containing invaluable primary sources for the late eighteenth and early nineteenth centuries. Curiously, few historians have mined these volumes.) Over the past fifteen or twenty years, however, a surge of historical and anthropological research has opened new perspectives on Andean highland societies in the transition from colony to nation. Many of these historical studies fold the nineteenth century into longer time frames, sometimes framing the "long nineteenth century" between 1780 and 1930, or between 1810 and 1930. In many ways, the Bourbon beginning of state centralization and modest free-trade reforms in the late eighteenth century anticipated what was to come later, just as Andean-state tensions that simmered during much of the nineteenth century might be seen as a long prelude to ethnic resurgence in the early twentieth century. Most of these studies center on specific regions or ethnic communities, and they combine "thick description" of everyday forms of cultural practice and meaning with broader structural analyses (e.g., the transitions to modern capitalist economies and nations). Over the late 1980s and early 1990s, historians and anthropologists have blended archival research, oral testimonies, and ethnological perspectives in order to capture a sense of Andean agencies, subjectivities, and historiographies. To date, most studies pertain to Peru and, secondarily, to Bolivia. Peruvian-based historiography has been especially prolific and creative in the past decade and a half, although Aymara historians based in La Paz have recently produced an extraordinary set of oral histories and historical interpretations. The most notable of these recent studies will be mentioned later, under sections pertaining to each republic.

There is still no overarching comparative study of the nineteenth-century Andean republics and their "Indian policies." It is worth remembering, of course, the relevant Cambridge volumes, edited by Leslie Bethell, on nineteenth-century Latin America, although indigenous history and experiences are largely neglected. Several recent collections, however, cut across the four republics and raise many crucial issues about Andean experiences and responses to republican policies and practices. The two-volume collection, J. P. Deler and Y. Saint-Geours, eds., *Estados y Naciones en los Andes: Hacia una historia comparativa: Bolivia, Colombia, Ecuador, y Perú* (Lima, 1986), intersperses illuminating, comparative commentary among solid essays on regional societies and Andean adjustments to external pressures. The recent historiographical turn, via Benedict Anderson's idea of national imagined communities, toward nation making as a contested political, discursive, and cultural project usually shies away from broad comparison. But see the illuminating exceptions to this rule, including Marie Danielle Demelas, *L'invention politique. Bolivie, Equateur, Pérou au XIX siècle* (Paris, 1992); Florencia Mallon, *Peasant and Nation: The Making of Postcolonial Mexico and Peru* (Berkeley, 1995); Sarah Radcliffe and Sallie Westwood, *Remaking the Nation: Place, Identity and Politics in Latin America* (London, 1996), the latter focused mainly on Ecuador; Greg Urban and Joel Sherzer, eds., *Nation-States and Indians in Latin America* (Austin, 1991); and Nils Jacobsen and Cristobál Aljovín, eds., *Political Cultures of the Andes, 1750–1950* (Durham, forthcoming). A more focused collection on Indian-state relations, *hacienda*-communal conflicts, and other nineteenth-century issues is developed in Alberto Flores Galindo, ed., *Comunidades campesinas: Cambios y permanencies* (Chiclayo, 1988), 2nd ed.; H. Bonilla, ed., *Los Andes en la Encrucijada. Indios, Comunidades, y Estado en el Siglo XIX* (Quito, 1991); and

H. Bonilla, *Un siglo a la deriva: Ensayos sobre el Perú, Bolivia y la guerra* (Lima, 1980). See also the relevant articles in the more anthropological volumes compiled by Segundo Moreno Yáñez and Frank Salomon, eds., *Reproducción y transformación de las sociedades andinas, siglos XVI–XX* (Quito, 1991), 2 vols. Two recent collected volumes are especially useful for the rich variety of Andean perspectives on the tensions and transitions between colonial rule and modern nation making: *El siglo XIX: Bolivia y América Latina* (La Paz, 1997), co-edited by Rossana Barragán, Dora Cajías, and Seemin Qayum, as well as the more theoretically cohesive compilation by Henrique Urbano, *Tradición y modernidad en los andes* (Cusco, 1997). See also the suggestive introductory essay and relevant articles in Steve J. Stern, ed., *Resistance, Rebellion, and Consciousness in the Andean Peasant World, 18th to 20th Centuries* (Madison, 1987), as well as the introductory and concluding essays in Brooke Larson and Olivia Harris, eds., *Ethnicity, Markets and Migration in the Andes: At the Crossroads of History and Anthropology* (Durham, 1995).

In lieu of richly documented or consistent serial government sources on nineteenth-century Andean societies, the student may tap the rich vein of foreign travel literature and embryonic social sciences, produced by Europeans, North Americans, and a few educated Creoles engaged in the discovery, exploration, and diagnosis of native inhabitants of the new nations. Scientific and literary excursions into the internal frontiers of the Andes served the cause of imperial and national "white civilizers" anxious to recolonize Andean territories and cultures. Travel books on the nineteenth-century Andes range from the scornful or patronizing (hopelessly marred by racism or romanticism) to sympathetic and insightful reports enriched by ethnographic imagery, both literary and visual. Of the latter, see the masterful work of Alexander von Humboldt, especially his *Vues des cordillères et monuments des peoples indigènes de l' Amériques* (Paris, 1810), and the monumental work of the French zoologist, Alcides D'Orbigny. He was commissioned by the French government to map the linguistic and physiological groupings of South America, which led to his report, *L'homme américain* (Paris, 1839). During his eight years in South America, he traveled extensively throughout the continent. See his monumental *Voyage dans l'Amérique Meridionale (Le Brasil, Uruguay, L'Argentine, Chili, Bolivia, Pérou, etc.) executé pendant les années 1823 à 1826*, 9 vols. (Paris, 1835–1847), for especially vivid descriptions of highland Bolivia. Valuable sources for the independence period include the travel diary of Colonel J. P. Hamilton, *Travels through the Interior Provinces of Colombia*, 2 vols. (London, 1827), and William Bennett Stevenson's sympathetic and ethnologically sensitive account, *Historical and Descriptive Narrative of Twenty Years' Residence in South America*, 3 vols. (London, 1825). The latter travel journal is especially insightful about highland Ecuador. Friedrich Hassaurek, an Austrian-born diplomat who served as Abraham Lincoln's ambassador to Ecuador, also wrote a fascinating travel memoir of highland Ecuador. Although flawed by racist remarks, his *Four Years Among the Ecuadorians* [1867] (Carbondale, 1967) sketches vivid scenes of many facets of rural life. Good travel reports on Colombia include A. Hettner, *Viajes por los andes colombianos, 1882–1884* [1888] (Bogotá, 1976), and Robert Cross, *Report by Robert Cross on his Mission to South America in 1877–1878* (London, 1879), the latter concerning the natural and social conditions of the quinine trade. By far, the most important exploratory field-research on rural Colombia was carried out by *La Comisión corográfica*, under the leadership of the Italian soldier and cartographer, Augustine Codazzi. He was contracted in 1850 to lead interdisciplinary expeditions into Colombia's hinterlands to survey and categorize the republic's resources, inhabitants, topographies, and boundaries. The expedition led to a series of studies and illustrations, some of them later published. On the *Comisión Corográfico* and the birth of Colombia's social sciences, see

O. Restrepo, "'La comisión corográfica' y las ciencias sociales," in J. Arocha and N. de Friedemann, eds., *Un siglo de investigación social. Antropología en Colombia* (Bogotá, 1984). Highland Peru, above all, attracted nineteenth-century European travelers, antiquarians, historians, geographers, and scientists. See Estuardo Núñez's important collection, *Antología de viajeros. Textos fundamentales sobre realidades peruanas* (Lima, 1994), and his *Viajes y viajeros por el Perú* (Lima, 1989). Historian William Hickling Prescott's interest in the Incas, and his grand narratives of the conquest of the Incas and the Aztecs, influenced his colleague, Ephraim George Squier, who set new standards of ethnological description in his work, *Peru: Incidents of Travel and Exploration in the Land of the Incas* [1877] (New York, 1973). Even more stunning for its naturalism, both visual and textual, is Charles Wiener's *Pérou et Bolivie: Recit du voyage* (Paris, 1880). Wiener was interested in the cultural continuities of Andean societies, and he seamlessly combined archaeological and ethnographic perspectives to encompass Peru's ancient and contemporary indigenous cultures in one field of vision. Other important travel memoirs and descriptions of highland Peru include: Sir Clements Markham, *Cuzco: a Journey to the Ancient Capital of Peru . . . and Lima . . .* (London, 1856), with excerpts recently republished in Peter Blanchard, ed., *Markham in Peru: The Travels of Clements R. Markham, 1852–1853* (Austin, 1991); the observations of Englishman, Edmond Temple, in his *Travels in Various Parts of Peru, including a Year's Residence in Potosí* (Bolivia), 2 vols. (Philadelphia, 1833); the journal of the Swiss naturalist, J. J. von Tschudi, *Travels in Peru during the Years 1838–1842 . . .* (London, 1847); and of course, the famous chronicle of discovery by Hiram Bingham, who first brought the "lost city" of Machu Picchu into the public eye, *Inca Land: Explorations in the Highlands of Peru* [1912] (Boston, 1922). Many of these ethnographies and travel accounts are exceptionally rich visual sources, as testified by many of the illustrations in this book.

See also the famous mid-nineteenth-century landscape painting by Frederick Edwin Church, "The Heart of the Andes" (1859), housed in the Metropolitan Museum of Art, in New York, and discussed by Deborah Poole, in her "Landscape and the Imperial Subject: U.S. Images of the Andes, 1859–1930," in Gilbert Joseph, C. Legrand, and Ricardo Salvatore, eds., *Close Encounters of Empire: Writing the Cultural History of US-Latin American Relations* (Durham, 1988), 107–38.

Traveler-reporters and artists were not all foreigners, of course. This book has argued that Creole elites borrowed and adapted the "machinery of representation" to manufacture their own landscapes, racial types, and historic icons – whether these elements were put to the service of Western narratives of progress and whitening, used to "discover" and celebrate their own authentic "races" and customs, or deployed "scientifically" to explain and essentialize biocultural differences. This book argues that Creole renderings of the Indian problem, and more generally the reification of racial difference, was a critical cultural enterprise in the forging of centralizing Andean states in the mid-to-late nineteenth century. Although the Andean region possessed no grand allegory, analogous to Domingo Faustino Sarmiento's *Facundo: civilización y barbarie* [1845] (Buenos Aires, 1958), the "Andean utopia" provided a powerful, yet extremely ambivalent symbol, which permeated Creole writings about the Peruvian nation, its ancient and colonial past, its contemporary social problems, and its future possibilities. On the interpenetration of Western racism and Andean utopianism in the Creole social imaginary, see Alberto Flores Galindo's incomparable study, *Buscando un Inca. Identidad y utopía en los andes* (Lima, 1988), 3rd ed.; and, more recently, the innovative book on racial and cultural essentialism in the writings of Cuzco's provincial intellectuals by Marisol de la Cadena, "Silent Racism and Intellectual Superiority in Peru," *Bulletin of Latin American Research* 17 (1998), 143–64; and her new book, *Indigenous Mestizos: The*

Politics of Race and Culture in Cuzco, Peru, 1919–1991 (Durham, 2000), chap. 1 and 2.

The recent turn toward cultural symbolism and meaning, especially as they interacted with material forms of power, contestation, and inequality, has led to an explosion of scholarly work on the politics of race, region, and culture – especially the construction of cultural-racial difference in the process of establishing exclusionary postcolonial nation-states. The nineteenth-century Andean context is an especially rich and dynamic context for historicizing the "representational machines" of informal empire, as Europeans and North Americans deployed all sorts of ways and means (travelogues, natural history exhibits, statistical reports, archaeological artifacts, paintings, engravings, photographs, and even world fairs) through which they could engage with, and import knowledge and images about, the indigenous cultures of South America. This point is succinctly explored in Ricardo Salvatore, "The Enterprise of Knowledge. Representational Machines of Informal Empire," in G. Joseph, C. Legrand, and R. Salvatore, eds., *Close Encounters of Empire: Writing the Cultural History of US–Latin American Relations* (Durham, 1988), 69–104. Among North Americans, of course, a rich resonance existed between the "picturing" of their own Western frontier and the expansionary impulse that many U.S. travelers and entrepreneurs brought to the Andes and the rest of Latin America toward the end of the century. See J. Valerie Fifer, *United States Perceptions of Latin America, 1850–1930: A 'New West' South of Capricorn?* (Manchester, 1991); and Mary Louise Pratt, *Imperial Eyes: Travel Writing and Transculturation* (London, 1992). To date, the masterful book by Deborah Poole, *Vision, Race, and Modernity: A Visual Economy of the Andean Image World* (Princeton, 1997), has set new standards for studying the technologies, aesthetics, and politics that went into making visual understandings of race, region, and nationhood. Although Poole concentrates on Peru, her landmark book engages broader issues of Andean culture, power, history, and race. See also the excellent study of nineteenth-century Ecuador through the eyes of European travelers by Jill Fitzell, "Cultural Colonialism and Ethnography: European Travelers in Nineteenth Century Ecuador," unpublished Ph.D. dissertation, University of British Columbia, 1994; a summary appears as "Teorizando la diferencia en los andes del Ecuador. Viajeros europeos, la ciencia del exotismo y las imágenes de los indios," in Blanca Muratorio, ed., *Imágenes e Imagineros: Representaciones de los indígenas ecuatorianos, siglos XIX y XX* (Quito, 1994), 25–74. Equally fascinating is Blanca Muratorio's richly detailed synthesis of Ecuadorian elites' variant nineteenth-century mythologies, discourses, and imageries of the Indian, in "Nación, identidad y etnicidad. Imágenes de los indios ecuatorianos y sus imagineros a fines del siglo XIX," in B. Muratorio, ed., *Imágenes e Imagineros. Representaciones de los indigenas ecuatorianos, siglos XIX y XX* (Quito, 1994), 109–96.

COLOMBIA

Among the four case studies of native Andean experiences and involvement in nineteenth-century nation making, Colombia and Ecuador are the least studied through the perspectives of ethnohistory. As a result, many of my own interpretive arguments about indigenous history in nineteeth-century Colombia and Ecuador in this book are drawn from a thinner and more fragmented documentary base than that which exists for Peru and Bolivia. Nevertheless, a few key studies have proven to be extraordinarily influential in my own attempt to probe the peculiar heritage and nature of Indian-state relations in these two northern republics and to draw broad comparative strokes between the North and South Andes (see the footnotes for chapters 2 and 3).

Colombian historiography is immeasurably enriched, for example, by the new synthesis co-authored by Frank Safford and Marco Palacios, *Colombia: Fragmented Land, Divided Society* (Oxford, 2002). It provides a fine-grained analysis of Colombian social, economic, and political contexts within which to place more focused studies of indigenous and African peoples over the ages. See also, David Bushnell, *The Making of Modern Colombia: A Nation in Spite of Itself* (Berkeley, 1993); and Anthony MacFarlane's *Colombia before Independence: Economy, Society and Politics under Bourbon Rule* (Cambridge, 1993). But no social history can grasp the complexity of Colombian popular cultures without encompassing its African populations. See, for example, William F. Sharp, *Slavery on the Spanish Frontier: the Colombian Chocó, 1680–1810* (Norman, 1976), and Nina de Friedemann, *De sol a sol: génesis, transformación y presencia de los negros en Colombia* (Bogotá, 1986).

Curiously, the historiography of indigenous-state relations under liberalism is extremely uneven. But I found Frank Safford's incisive essays on elite policies and representations to be particularly helpful. See especially, "Race, Integration and Progress: Elite Attitudes and the Indian in Colombia 1750–1870," *Hispanic American Historical Review* 71: 1 (1991), 1–34; and "The Emergence of Economic Liberalism in Colombia," in J. Love and N. Jacobsen, eds., *Guiding the Invisible Hand: Economic Liberalism and the State in Latin American History* (New York, 1988), 32–62. On racial discourses among nation builders, see Leon Helguera, *Indigenismo in Colombia: A Facet of the National Identity. Search, 1821–1973* (Buffalo, 1974); and Peter Wade, "The Language of Race, Place, and Nation in Colombia," *América Negra* 1 (1991), 41–65. Recently, Peter Wade placed the Colombian case in broader hemispheric perspective, with his crucial synthesis on the historically different racial positioning of blacks and Indians in relationship to Latin American nation-states;

see his influential primer, *Race and Ethnicity in Latin America* (London, 1997). In his study of lowland native peoples and the rubber boom, Michael Taussig discusses the real and rhetorical violence of extractive capitalism and imperial-civilizing projects in his provocative, somewhat eccentric study, *Shamanism, Colonialism, and the Wild Man: A Study in Terror and Healing* (Chicago, 1987).

Research on the Chibcha peoples of Colombia's northeastern highlands is still spotty. Much of it revolves around the conflict over *resguardo* lands under late colonial and liberal regimes. Classic studies include Juan Friede, *El indio en la lucha por la tierra. Historia de los resguardos del macizo central colombiano* (Bogotá, 1944), and Hermes Tovar Pinzón, *La formación social chibcha* (Bogotá, 1980), but the student will find a quick overview in Orlando Fals Borda's article, "Indian *Congregaciones* in the New Kingdom of Granada: Land Tenure Aspects, 1595–1850," *The Americas* 13 (1957), 331–51. For specifically nineteenth-century anti-*resguardo* policies and conflicts, see Glen Curry, "The Disappearance of the Resguardo *Indígenas* of Cundinamarca, Colombia, 1800–1863," unpublished Ph.D. dissertation, Vanderbilt University, 1981, as well as the works by Friede and Tovar Pinzón, cited earlier in this paragraph. See also, Silvia Broadbent, *Los Chibchas: Organización socio-política* (Bogotá, 1964). For broader historical studies of land tenure, peasant societies, and agrarian change in nineteenth-century Colombia, see Marco Palacios, *Coffee in Colombia: An Economic, Social, and Political History* (Cambridge, 1980); Charles Bergquist, *Coffee and Conflict in Colombia, 1886–1910* (Durham, 1968); Catherine Legrand, *Frontier Expansion and Peasant Protest in Colombia, 1850–1936* (Albuquerque, 1986); Jane Rausch, *A Tropical Plains Frontier: The Llanos Frontier in Colombian History, 1830–1930* (Albuquerque, 1993); and Silvia Broadbent, "The Formation of Peasant Society in Central Colombia," *Ethnohistory* 28: 3 (1981), 258–77. *Minifundia-latifundia* dynamics at the micro-level is examined in Orlando Fals Borda's monograph, *Peasant Society in the Colombian Andes: A Sociological Study of Saucio* (Gainesville, 1955). A general ethnological introduction to Colombia's native peoples is found in Roberto Pineda, ed., *Introducción a la Colombia indígena* (Bogotá, 1987).

Some of the most innovative historical anthropology on Colombia in recent years has come from Joanne Rappaport's two case studies of the southern Páez and Pasto peoples in, respectively, *The Politics of Memory: Native Historical Interpretation in the Colombian Andes* (Cambridge, 1990; reprinted by Duke University Press, 1997); and *Cumbe Reborn: An Andean Ethnography of History* (Chicago, 1994). In both works, Rappaport explores the contours of native historical consciousness and ethnic politics in the struggle over territory, community, and identity. Her study of the Páez peoples, in particular, traces the social, economic, and cultural forces and counterforces of change under the pressures of republican land reform, white colonization, and extractive capitalism during the second half of the nineteenth century. More traditional but informative studies of the Páez may be found in Elías Sevilla-Casas, *Estudios antropológicos de Tierradentro* (Cali, 1976); and M. T. Findji and J. M. Rojas, *Territorio, economía, y sociedad páez* (Cali, 1985). Essential to the study of the Paéz political mobilization in the early twentieth century is the direct testimony of the indigenous leader and writer, Manuel Quintín Lame, *En defensa de mi raza* [1939] (Bogotá, 1971), with its English translation in *Liberation Theology From Below* (Maryknoll, 1987); see also his *Las luchas del indio que bajó de la montaña al valle de la 'civilización'* (Bogotá, 1973). In addition, see María Teresa Findji, "From Resistance to Social Movements: The Indigenous Authorities Movement in Colombia," in A. Escobar and S. Alvaréz, eds., *The Making of Social Movements in Latin America* (Boulder, 1992), 112–33; and the splendid synthesis of Andean political movements in Colombia, and across the whole Andean region, during the twentieth century in Xavier Albó, "Andean People in the Twentieth Century," in F. Salomon and S. Schwartz, eds., *Cambridge History of the Native People of the Americas: South America* (Cambridge, 1992), III: 2, 765–871.

ECUADOR

In recent years, several U.S. social historians have advanced the field of pre-Hispanic and colonial Ecuador study in significant ways. No literature review can ignore the pathbreaking ethno-history of Frank Salomon, who tested the classic anthropological models of Andean social organization against the northern ethnic chiefdoms on the eve of the Spanish conquest in his book *Native Lords of Quito in the Age of the Incas: The Political Economy of the North-Central Chiefdoms* (Cambridge, 1986). Important new works on indigenous people under colonial rule include Martin Minchom, *The People of Quito, 1690–1810* (Boulder, 1994); Karen Powers, *Andean Journeys: Migration, Ethnogenesis, and the State in Colonial Quito* (Albuquerque, 1995); and Kenneth Andrien, *The Kingdom of Quito, 1690–1830: The State and Regional Development* (Cambridge, 1995).

Ecuadorian scholars have taken the lead in research on nineteenth- and twentieth-century social and cultural issues of Indians and nation making. Emerging historical interest in peasant politics and political consciousness was sparked by the 1990 Indian uprising in highland Ecuador and nurtured by a network of young Andeanists drawn to the former Facultad Latinoamericana de Ciencias Sociales (FLACSO) program in Andean history and anthropology, based in Quito. Several important collections have begun to bring this new research to light: see especially, I. Almeda et al., eds., *Indios: Una reflexión sobre el levantamiento indígena de 1990* (Quito, 1991), particularly the contribution by Hernán Ibarra, "La identidad devaluada de los 'Modern Indians,'" 319–49;

various contributions in the anthologies, Centro de Documentación e Información de los Movimientos Sociales del Ecuador (CEDIME), *Sismo étnico en el Ecuador* (Quito, 1993); Gonzalo Rubio Orbe, *Los indios ecuatorianos. Evolución histórica y políticas indigenistas* (Quito, 1987); and H. Bonilla, ed., *Los Andes en la Encrucijada: Indios, Comunidades, y Estado en el Siglo XIX* (Quito, 1991); see also, Leon Zamosc, "Agrarian Protest and the Indian Movement in the Ecuadorian Highlands," *Latin American Research Review* 29 (1994), 37–68.

An older historical literature on Ecuadorian Indians and the nation begins with the classic *indigenista* studies by the noted Mexican anthropologist and ambassador to Ecuador, Moises Sáenz, *Sobre el indio ecuatoriano y su incorporación al medio nacional* (Mexico, 1933), and by Pío Jaramillo Alvarado, *El indio ecuatoriano: Contribución al estudio de la sociología indo-americano* (Quito, 1936). The famous muckraking novel by Jorge Icaza, *Huasipungo* (Quito, 1934) also belongs to this foundational literature of early twentieth-century *indigenismo*. But until recently, few Ecuadorian historians have studied Indian political movements, except as discrete and largely insignificant uprisings (see O. Albornoz, *Las luchas indígenas en el Ecuador* [Guayaquil, 1971]), or as subordinate factions of larger intra-elite political struggles (see Victor A. Jaramillo, *Participación de Otavalo en la Guerra de Independencia* [Otavalo, 1933] and V. Goncharov, "Los indígenas en la revolución liberal de Eloy Alfaro," *Los pueblos autóctonos en América latina: Pasado y presente*, 2 vols. [Moscow, 1984], 2: 19–206). In contrast, see the recent study of the 1871 Daquilema rebellion in Hernán Ibarra, *'Nos encontramos amenazados por todita la indiada.' El levantimiento de Daquilema*: Chimborazo 1871 (Quito 1993). Other recent studies cultivate fine-grained analyses of peasant politics, the problem of political authority, everyday forms of resistance, popular discourses, and discontentment. See especially the three Ecuadorian contributions in H. Bonilla, ed., *Los Andes en la*

Encrucijada: Indios, Comunidades, y Estado en el Siglo XIX (Quito, 1991): Martha Moscoso, "La tierra: Espacio de conflicto y relación entre el Estado y la comunidad en el siglo XIX," 367–90; Silvia Palomeque, "Estado y comunidad en el siglo XIX. Las autoridades indígenas y su relación con el Estado," 391–418; and Galo Ramón, "Los indios y la constitución del estado nacional," 419–56. As part of his broader forthcoming study of ethnic politics and nineteenth-century nation building in Ecuador, Andrés Guerrero published an important article on the clashes between folk-legal and republican concepts of land and authority in nineteenth-century Otavalo: "Curagas y tenientes políticos: La ley de la costumbre y la ley del estado (Otavalo, 1830–1875)," *Revista Andina* 7: 2 (1989), 321–65. For a fine-grained social history of urban life in Guayaquil, see Camilla Townsend, *Tales of Two Cities: Race and Economic Culture in Early Republican North and South America* (Austin, 2000). Also suggestive is Martha Moscoso's short essay on gendered processes of transculturation among women migrants to Quito: "Mujeres indígenas, mestizaje y formación de los sectores populares urbanos en Quito, segunda mitad del siglo XIX," in R. Barragán et al., eds., *El siglo XIX. Bolivia y América Latina* (La Paz, 1997), 487–96. This theme is developed in a brilliant new study of Andean gender and racial identities, especially for the case of contemporary Ecuador, by Mary Weismantel in her *Cholas y Pishtacos: Stories of Race and Sex in the Andes* (Chicago, 2001). See also the special issue of the *Bulletin of Latin American Research* 17 (1998) on "Race and Ethnicity in the Andes," edited by Weismantel.

On the social interaction between peasants, landlords, and state policies in different regions of nineteenth-century Ecuador, see Juan Maiguashca, ed., *Historia y región en el Ecuador, 1830–1930* (Quito, 1994). Especially useful to my analysis of tributary relations in republican Ecuador was Mark J. Van Aken's article, "The Lingering Death of Indian Tribute in Ecuador," *Hispanic*

American Historical Review 61: 3 (1981), 429–45. A new work on Indian-state relations in the northern Imbabura region is by Derek Williams, "Negotiating the State: National Utopias and Local Politics in Andean Ecuador, 1845–1875," unpublished Ph.D. dissertation, Stony Brook University, 2001. Williams's fine-grained study of President García Moreno's regime of "Catholic Modernity" and its regulation of popular religion and other aspects of "Indian morality" is especially insightful: "Assembling the 'Empire of Morality': State Building Strategies in Catholic Ecuador, 1861–1875," *Journral of Historical Sociology* 14 (2001), 149–74. Republican discourses, laws, and policies vis-à-vis Indian labor, land, and markets are also explored in three important articles: Andrés Guerrero, "Una imagen ventrílocua: el Discurso Liberal a la 'Desgraciada Raza Indígena' a fines del siglo XIX," in B. Muratorio, ed., *Imágenes e Imagineros: Representaciones de los indigenas ecuatorianos, siglos XIX y XX* (Quito, 1994), 197–252; Rosemary Bromley and Robert Bromley, "The Debate on Sunday Markets in Nineteenth-Century Ecuador," *Journal of Latin American Studies* 7 (1975), 85–108; and Kim Clark, "Indians, the State and Law: Public Works and the Struggle to Control Labor in Liberal Ecuador," *Journal of Historical Sociology* 7 (1994), 49–72.

Ecuador's entrenched *hacienda* regime, and its servile labor institutions, were traditional topics of early *indigenista* and a later genertion of Marxist social science. A fine example of the latter is Andrés Guerrero, *Haciendas, capital y lucha de clases andina* (Quito, 1984). More recently Ecuador's land tenure regime, both its *hacienda*-styled feudalism and pockets of peasant-styled *minifundismo*, have come under the scrutiny of social historians, who are more interested in the subtle dynamics of Indian-landlord paternalism and indigenous strategies of resistance. For an overview of recent studies, as well as a suggestive methodological discussion of peasant negotiations of paternal power on a highland Ecuadorian estate, see Mark Thurner, "Peasant Politics and

Andean Haciendas in the Transition to Capitalism: An Ethnographic History," *Latin American Research Review* 28 (1993), 41–82. On the symbolic power of landlord paternalism, see Andrés Guerrero, *La semántica de la dominación: el concertaje de indios* (Quito, 1991).

Communities of Otavalan farmers, weavers, and merchants have long attracted anthropological interest in their cultural strategies of social reproduction and selective adaptation. Among Ecuador's native highland peoples, the Otavalans stand out for their ethnic cohesion, pride, and prosperity. An early ethnographic classic is Elsie Clews Parsons's *Peguche, Cantón of Otavalo, Province of Imbabura, Ecuador: A Study of Andean Indians* (Chicago, 1945), but see also Lynne Meisch, *Otavalo: Weaving, Costume and the Market* (Quito, 1987). Two recent studies in Norman E. Whitten, Jr., ed., *Cultural Transformations and Ethnicity in Modern Ecuador* (Urbana, 1981), provide very useful orientations to Otavalan cultural history: Frank Salomon, "Weavers of Otavalo," 420–49; and Joseph B. Casagrande, "Strategies for Survival. The Indians of Highland Ecuador," 260–77. The latter article studies six highland communities, including the Otavalan town of Pugaje. More generally, Whitten's volume includes a rich variety of ethnohistorical and ethnographic studies of contemporary Ecuador, besides the two articles mentioned. See especially the provocative study on the erasure of Indianness under Ecuador's modern project of racial assimilation in the article by Ronald Stutzman, "El *mestizaje*: An All-Inclusive Ideology of Exclusion," 45–94. Illustrative of new research currents on race, sexuality, and bodily discipline in the Andes is Rudi Colloredo-Mansfeld's study of the Otavalan people, both at "home" in Imbabura and in a trade diaspora now stretching from Quito to New York to Amsterdam. See his article, "'Dirty Indians,' Radical *Indígenas*, and the Political Economy of Social Difference in Modern Ecuador," *Bulletin of Latin American Research* 17 (1998), 121–42.

PERU

The resources on nineteenth-century Peru are far more extensive and layered than those related to the other Andean republics. Several streams of historiography, ethnohistory, and published documentary collections feed into the study of nineteenth-century Peruvian social history and, more recently, into ethnohistorical research on indigenous societies in the transition from colony to nation. To begin with, there are several fine synthesis of Peru's national history. See, for example, Peter Klarén, *Peru: Society and Nationhood in the Andes* (Oxford, 1999); and H. Dobyns and P. Doughty, *Peru: A Cultural History* (Oxford, 1976); and the classic anthology, *The Peru Reader. History, Culture, Politics*, eds., O. Starn et al. (Durham, 1995). Second, nineteenth-century Peruvian historiography rests on a solid foundation of research into Andean societies under Spanish rule. A core of regional-ethnic studies provides deep historical perspective on cultural continuities, changes, and diversities in the plural Andean world. Furthermore, long-term temporal frameworks often bridge the conventional political divide between the late-colonial and republican periods. While some colonial-Andean histories discuss the implications of "colonial legacies" for recent patterns of Indian cultural adaptation, resistance, and poverty (for example, Steve J. Stern, *Peru's Indian Peoples and the Challenge of Conquest: Huamanga to 1640* [Madison, 1982]), others trace long-term sociocultural trends and/or ideologies across colonial and postcolonial periods of time (such as, Bruce Mannheim, *The Language of the Inca since the European Invasion* [Austin, 1991]; Luís Miguel Glave, *Vida, símbolos y batallas* [Lima, 1993]; Karen Spalding, *Huarochirí: An Andean Society under Inca and Colonial Rule* [Stanford, 1984]; and Manuel Burga, *Nacimiento de una utopía: Muerte y resurrección de los incas* [Lima, 1988]).

Third, modern anthropological research on Peru's highland indigenous peoples has flourished since the Second World War, branching off in the 1960s and 1970s into a host of subfields and dialogues (see Frank Salomon, "The Historical Development of Andean Ethnology," *Mountain Research and Development* 5: 1 [1985], 79–98, for a detailed overview). Peruvian ethnologist Luís E. Valcárcel, and later the ethnographic and literary works of José María Arguedas, inspired an international group of ethnological researchers and activists to write and lobby against modernizing models of forced assimilation. These ethnological studies of contemporary Andean societies drew much of their inspiration from older ethnohistorians like John V. Murra, John Rowe, Franklin Pease, and R. Tom Zuidema, who documented the adaptability and diversity of Andean cultural traditions and social organization under Inca and early colonial rule. Until recently, however, ethnologists have concentrated on contemporary Andean societies, while ethnohistorians have focused on Inca, European conquest, and postconquest periods, leaving the study of nineteenth-century rural Peru to others.

Indeed, until the late 1970s, research on nineteenth-century Peru was virtually monopolized by socioeconomic and political historians, many of them grounded in Marxist concerns of political economy, dependency, and the transition to capitalism. A third research tradition, then, which sometimes diverted attention from highland rural society, Andean agency, and cultural themes, was the rise of a (mostly Peruvian-based) Marxian historiography of nineteenth-century Peru. The logic of the world capitalist market (and its human agents), creating its own peculiar conflicts and contradictions in precapitalist societies, determined the forces of historical change, leaving the Peruvian peasantry almost passive and impervious to social change (see Jean Piel, "The Place of the Peasantry in Nineteenth-Century Peru," *Past and Present* 46 [1970], 108–33, for an extreme example of this position). But out of this historiography also came a clarifying synthesis of nineteenth-century Peru: Manuel Burga and Alberto Flores-Galindo, *Apogeo y Crisis de la República*

Aristocrática (Lima, 1984), 3rd ed. It still stands as a classic interpretation of three related trends: the persistence of Andean-colonial forms of landed paternalism in the twentieth century; the power of mercantile capitalism to reorganize rural society in the southern highlands during the wool boom; and the rise of agrarian capitalism in the northern sugar zones, the site of militant syndicalism.

Still fundamentally untapped by sociocultural historians of nineteenth-century Peru for suggestive areas of future research is the monumental 17-volume work by Jorge Basadre, *Historia de la República del Perú* (Lima, 1968–9), 6th ed.; his pathbreaking work on the social history of the republic, *La multitud, la ciudad, y el campo en la historia del la República* (Lima, 1947); and his documentary collection, *Introducción a las bases documentales para la historia de la República del Perú con algunas reflexiones*, 2 vols. (Lima, 1971). Researchers interested in official demographic statistics on Peruvian Indians may also count on a preliminary documentary base. George Kubler first outlined Indian population trends in his Smithsonian-sponsored study, *The Indian Caste of Peru, 1795–1910: A Population Study Based upon Tax Records and Census Reports* (Washington, D.C., 1952). His major finding, that Indians remained a statistical majority of the nation's population during the nineteenth century, was recently reinforced and modestly revised by Paul Gootenberg's enlightening socio-demographic analysis, "Population and Ethnicity in Early Republican Peru: Some Revisions," *Latin American Research Review* 26: 3 (1991), 109–58.

Recent research on rural highland peasantries during and after Peruvian independence clusters around several major topics. Defining the new historiographic landscape is a group of historical-anthropological studies that situate the particularities of peasant or ethnic involvement in postcolonial nation making, regional change, and local cultural adaptation within larger frameworks of long-term regional change (usually organized around periods of upheaval and/or economic transition – the Independence wars, the War of the

Pacific, regional uprisings, the expansion of commercial capitalism and territorial incursions, etc.). Although they differ in important ways, these studies embrace a range of interlocking themes and perspectives, emphasizing Andean peasant social experiences, understandings, and inroads into hegemonic relations of power and representation. These keystone works include: Alberto Flores-Galindo, *Arequipa y el sur andino. Siglos XIII–XX* (Lima, 1977); Florencia Mallon, *The Defense of Community in Peru's Central Highlands: Peasant Struggle and Capitalist Transition, 1860–1940* (Princeton, 1983); Nelson Manrique, *Yawar mayu: Sociedades terratenientes serranas, 1879–1910* (Lima, 1988); Gavin Smith, *Livelihood and Resistance: Peasants and the Politics of Land in Peru* (Berkeley, 1989); Nils Jacobsen, *Mirages of Transition: The Peruvian Altiplano, 1780–1930* (Berkeley, 1993); Carlos Contreras, *Mineros y campesinos en los andes* (Lima, 1988); Ernesto Yepes del Castillo, *Perú, 1820–1920: Un siglo de desarrollo capitalista* (Lima, 1972); Alejandro Diez Hurtado, *Comunes y haciendas: Comunalización de Piura (siglos XVIII al XX)* (Cuzco, 1998); Henrique Urbano, ed., *Poder y violencia en los Andes* (Cuzco, 1991); and Mark Thurner, *From Two Republics to One Divided: The Contradictions of Postcolonial Nationmaking in Andean Peru* (Durham, 1997).

Peasant participation in the War of the Pacific has been the subject of ongoing debates over broader issues of peasant political consciousness and imagined national projects in predominantly precapitalist societies. Beyond the polemics (see the debate crystallized in articles by F. Mallon and H. Bonilla in Steve J. Stern, ed., *Resistance, Rebellion, and Consciousness in the Andean Peasant World, 18th to 20th Centuries* [Madison, 1987]), historians have begun to rewrite the history of Peru's national crisis in the 1880s from the "bottom up" and from a comparative regional perspective. Focusing more on regional particularities of preexisting relations of power, and on peasant experiences, visions, and voices captured in fragmented form during the crisis of war, these recent histories are opening windows on rural Andean worlds usually lost to view. See especially Florencia Mallon, *The Defense of Community in Peru's Central Highlands: Peasant Struggle and Capitalist Transition, 1860–1940* (Princeton, 1983), chap. 3, and her comparative study, *Peasant and Nation: The Making of Postcolonial Mexico and Peru* (Berkeley, 1995), and Nelson Manrique, *Campesino y nación: Las guerrillas indígenas en la guerra con Chile* (Lima, 1981), and his *Yawar mayu Sociedades terratenientes serranas, 1879–1910* (Lima, 1988). A second focal point of insurgent peasant politics and political aspirations revolves around the 1885 rebellion in the Huaylas region. See especially Mark Thurner, *From Two Republics to One Divided: The Contradictions of Postcolonial Nationmaking in Andean Peru* (Durham, 1997), chap. 5; and William W. Stein, *El levantimiento de Atusparia* (Lima, 1988); and his essay, "Myth and Ideology in a Nineteenth-Century Peruvian Uprising," *Ethnohistory* 2 (1982), 237–64. There is another cluster of historical work focused on the insurgent peasant movements of Puno, Cuzco, and Ayacucho around the turn of the twentieth century. Flores Galindo's *Buscando un Inca: Identidad y utopia en los andes* (Lima, 1988), 3rd ed., chap. 9, captures the "utopian horizon" of the rebel leader, Gutiérrez Cueva (alias Rumi Maqui), in the province of Puno in the early twentieth century, as well as the racist discourse informing government policies and repression. See also Nils Jacobsen, *Mirages of Transition: The Peruvian Altiplano, 1780–1930* (Berkeley, 1993), as well as the dated, unpublished, but still incomparable study by Dan Hazen, "The Awakenening of Puno: Government Policy and the Indian Problem in Southern Peru, 1900–1955," unpublished Ph.D. dissertation, Yale University, 1974. A useful synoptic overview is Michael González, "Neocolonialism and Indian Unrest in Southern Peru, 1867–1898," *Bulletin of Latin American Research* 6 (1987), 1–26.

Research on Andean participation in the wars between patriots and royalists during the 1810s and 1820s is thinner. Until recently, many historians tended to focus on the Andean civil wars during the 1780s, dismissing the formal independence wars as intra-elite civil wars between the invading armies of foreign patriots and local Peruvian royalists. Christine Hunefeldt's pathbreaking study of the independence era was the first major work to shatter elite-centric perspectives, by studying local peasant reactions to Spanish constitutionalism and later Bolivar-styled liberalism, simmering tax- and land-based conflicts, and spin-off rebellions like the 1812 Indian uprising of Huánuco; see her *Lucha por la tierra y protesta indígena: Las comunidades indígenas entre la colonia y república* (Bonn, 1982). On peasants, *caudillo* politics, and banditry before and after independence, see Charles Walker's important regional study, *Smoldering Ashes: Cuzco and the Creation of Republican Peru, 1780–1840* (Durham, 1999), and several articles in Carlos Aguirre and Charles Walker, eds., *Bandoleros, Abigeos y Montoneras: Criminalidad y Violencia en el Perú, siglos XVIII–XX* (Lima, 1990). For innovative research on peasant royalists in the Ayacucho region, see Cecilia Méndez-Gastelumendi, "Los campesinos, la independencia y la iniciación de la república. El caso de los iquichanos realistas: Ayacucho, 1825–1828," in H. Urbano, ed., *Poder y Violencia en los Andes* (Cuzco, 1991), 65–188; this is part of her larger study, "Rebellion Without Resistances: Huanta's Monarchist Peasants in the Making of the Peruvian State: Ayacucho, 1825–1850," unpublished Ph.D. dissertation, Stony Brook University, 1996.

Other studies are beginning to focus attention on the processes by which republican authorities tried to impose new tax, land, and other policies on Indian communities. For an early institutional study, see Thomas M. Davies, *Indian Integration in Peru: A Half Century of Experience, 1900–1948* (Lincoln, 1974), chaps. 1 and 2, on nineteenth-century background. A spate of recent books and articles deal with Indian tributary policies and politics, for example: Victor Peralta Ruíz, *En pos del tributo en el Cusco rural, 1826–1854*

(Cusco, 1991); and Carlos Contreras, "Estado republicano y tributo indígena en la sierra central en la postindependencia," *Histórica* 13: 1 (1989), 9–44. Recently, Nils Jacobsen has reconsidered liberal land reform policies in his sweeping synthesis, "Liberalism and Indian Communities in Peru, 1821–1920," in R. Jackson, ed., *Liberals, the Church, and Indian Peasants: Corporate Lands and the Challenge of Reform in Nineteenth-Century Spanish America* (Albuquerque, 1997), 123–70. An indispensable book on peasant household economies in the Peruvian highlands, from Inca times to the present, is anthropologist Enrique Mayer's *The Articulated Peasant: Household Economies in the Andes* (Boulder, 2001).

Following Flores Galindo's provocative essay, "República sin ciudadanos," (in his book, *Buscando un Inca: Identidad y utopia en los andes* [Lima, 1988], 3rd ed., chap. 8), scholars turned to study the Creole political imaginary and its essentialization, or erasure, of "indigeneity." Already mentioned is Deborah Poole's study of visual representations of gender, race, and nation in her book, *Vision, Race and Modernity: A Visual Economy of the Andean Image World* (Princeton, 1997). But race, geography, history, and nationality are also explored in several recent essays, which serve as invitations for future research. On the construction of Peru's racialized geography, see the little-cited but splendid article by Benjamin Orlove, "Putting Race in Place: Order in Colonial and Postcolonial Peruvian Geography," *Social Research* 60 (1993), 301–36. On the ways that highland peasant political claims and actions "destabilized liberal notions of 'republic' . . . and eventually challenged the teological historicity of Creole nation-building itself," see the complementary essays by Mark Thurner ("'*Republicanos*' and 'la Comunidad de Peruanos.' Unimagined Political Communites in Postcolonial Andean Peru," *Journal of Latin American Studies* 27 [1995], 291–318; quote on 291), and Cecilia Méndez-Gastelumendi ("República sin indios: La comunidad imaginada del Perú," in H. Urbano, ed., *Tradición y Modernidad en los Andes* [Cuzco, 1992], 15–41).

See also Méndez's penetrating recent article on the mutual construction of ethnic and national identities at a local level, "The Power of Naming, or the Construction of Ethnic and National Identities in Peru: Myth, History and the Iquichanos," *Past and Present* 171 (2000), 127–60. Worth mentioning here is Paul Gootenberg's *Imagining Development* (Berkeley, 1993) for a view of coastal Creole teleologies of economic progress, which fundamentally effaced indigenous communities, claims, and identities from the nineteenth century.

There is a rich scholarly literature, of course, on the rise of *indigenismo* and its articulation with political movements, ideologies, regionalism, and nation making after the turn of the twentieth century. Most of this literature is focused on the foundational texts of literary critics, activists, and reformers, such as C. Matta de Turner, M. González Prada, J. de la Riva Agüero, J. C. Mariátegui, L. E. Valcárcel, Haya de la Torre, and J. M. Arguedas, although many scholars cast their studies more broadly. The late literary scholar, Angel Rama, laid the conceptual foundations in his fundamental article, "El area cultural andina (hispanismo, mesticismo, indigenismo)," *Cuadernos Americanos* 33 (1974), 136–73. For standard overviews of Creole mediations on the Indian problem and its challenges to modernization and nation making, see Efraín Kristal, *The Andes Viewed from the City: Literary and Political Discourse on the Indian in Peru, 1848–1930* (New York, 1987), and L. E. Tord, *El indio en los ensayistas peruanos, 1848–1948* (Lima, 1978). For strong social, political, and regional contextualization of indigenist ideologies, see the following studies: Carlos Iván Degregori, et al., *Indigenismo, clases sociales y problema nacional* (Lima, 1979); José Deustua and José Luís Réñique, *Intelectuales, indigenismo, y descentralismo en el Perú, 1897–1931* (Cuzco, 1984); and José Tamayo Herrera's various books, *Historia social del Cuzco republicano* (Lima, 1981), *Historia del indigenismo cuzqueño, siglos XVI–XX* (Lima, 1980), *El pensamiento* indigenista (Lima,

1981), and *Historia social e indigenismo en el Altiplano* (Lima, 1982). Deborah Poole offers an insightful study of positivist race science, "Ciencia, peligrosidad y repression en la criminología indigenista peruana," in Carlos Aguirre and Charles Walker, eds., *Bandoleros, Abigeos y Montoneros: Criminalidad y Violencia en el Perú, siglos XVIII–XX* (Lima, 1990), 335–67. As mentioned earlier, Marisol de la Cadena takes the study of Cuzco's indigenist movement in new theoretical and methodological directions in her book, *Indigenous Mestizos: The Politics of Race and Culture in Cuzco, 1919–1991* (Durham, 2000). Nelson Manrique also investigates the advent of modern racial essentialism in his recent book, *La piel y la pluma. Escritos sobre literatura, etnicidad y racismo* (Lima, 1999). On the folklorization of Peru's Andean cultures, see Zoila Mendoza, "Defining Folklore: Mestizo and Indigenous Identities on the Move," *Bulletin of Latin American Research* 17 (1998), 165–83.

Fine-grained socioeconomic and cultural research on Andean rural society, agrarian power relations, and the changing contours of class and ethnic identity are to be found in an older generation of studies (e.g., Pierre Van den Berghe, ed., *Class and Ethnicity in Peru* [Leiden, 1974]), as well as in many of the studies cited earlier. One particular theme, however, has been reexamined in recent studies: the power, politics, and political culture of regional landowning power holders (*gamonales*). Studies by Flores Galindo (*Arequipa y el sur andino: siglos XIII–XX* [Lima, 1977]), Francois Bourricaud (*Cambios en Puno* [Mexico City, 1967]), and, more recently, Nils Jacobsen (*Mirages of Transition: The Peruvian Altiplano, 1780–1930* [Berkeley, 1993]) have put sociological and historical content into flat stereotypes of *gamonalismo* (first characterized by José Carlos Mariátegui). Some researchers, like Juan Martínez Alier (*Los huachilleros el Perú* [Lima, 1973]), have deemphasized landlords' monopoly of power over Indian sheep herders, who fashioned their own strategies of resistance to modern property relations and the efforts to modernize sheep ranching. In the last few years, a new group of anthropologists and historians has renewed interest in the idioms, routines, and rituals of power and violence in regional highland cultures. See, for example, Deborah Poole, ed., *Unruly Order: Violence, Power, and Cultural Identity in the High Provinces of Southern Peru* (Boulder, 1994).

BOLIVIA

Research on Bolivia's nineteenth-century Indian peasants has been at the intersection of politics, history, and anthropology for almost two decades. Several factors account for this: the simple fact that Bolivia's Indian problem was always central to republican state-making, given the numerical predominance of communal-based indigenous peoples; the creative ethnohistorical work of John Murra, Tristan Platt, Sinclair Thomson, Olivia Harris, Xavier Albó, Thomas Abercrombie, Nathan Wachtel, Jorge Dandler, Silvia Rivera Cusicanqui, Roger Rasnake, Carlos Mamani, Rossana Barragán, Esteban Ticona, Roberto Choque, myself, and others, which set interdisciplinary field/archival standards of scholarship on Andean *ayllus* under colonial and republican rule; and the rise of activist historians and anthropologists in Bolivia, whose work has placed Aymara and Quechua interests, narratives, and memories at the center of their historical research. Among the latter, the collective oral history projects of the Taller de Historia Oral Aymara (THOA), together with the activist anthropology of the Centro de Investigación y Promoción del Campesino (CIPCA), have produced important bodies of oral documentation, field studies, and indigenous histories written in Quechua, Aymara, and Spanish (see following).

Although Bolivia has no equivalent to Peru's Jorge Basadre, Josep Barnadas' bibliographic guide is still very useful (though dated): *Introducción a los estudios bolivianos contemporaneos, 1960–1984* (Cusco, 1987). A broad chronological synthesis of peasant history is Xavier Albó and J. Barnadas' *La cara india y campesina de nuestra historia* (La Paz, 1984). See also the wonderful socio-economic and political synthesis by Herbert Klein, in his *Bolivia: Evolution of a Multi-Ethnic Society* (Oxford, 1982); and the edited volume by Fernando Calderón and Jorge Dandler, *Bolivia: La fuerza histórica del campesinado* (La Paz, 1984). A basic primary source for early nineteenth-century Bolivia, with suggestive census data and descriptions of Indian societies, is John B. Pentland, *Report on the Bolivian Republic, 1827* (United Kingdom, Foreign Office), 61/12; and José María Dalence's compendium, *Bosquejo estadístico de Bolivia* [1846] (La Paz, 1975). A visual counterpart to Dalence's statistical portrait of mid-nineteenth-century Bolivia is the magnificent *costumbrista* paintings of Melchor María Mercado, *Album de paisajes, tipos humanos y costumbres de Bolivia* (Sucre, 1991). Working with nineteenth-century tributary population records (*padrones*), Erwin P. Grieshaber compiled an aggregate overview of official Indian population trends in his important article, "Survival of Indian Communities in Nineteenth Century Bolivia: A Regional Comparison," *Journal of Latin American Studies* 12 (1980), 223–69. As did Kubler for Peru, Grieshaber found remarkable demographic stability among high-land Indians over the nineteenth century; moreover, the proportion of landholding *comunarios* increased during the postindependence decades. (Bolivia was the one republic to preserve the status of corporate Indian lands until the 1870s.) There is still very little research on Andean rural societies during the wars for independence in Alto Peru (later, Bolivia), although see the preliminary study by René Arze, *Participación popular en la independencia de Bolivia* (La Paz, 1979); on Indians, *caudillos*, and republican law and policy see Rossana Barragán, *Indios, mujeres y ciudadanos. Legislación y ejercicio de la ciudadanía en Bolivia (siglo XIX)* (La Paz, 1999); and Victor Peralta Ruíz and Marta Irurozqui, *Por la Concordia, la fusion, y el unitarismo. Estado y caudillismo en Bolivia, 1825–1880* (Madrid, 2000), esp. chap. 5.

One of the richest veins of research on indigenous politics, culture, and thought has been pursued by anthropologist Tristan Platt, since the publication of his study, *Estado boliviano y ayllu andino. Tierra y tributo en el Norte de Potosí* (Lima, 1982). In that book and in later articles, Platt posed the *ayllus* of northern Potosí as historical subjects, negotiating the terms of their own integration into the postcolonial (but still tribute-collecting) republic of Bolivia. He framed the issue in terms of Indians' moral evaluations of their "tributary pact" with the fledgling republican state and their insurgent reactions when that pact broke down in the late nineteenth century. See his articles, "Liberalism and Ethnocide in the Southern Andes," *History Workshop* 17 (1984), 3–18, and "The Andean Experience of Bolivian Liberalism, 1825–1900: The Roots of Rebellion in Nineteenth-Century Chayanta (Potosí)," in Steve J. Stern, ed., *Resistance, Rebellion, and Consciousness in the Andean Peasant World 18th to 20th Centuries* (Madison, 1987), 280–326. More recently, Platt has explored popular Andean conceptions of nationalist symbols and ideas in his provocative essays, "Simón Bolivar, the Son of Justice and the Amerindian Virgin: Andean Conceptions of the *patria* in Nineteenth-Century Potosí," *Journal of Latin American Studies* 25 (1993), 159–85; and "The Sound of Light. Speech, Script and Metaphor in the Southern Andes," in S. Arze et al., eds., *Etnicidad, economía, y simbolismo en los Andes* (La Paz, 1992), 439–66. Platt's ethnohistorical work on northern Potosí *ayllus* is complemented by the historically sensitive ethnologies by Olivia Harris (see her "Labour and Produce in an Ethnic Economy; Northern Potosí, Bolivia," in David Lehmann, ed., *Ecology and Exchange in the Andes* [Cambridge, 1982]), Ricardo Godoy (see his *Mining and Agriculture in Highland Bolivia: Ecology, History, and Commerce among the Jukumanis* [Tucson, 1990]), and Silvia Rivera Cusicanqui and THOA, *Ayllus y proyectos de desarrollo en el norte de Potosí* (La Paz, 1992).

Other works on Bolivia, produced by both anthropologists and historians, offer local-ethnic or regional perspectives on cultural change. Roger Neil Rasnake's *Domination and Cultural Resistance: Authority and Power among an Andean People* (Durham, 1988) traces the transformation of hereditary chiefdoms into fragmented, rotative ethnic authorities and the changing contours of ritual life among the Yuras near the mining town of Potosí. Sinclair Thompson historicizes this process in an insurgent context, in his *We Alone Will Rule. Native Andean Politics in the Age of Insurgency* (Madison, 2002). A panoramic historical vision of the Urus, living on the margins of the *altiplano*, is offered by the French ethnohistorian, Nathan Wachtel, in his *Le retour des ancetres. Les indiens urus de Bolivie, XXe–XVIe siècle: Essai d'histoire regressive* (Paris, 1990). Equally sweeping is Thomas Abercrombie's study of the K'ulta people, *Pathways of Memory and Power: Ethnography and History among an Andean People* (Madison, 1998). See the salient articles in two important conference volumes: Silvia Arze et al., eds., *Etnicidad, economía y simbolismo en los Andes* (La Paz, 1992); and Rossana Barragán, D. Cajías, and S. Qayum, eds., *El siglo XIX. Bolivia y América Latina* (La Paz, 1997).

Social and ethno-histories of the Quechua-speaking communities in their regional contexts have focused on the eastern valleys of Chuquisaca and Cochabamba. Erick D. Langer's *Economic Change and Rural Resistance in Southern Bolivia, 1880–1930* (Stanford, 1989) examines the cultural and social diversity of rural society in Chuquisaca during the rise and decline of the region's *hacienda*-silver mining complex. Several studies explore the heterogeneous rural subcultures of ethnically mixed Cochabamba in the nineteenth century, including Brooke Larson, *Cochabamba. 1550–1900: Colonialism and Agrarian Transformation in Bolivia* (Durham, 1998), expanded ed.; Gustavo Rodríguez Ostría and Humberto Solares Serrano, *Sociedad Oligárquica, Chicha y Cultura Popular* (Cochabamba, 1990); Rodríguez, "Entre reformas and contrareformas. Las comunidades indígenas en el Valle Bajo cochabambino (1825–1900)," in H. Bonilla, ed., *Los Andes en la Encrucijada* (Quito, 1991), 277–335; Robert H. Jackson, *Regional Markets and Agrarian Transformation in Bolivia: Cochabamba, 1539–1960* (Albuquerque, 1994); and María Lagos, *Autonomy and Power: The Dynamics of Class and Culture in Rural Bolivia* (Philadelphia, 1994).

Recent studies of Aymara regions of northern highland Bolivia chart a landscape of violence, conflict, and mobilization during the late nineteenth and early twentieth centuries. See Tomás Huanca, "Los procesos de desestructuración en las comunidades andinas a fines del siglo XIX: el altiplano lacustre," *Coloquio Estado y Región en los Andes* (Cusco, 1987), 45–86; Silvia Rivera Cusicanqui, "La expansión del latifundio en el altiplano boliviano," *Avances* 2 (1978), 95–118; Herbert S. Klein, *Haciendas and Ayllus: Rural Society in the Bolivian Andes in the Eighteenth and Nineteenth Centuries* (Stanford, 1993); and Erick Langer and R. Jackson, "Liberalism and the Land Question in Bolivia, 1825–1920," in R. Jackson, ed., *Liberals, the Church, and Indian Peasants: Corporate Lands and the Challenge of Reform in Nineteenth-Century Spanish America* (Albuquerque, 1997), 171–92.

Aymara political movements are of particular interest. See especially the seminal work by Silvia Rivera Cusicanqui, '*Oprimidos pero no vencidos.' Luchas del campesinado aymara y qechwa, 1900–1980* (La Paz, 1986); but see also Ramiro Condarco Morales, *Zárate, el "Temible" Willka. Historia de la rebelión indígena de 1899* (La Paz, 1982), 2nd. ed.; Carlos Mamani Condori, *Taraqu. Masacre, Guerra, y 'Renovación' en la biografía de Eduardo L. Nina Qhispi* (La Paz, 1991); and Victor Hugo Cárdenas, "La lucha de un pueblo," in Xavier Albó, ed., *Raíces de América. El Mundo Aymara* (Madrid, 1988), 495–534. Particularly important is the oral history work on the *cacique* movement of the early twentieth century by the Aymara collective, THOA. See especially their books: *El indio Santos Marka T'ula. Cacique principal de los ayllus de Callapa y apoderado general de la comunidades originarias de la República* (La Paz, 1988); *El escribano de los caciques apoderados. Kasikinakan purirarunakan qillqiripa. Testimonios* (La Paz,1991), on the testimony of Marka T'ula's scribe; and *Mujer y resistencia comunaria. Historia y memoria* (La Paz, 1986), on the participation of Indian women in communal movements.

An incipient ethno-historical literature exists on the more elusive themes of Indians in mining towns and cities, Aymara- and Quechua-based trading-kinship circuits, and popular meanings and uses of ethnic and gender identity in different ritual, social, and political settings. See, for example, Silvia Rivera Cusicanqui, ed., *Ser mujer indígena, chola o birlocha en la Bolivia postcolonial* (La Paz, 1996); Marcia Stephenson, *Gender and Modernity in Andean Bolivia* (Austin, 1999); and Leslie Gill, *Precarious Dependencies: Gender, Class and Domestic Service in Bolivia* (New York, 1994). But these themes also beckon nineteenth-century ethnohistorians. On urbanized Aymara and cultural forms of *mestizaje*, ethnic, and gendered boundaries, see Rossana Barragán, *Espacio urbano y dinámica étnica; La Paz en el siglo XIX* (La Paz, 1990); and her article, "Entre polleras, lliqllas y ñañacas. Los mestizos y la emergencia de la tercera república," in Silvia Arze et al., eds., *Etnicidad, Economía, y Simbolismo en los Andes* (La Paz, 1992), 85–128. Through the lens of ritual performance, Thomas Abercrombie's articles explore urban Indianness and national identity in the mining town of Oruro: "La fiesta del Carnaval postcolonial en Oruro. Clase, etnicidad y nacionalismo en la danza folklórica," *Revista Andina* 20 (1992), 279–352, and "To Be Indian, to Be Bolivian: 'Ethnic' and 'National' Discourses of Identity," in G. Urban and J. Sherzer, eds., *Nation-states and Indians in Latin America* (Austin, 1991), 95–130. On ethnic identities, market participation, and class relations, see Olivia Harris, "Ethnic Identity and Market Relations: Indians and Mestizos in the Andes," in B. Larson and O. Harris, eds., *Ethnicity, Markets and Migration in the Andes*, 351–90; and Tristan Platt, "Ethnic Calendars and Market Interventions among the Ayllus of Lipes during the Nineteenth Century," in B. Larson and O. Harris with E. Tandeter, eds., *Ethnicity, Markets, and Migration in the Andes*, 259–96.

Curiously, we still lack a synthetic study of the political, institutional, or discursive relations between Andean peasants and the republican state in nineteenth-century Bolivia. This theme informs many local or regional studies but has not yet been examined from a comparative or national perspective. For narrower studies on nineteenth-century tribute policy, however, see Jorge Alejandro Ovando Sanz, *El tributo indígena en las finanzas bolivianas del siglo XIX* (La Paz, 1986); Nicolás Sánchez-Albornoz, *Indios y tributos en el Alto Perú* (Lima, 1978), chap. 5; and Tristan Platt, *Estado tributario y librecambio en Potosí (siglo XIX)* (La Paz, 1986). Erick D. Langer examines liberal land reform rhetoric and policy in his "Liberalismo y la abolición de la comunidad indígena en el siglo XIX," *Historia y Cultura* 14 (1988), 59–95.

A curious lag exists in the Bolivian historiography on the formation of racial discourses and imagery in the liberal, positivist, and nationalist imaginaries of Creole elites. This is especially puzzling given the extraordinary body of diagnostic and allegorical work on the Indian problem produced in Bolivia in the late nineteenth and early twentieth centuries. We need only mention Alcides Arguedas' *Pueblo enfermo* [1909] (La Paz, 1936), 3rd ed., which became a foundational text of Bolivian racial pessimism and national self-critique, or Bautista Saavedra's pioneering ethnography, *El ayllu* (La Paz, 1904), to underline the growing Creole obsession with its Indian problem in the immediate aftermath of the 1899 Aymara rebellion. Certainly, a pioneering work on Bolivia's politics of racial and national identity is Marie-Danielle Demelas' *Nationalisme sans nation? La Bolivie aux XIXe–XXe siecles* (Paris, 1980). New historical and literary scholarship is now beginning to turn its attention to

Bolivia's literary and visual *indigenismo*, although it is not always well contextualized or articulated to contemporary Aymara and Quechua political mobilizations and moral claims, which had such a shaping impact on the Creole racial imaginary. See, for example, Marta Irurozqui, *La armonía de las desigualdades. Elites y conflictos de poder en Bolivia, 1880–1920* (Cusco, 1994), and her more comprehensive follow-up study, *'A Bala, Piedra y Palo.' La construcción de la ciudadanía política en Bolivia, 1826–1952* (Seville, 2000), which integrates "political history from below" into her overarching study of Creole political and racial ideologies. See also the new work on racial discourses, law, and public policy: Laura Gotkowitz, *Within the Boundaries of Equality: Race, Gender and Citizenship in Cochabamba, Bolivia, 1880–1953* (Durham, forthcoming); Seemin Qayum, "Creole Imaginings: Race, Space, and Gender in the Making of Republican Bolivia," unpublished Ph.D. dissertation, Goldsmith's College, University of London, 2002; Brooke Larson, "Redeemed Indians, Barbarianized Cholos: Crafting Neocolonial Modernity in Liberal Bolivia," in N. Jacobsen and C. Aljovín, eds., *Political Cultures of the Andes, 1750–1950* (Durham, forthcoming); and Ann Zulawski, "Hygiene and the 'Indian Problem': Ethnicity and Medicine in Bolivia, 1910–1920," *Latin American Research Review* 35 (2000), 107–29. Also noteworthy is the new work by Bolivia literary scholars, such as Josefa Salmón, *El espejo indígena. El discurso indigenista en Bolivia, 1900–1956* (La Paz, 1997); and Isabel Bastos, "El indigenismo en la transición hacia el imaginario populista," *Estudios bolivianos* 2 (1996), 19–47. In my view, the most important historical synthesis of Bolivia's political and ideological struggle to come to grips with its pluriethnic heritage is the little cited but sweeping historical essay by Silvia Rivera Cusicanqui, "La raíz. Colonizadores y colonizados," in Xavier Albó and Raúl Barrios, eds., *Violencias encubiertas en Bolivia. Cultura y Política* (La Paz, 1993), 27–139.

Index

CPSIA information can be obtained
at www.ICGtesting.com
Printed in the USA
LVHW031133010921
696661LV00002B/136